Jesus the Evangelist

Doing it his way in my world

ROBIN GAMBLE

David C Cook

First published 2009

Published by David C. Cook
Kingsway Communications Ltd
26–28 Lottbridge Drove, Eastbourne BN23 6NT, UK

David C. Cook
4050 Lee Vance View, Colorado Springs, CO 80918, USA

David C. Cook Distribution Canada
55 Woodslee Avenue, Paris, Ontario, Canada N3L 3E5

Cover design by PinnacleCreative.co.uk

ISBN 978 1 84291 403 8

Typeset in India by Alliance Data Technology

Printed in Italy

Contents

This book is dedicated to

Christopher Byward – *who taught me to love the Bible*

Denis Shepheard – *who taught me to love Jesus*

and to my wife Maureen – *who taught me how to love people*

INTRODUCTION

Jesus – an Evangelist?

Jesus is the heavyweight world champion and gold medallist of all truly great historical celebrities. It is not so much that he is top of his division, but rather that he is the only one in it, and it is not just that everyone knows about him, but they all seem to like him too. Even the ones who do not believe in God, and the many who despise all things Christian, all think that Jesus was a really good guy. He is seen as a sort of Nelson Mandela, Gandhi, Bono, Mother Teresa and Peter Kaye character all rolled into one.

Once upon a time he was known as 'Prophet, Priest and King' or as 'Master and Lord'. This was after starting out as 'Messiah', 'Immanuel' and 'Son of Man'. He has come and gone and come again as both the 'Historical Jesus' and the 'Existentialist Christ of Faith'. He has been painted and patronised as the 'Gentle Galilean Carpenter'. For a while he was known as the 'Founder of Christianity', before becoming first a 'Superstar' and then a 'God-Clown'. In recent years he has been a hippie, a husband, a Che-Guevara revolutionary, a feminist and even the father of French medieval kings. Yet throughout this constant shape-changing, Jesus has maintained his position as the number one saint and saviour.

Contemporary 'Life of Jesus' theologians stress that first and foremost Jesus must be understood as a first-century Jew. Living in Galilee, the most northerly and Gentile-influenced part of Israel, he would have picked up plenty of Hellenistic and Roman thinking, but his big identity components were his Jewish religion, culture, family and friendships. So then, we can draw a picture of him as a passionate 'of the people' preacher, with a strong northern accent, wandering around in his homeland from town to village, teaching, healing, proclaiming, and driving out evil spirits. He operated out in the fields, on the lakeside, in the synagogue and in homes. Sometimes he gathered great crowds and on other occasions he worked in secret with his disciples. He mixed with rich and poor, men and women, religious and irreligious, Jew and Gentile.

As with all creative and innovative people, Jesus is impossible to pigeonhole. If we want to complete the sentence 'Jesus was a. . .', then we are going to need more than one ending. In fact, today's scholars seem to have two. One group see him as a great wisdom teacher, a sort of 'super-rabbi' loaded with spiritual and ethical insight. For the second, scholarly tendency, Jesus is a reforming and popular people's prophet, with a red-hot message or oracle from God calling the masses back to true religion and warning of a coming judgement. And for Wolfhart Pannenberg, he is much more than just a teacher or prophet: 'Jesus not only issued a call to repentance, but with full authority he granted to the men he met the salvation expected in the future' (*Jesus: God and Man*, p. 215). He did not just talk about it, he actually delivered – he led people into a full existential experience.

So we can see the Jesus of the Gospels as both a deep wisdom teacher and a passionate 'turn-back-to-God' prophet. And yet I think we can add a third ending to our sentence. Jesus was also a 'making-it-happen' evangelist. I say this knowing that the New Testament nowhere actually calls him an evangelist, but the big words 'evangel', 'gospel' and 'good news' are all there. He has evangelism in his genes and in his vocation, his sense of calling from the Father.

The four functions of evangelism

Evangelists do four things:

- Firstly, they put into words and proclaim the gospel message, the evangel.
- Secondly, they try to encourage and persuade their listeners to believe in and respond to the message. They catch fish and grow healthy plants. Evangelists are not content simply to offer the 'good news': they also want to see people receive and enjoy it.
- Thirdly, they introduce the listeners who have responded to a community of the like-minded, or, if such a group does not exist, they try to build one. Evangelists are church planters and builders.
- Fourthly, they teach and mentor their respondents to become evangelistically active themselves.

In other words, in the loving hands of evangelists, responding men and women go through four steps or movements in a spiritual journey. They begin as interested searchers, and become firstly serious enquirers and then committed learners. They move into deep discipleship and membership and then go out themselves as apostolic life-changers.

The importance of this long-term journey, pilgrimage or process is nicely illustrated in Rick Warren's *The Purpose-Driven Church*: 'We developed a workable process to turn seekers into saints, turn consumers into contributors, turn members into ministers, and turn an audience into an army.'[1]

Evangelists are committed to these four aspects of work because these were what Jesus did. Jesus the evangelist never lost sight of that elusive element: the final product. Too much of our evangelising energy today is dedicated almost entirely to the first part of the process, the scattering of the seed. The idea of a harvest that can be counted and evaluated often frightens us with a sense of possible or even likely failure. Jesus' final product may not have been as big or numerous as he hoped (Luke 10:13), but it was of such a quality and depth that it – or rather they – went on to change the world.

> Jesus went throughout Galilee, teaching in their synagogues, preaching the good news of the kingdom, and healing every disease and sickness among the people. (Matthew 4:23)

Put simply, Jesus was the very first, and possibly the best ever, proclaimer of the word outwards, gatherer of the people inwards, and launcher into the next generation onwards. He was an evangelist.

Why is it, then, that bookshops and libraries are full of Jesus books that cover every conceivable aspect of his life, but never use

[1] Rick Warren, *The Purpose-Driven Church*, Zondervan 1996, page 46.

the words 'evangelism' or 'evangelist' in their titles or even in their contents pages? Whether coming from a fairly conservative stable, with the likes of Tom Wright or James Dunn, or from the more liberal 'Jesus Seminar' of John Dominic Crossan, be they serious heavyweights or popular paperbacks, still we search in vain to see the big 'E' and the even bigger 'J' brought together.

Thinking about evangelism in the New Testament usually begins with the Acts of the Apostles. Sometimes it goes a bit further back to the sending out of the Twelve and the Seventy-two. In this version the 'Great Commission' and Pentecost are seen as the beginning of something that starts in Jerusalem and moves on towards Samaria, Antioch, Athens and Rome. Here the major personalities are Peter and Philip, Paul and Barnabas. Yet all of this is actually second- and third-phase development. The genesis and formative first steps can only be discovered when we look at Jesus himself. What was he really like? How did he frame his message? Did he have a plan? How effective was he? Or (for those who love this sort of thing) we might say we need to examine the man, the message and the methods. Only then can the Proclaimed become once again the pioneer for all subsequent proclaimers.

Thinking about evangelists

Calling Jesus an evangelist may seem a bit strange, because in the popular imagination evangelists seem to be everything that he is not. Evangelists are loud, 'in yer face', full of themselves, pushy and sometimes even aggressive. Their theology is often narrow and not well thought through, and they can often be prickly and egotistical. Jesus is a million miles away from all this. He is gentle and patient, values people as unique individuals and has a huge soft spot for the unloved and unsuccessful. Everybody loves Jesus, but who loves evangelists?

In *The Simpsons*, it is Bart's next-door neighbour Ned Flanders, an enthusiastic evangeliser, who is the most despised person in the whole show. We find something similar, though somewhat darker, in Michael Arditti's novel *Easter*. This is a serious piece of work, examining the state of Western Christianity and in particular the Church of England. Amongst a huge cast list of largely unsavoury characters, it is the evangelising bishop who stands out as the least likeable and most deranged. For one reason or another, we just do not like evangelists.[2]

Of course evangelists are odd and often difficult characters with lots of sharp edges. But the edges are crumbly and at their centre they are frequently massively insecure, driven personalities living on the frontier between church and world, success and failure. They are performers with bags of temperament, swinging in a flash from high to low, light to dark. Evangelists hardly ever turn off, it is always there. I am constantly finding myself at a football match, in a crowded shopping street or wandering round an art gallery and instead of simply enjoying the football or the pictures, my mind is consumed by the crowds and thoughts of how I could reach them.

Operating as an evangelist within Anglican structures, I keep having to field sharp accusations of 'manipulation', 'exploiting vulnerability', 'pressurising' and 'playing the numbers game'. Such talk may well derive from bad personal experiences, but I wonder how much of it comes also from a sort of blind prejudice fuelled by old-fashioned churchmanship and shallow theology.

---

[2] Michael Arditti, *Easter*, Arcadia Books 2000.

Some have such a problem with the 'E' word that they reinvent it, referring to 'my understanding of evangelism' or 'my theology of evangelism' in an *Alice in Wonderland* sort of way: 'When I use a word,' Humpty Dumpty said, in rather a scornful tone, 'it means just what I choose it to mean – neither more nor less.' Language, if it is to work as a shared system of communication and understanding, does not allow us to have our own private definitions. The words 'evangelise', 'evangelism' and 'evangelist' have already got their own meanings, which, according to the *Oxford English Dictionary*, are:

- to proclaim or preach the gospel or good news;
- to seek to convert people to Christianity;
- to imbue with the spirit of the gospel.

If, in our sophistication, we distance ourselves from evangelists and the work of evangelism, we are moving away from the values, priorities and patterns of Jesus' own ministry.

We can identify two passions in our four functions of evangelism. First, evangelists proclaim or articulate the good news. Second, following on from that, they encourage as many people as possible to believe in and live by this proclamation, to join with others and give themselves to the evangelism adventure. This is exactly what Jesus did, sharing the gospel in word and act, and calling men and women to follow him. His was an explicit rather than an implicit communication. It is virtually impossible to imagine him being content with a soft-focused, word-shunning sort of 'presence' mission. He viewed his evangelism as a loving, people-friendly, life-transforming and massively important work, and we should do the same.

The issue then is, can we begin to do it, and to do it his way? This, of course, begs the question: 'Who are the *we*?' Is Jesus-type evangelism the task of the strange individuals who are called or even employed as evangelists? Should it be the ministry, or at least part of the ministry, of all Christian leaders, be they lay or ordained? Or is it an inclusive and heavy responsibility that all Christians should pick up together? As a practising evangelist and a careful reader of the New Testament, I would want to answer 'all three', except that I would want to use the term 'huge and exciting possibility', rather than 'heavy responsibility'.

• The term 'evangelist' is used massively and everywhere in today's church, but surprisingly it appears only three times in the New Testament. Philip is described as 'the evangelist' in Acts 21:8; evangelists are mentioned in the list of ministries in Ephesians 4:11; and finally, Timothy is encouraged to 'do the work of an evangelist' in 2 Timothy 4:5. We can think of the New Testament time scale as roughly dividing into three periods: firstly, that of Jesus' ministry; secondly, the apostolic era of evangelism and church planting; and thirdly, a phase when established churches were organising their structures and patterns of ministry. It seems that it was only in this final historical period that what we think of as 'evangelists' emerged. Jesus himself never used the word. In contrast he seemed to be more interested in the 'evangel' itself and on building a movement to share the 'good news'.

Clearly, there are certain people with a whacking great 'E' in their DNA. They are supposed to have a gift, an expertise. They are there to be available to the wider church as servants, and perhaps as demonstrators and thus enablers. This strange little 'E' tribe has suffered in the recent past from being almost exclusively male. Now, however, a new generation of women evangelists are coming to the fore. Jan Harney, a colleague of mine in Manchester, is a superb example. She is just as bold and courageous as the men are supposed to be, but she also brings a strain of womanly gentleness and 'working togetherness' that male evangelists sometimes lack. Jan has a fantastic awareness of women's issues such as relationships, dress and appearance, foods and crafts, which she develops with a great sense of fun. There are lots of men who will listen more intently to, and perhaps feel a bit less got at by, a female rather than a male evangelist. The reverse is, of course, equally true, in that there are many women who prefer listening to men.

Evangelists are frontier people. They live with one foot in the church and one foot in the world, never quite fitting in or being at home in either. Many are insecure, vulnerable and easily damaged, needing lots of encouragement and affirmation. They look and sound as if they are big, tough and confident, but much of that is front. They can be hard work to live with, yet they bring something which is vital and Christ-like to the table.

- So much for evangelists. What about the great crowd of clergy, of all denominations, church leaders and full-time staff? For Anglican clergy, evangelism is part of our basic job spec., laid out for us in the Ordinal, in which we are encouraged to go out into 'the wilderness of this world and find the Father's lost children'. As such it is nothing to do with gifting or ability, but is all about vocation and the incredible opportunity that is open to us, even in our post-Christendom culture. In his *Finding Faith Today*[3] (one of the most carefully researched books on how and why people actually become Christians) John Finney states, 'The research also showed that ministers are significant not only

---

3 John Finney, *Finding Faith Today*, Bible Society 1992.

in the running and morale of the church but also in the personal lives of the people they encounter.' He then goes on to point out that of all new converts interviewed, '17% said a minister was the main factor for their becoming a Christian and no less than 43% said they were an important supporting factor.' Clergy and pastors of all denominations, those who work in Christian social, community, charity, educational and even organisational ministry, and all who are involved in local church lay leadership have a very open field in front of them. But with the opportunity comes a responsibility.

- Apart from evangelists and leaders, what about the potentially largest and most important group of would-be evangelisers, i.e. the mass (and I use that word purposefully) of all our church members? For most Christians, evangelism is a turn-off rather than a turn-on. It has become a de-skilling term which sparks off our sense of inadequacy rather than our simple, disciple-like willingness to follow and offer. It is a word that discomforts and frightens rather than invites and encourages. It is not surprising, then, that many of us, both lay and ordained, breathe a collective sigh of relief at the thought that we have not been called to this work.

For far too long our concept of 'evangelist' has been based too heavily on Paul's writings with their attendant ideas of a select group of individuals, each with a specific gift and defined ministry. Jesus seems to have operated a more open system rooted in the deep soil of shared vocation and following. While we can see that some sort of specific evangelistic ministers had emerged by the time of Paul's writings, the Gospels seem to show a simpler picture. Here the Twelve are central, and will become leaders and the essential witnesses, but the catching of fish, shining of light and scattering of the seed/word seems to rest with all of Jesus' followers. In Matthew the 'Great Commission' is given to the Eleven, but in Luke we see that the recipients of the commission and the mission-empowering Holy Spirit include the disciples and their companions (Luke 24:33). Thus, while there are certain key evangelism people, the calling applies to all Jesus' followers.

So, then, the evangelistic opportunity and ministry derive from Jesus. He did it first, and remains the best model for us to learn from. He shared his mission and his evangel with the people he evangelised, and asked them to share it with his world.

Thinking about Jesus and me

In thinking about Jesus, my first port of call will be the Synoptic Gospels, Matthew, Mark and Luke. Their overlapping stories of his works and words have a remarkable level of unity and consistency. John's Gospel adds a Greek philosophical element to the Aramaic and Hebrew thinking. Much of the shared Synoptic material is omitted by John, while new episodes are introduced, such as Jesus' meetings with Nicodemus and the woman at the well. John will therefore be a key secondary place to visit. The historical reliability of the Gospels took a real battering in the late nineteenth and twentieth centuries. Over the last twenty or so years, however, scholars have critiqued much of that approach. New work done on oral tradition and on the Gospels as written down and accurately remembered communal tradition is recasting them as reliable historical accounts which go right back to the living Jesus.

> What we today are confronted with in the gospels is not the top layer (last edition) of a series of increasingly impenetrable layers,

> but the living tradition of Christian celebration which takes us with surprising immediacy to the heart of the first memories of Jesus.[4]

Over the years, much of my thinking and working has been greatly influenced, even formed, by that of other evangelists. They, in turn, were often similarly moulded by their predecessors and betters. I am tremendously grateful for this system and for those who have had an impact on me through it, but increasingly I feel the need to go right back to the root.

Many evangelists love to use the metaphor of 'asking Jesus into our heart', which of course derives from Revelation 3:20. It is a beautiful and moving picture, and I have used it myself many times. It is, however, an essentially egotistical image and represents only half of the conversion or transformation process. The other half is about us entering into *his* heart, his hopes, plans and dreams. As evangelists, we each need to enter the very heart of Jesus' humanity, his message and his way of doing things. I want now to be shaped by the very first evangelist. I need to discover what he was like as a man, what his message was, and what methodologies he developed.

This is not a book about the theology of Jesus' incarnation, nor even the efficacy of his cross. It is about the central thread or core of his ministry as the first and greatest evangelist, an area of thought that has been too long neglected. As a working, and hopefully thinking, evangelist, I want to do two things: firstly, I want to look deeply into Jesus, who he was, what he did and how it worked; and secondly, I want to reflect on the sort of world I live in. Mine is a very different world from his. His was based around

---

4 James Dunn, *Jesus Remembered*, Eerdmans 2003.

settled agricultural and fishing communities and families; it was pre-modern, religious and generally impoverished. My world is fast and mobile, urban and affluent, gadget rich and time poor; it is postmodern, multi-cultural and shops till it drops. There is a need to bring those two worlds together – his world and my world, his experiences and mine, his ministry then and his ministry now, in me. I want to find out about Jesus the evangelist and then do it his way in my world.

Within the relativity of our time and place
We cannot move forward,
Until we have
First travelled backward.

So, before we flock to our conferences,
                                turn on to our DVDs,
                           and consult our advisors,
Let us first look back to His stories.

And, before we contextualise,
                                       strategise,
                                and revitalise,
Perhaps first we should simply now Jesus-ise.

Then, before we become so post-modern,
                                                richly-western,
                                      and stressfully-urban,
We can first be again ancient,
                             simply-eastern,
                    and peacefully-rural.

So may our sitting at His feet
be the seeing of our first steps,
      the source of our resource,
      the root of our fruit,
      the beginning of our becoming.

CHAPTER ONE

Behold the Man

'Behold the man
Look and see for yourself

Look at the face the eyes the mouth
See the life the laughter the tears
Look at the body the shoulders the feet
See the strength the poise the weariness
Behold the man'

So said the baptiser and the procurator
Like echoing bookends
One at the beginning and one at the ending.

Evangelistic people tend to be fascinated, even gripped, by two questions: 'What shall we do?' and 'What are we going to say?' The first is all about activity, strategy, plans and projects, while the second concerns our message, words and presentation. But I believe there is a third question which precedes these two and is probably more important: 'What sort of person am I going to be?' This is a question not so much about doing and communicating, but about being; as such it revolves not around 'my ministry' but around 'my me'!

Now, I am absolutely fascinated and gripped by all the speaking and doing models developed by Jesus. I want to know what he said, to whom and why. I am hungry to discover what he did, what his plan was and how well it all worked out. Yet there is a preliminary and, I think, deeper and more intriguing matter: 'What was he actually like as a person?' So, before launching into all the message and ministry issues, I want first to have a few thoughts about the man who was Jesus the evangelist.

In effect I am going to paint a picture, but in doing so I shall limit myself to just seven strokes of paint on the canvas. It certainly will not be an all-encompassing portrait of Jesus. This has already been done countless times and by much better painters/writers than me. Mine will be a fairly minimalist, impressionistic sort of work, in which I shall be trying to bring out the evangelist in Jesus. It takes one to know one.

Before beginning on the actual canvas, however, there are two massive theological ideas about Jesus as 'messiah' and 'incarnation' that we need to note briefly. By doing so we shall be creating a context, or frame, for the picture.

In calling Jesus the Messiah, we are saying that he was the long-awaited Jewish saviour, leader and transformer sent by God. He was sent to save and transform not just the Jewish nation and religion, but each individual Jewish person within it. More than this, however, Jesus came to see himself as the world-inclusive Messiah or Christ, and this universal, international view of his messiahship came to be adopted by his followers.

> The Son of Man came to seek and to save what was lost. (Luke 19:10)

> Therefore go and make disciples of all nations. (Matthew 28:19)

These are two of Jesus' most striking sayings, which spring out of his awareness of himself as 'world Messiah'.

It is very interesting to note how many of our mystical adventure tales derive from this idea of messiahship. King Arthur, Robin Hood, Peter Pan, Aslan, Frodo Baggins and Luke Skywalker all fit the same pattern. The people are oppressed, the evil is growing, some sort of supernatural help is needed, there are prophecies of a future liberator whose birth and early childhood are hidden in obscurity, and then: hey presto! The latest manifestation of the story is, of course, Harry Potter. Voldemort and his Death Eaters are a cross between Hitler and the Nazis and the devil and his demons. Harry is the long-expected messiah and the final enemy is death itself. It is not so much that Jesus fits into the pattern, but rather that he establishes it for all the others to follow.

> The Word became flesh and made his dwelling among us. (John 1:14)

This is pure incarnationalism: the glory and light, joy and laughter, music and creativity of heaven squeezed into human form. Somehow he became the 'incredible shrinking God'. Imagine a great scientist who loves cockroaches and spends his life studying them so that he can make their lives better. Eventually the scientist leaves his friends, family and life behind and becomes a cockroach himself so that he can share in and transform their lives from the inside. So Jesus, in a shocking sort of carnal way, actually became 'enfleshed', or incarnated, as a human being.

The painful reality of incarnation is brought out powerfully in Nikos Kazantzakis's novel, *The Last Temptation.*[1] There, the great tectonic plates of Jesus' humanity and divinity are continually in collision, producing tremors of doubt, loneliness and inner anguish. The collision is nowhere more grating than in his sexuality. In this section of the story, an elderly rabbi trying to help a teenage Jesus is asking the sort of direct question that we would never dare to voice.

> 'But I should like to ask you just one thing more: Jesus, have you ever slept with a woman?'
>
> 'No,' the youth answered softly.
>
> 'And you don't want to?' the old man asked once more.
>
> 'I do,' the youth answered, so softly that the rabbi could hardly hear. 'No I don't, I don't!'
>
> 'Why not?' asked the rabbi.
>
> 'It's not enough for me,' the youth said. 'I need something bigger.'

One of the most alluring stories of modern missionary incarnationalism is provided by Vincent Donovan, an American Roman Catholic missionary who worked amongst the Masai in East Africa. Having tried, unsuccessfully, to operate from within his comfort zone of the mission compound, he wrote in frustration to his bishop:

> I suddenly feel the urgent need to cast aside all theories and discussions, all efforts at strategy – and simply go to these people and do the work among them for which I came to Africa.

---

[1] Nikos Kazantzakis, *The Last Temptation*, Bantam Books 1961.

> I would propose cutting myself off from the schools and the hospital, as far as these people are concerned – as well as the socializing with them – and just go and talk to them about God and the Christian message.[2]

And that is what he did!

'Son of Man', Jesus' favourite name (or theological tag) for himself, blends together his messiahship and his incarnation. By continually referring to himself in this way, he was stressing his human ordinariness. He was describing himself as 'one of you', but he was also hinting at something else in the background. He was not just 'the man of the people', but also 'the man *for* the people', with something special and unique to give that could change the lives of all men and women.

Here, then, are two massive theological ideas. One is about offering salvation to everybody, and the other is about being part of everybody. Both are held together in Jesus' description of himself as the 'Son of Man'.

Well, so much for the picture frame; now for the seven daubs of paint.

1. Focused

> For even the Son of Man did not come to be served, but to serve, and to give his life as a ransom for many. (Mark 10:45)

Jesus was a man on a mission. He had a mission because he first had a vocation, a calling from his Father.

---

[2] Vincent Donovan, *Christianity Rediscovered*, SCM Press 1978, page 15.

A good evangelist is like an Olympic sprinter, bending down at the start of the race, attention riveted on the finishing line. This metaphor is not mine, but Gavin Reid's, who thought more and learnt more about evangelism and evangelists than most of the rest of us put together.

Focus is about knowing precisely what it is that you want to achieve, so it is all about destination, goals and objectives. Creative artists, high-achieving sports stars and successful business people all need focus. Jesus was focused up to the eyeballs. He knew why he was here and exactly what he wanted to achieve. He had vision, a tight mission statement and a crystal-clear plan.

Jesus' clear strategic plan of action began in the festival-like atmosphere of his 'springtime' Galilean ministry. Here the constant travelling, healing and proclaiming looks to have been free, spontaneous and even messy, yet we get the impression that Jesus knew what he was about, retained control and never lost himself in all the excitement. He had a conviction, an interior map and compass and even a timetable. His hands were on the steering wheel; he knew where and when he was going. The disciples probably expected things simply to keep going on in that Galilean way, with ever-larger crowds and growing acclaim, all neatly within their northern comfort zone. Suddenly, however, Jesus ended it when he 'resolutely set out for Jerusalem' (Luke 9:51). This was a sharp direction change, and it shows us a very focused man who can tear himself away from the party to follow his own road.

In the middle, or transitional, phase of the mission there were three occasions when Jesus tried to explain the 'Jerusalem and cross' plan to the disciples. They never got it. Being a focused evangelist/leader can be a very lonely place, especially if you are the only one who can read the map. He had already become isolated from his family; now he was to become disjointed from his followers. In more ways than one, he 'had nowhere to lay his head'. Perhaps he had been speaking to himself when he said, 'No one who puts his hand to the plough and looks back is fit for service in the kingdom of God' (Luke 9:62).

The final act took place in Jerusalem. Everything seems to have been prepared – instructions were given concerning donkeys and meal preparations, booby traps were knowingly entered, other people's words and betrayals were all anticipated. By this time Jesus was so focused that we can speak of him as a driven man, driven not by personal ambition or obsession, but by obedience and compassion. Towards the end, there were three opportunities to do it a different way or simply bail out altogether: in the garden, before the priests, and before Pilate. In a strange way, these opportunities balance the three temptations which had come right at the beginning (see Luke 4:1–13). In both cases he was a man who had worked it out and was focused on his destination.

Today we are increasingly (and quite rightly) being urged by the likes of Rick Warren to have purpose-driven churches and lives. I think we can use this sort of language of Jesus as the ultimate 'purpose-driven evangelist'.

The thing about being focused or purpose driven is that not only does it tell you what to do, it also tells you what not to do.

- As Jesus became increasingly successful during the early stages of his ministry, there must have been various enticing and worthwhile possibilities that opened up to him. With people coming to him from Syria and the northern Galilee towns, he could have responded with an extended healing and evangelising mission to those parts, but he didn't.

- With the great popularity that he achieved, and with growing support from a handful of wealthy and well-placed followers, he could have made a few moves aimed at bringing about more social and political justice, but he didn't. He purposefully kept away from the Roman Galilean cities with their Roman administrators such as Sephardis and Tiberias, and avoided even talking about the Romans, and whenever he got too close to Herod he moved away, thus avoiding political conflict.
- Or would it have really mattered if he had put the Jerusalem part of the plan on hold for a few years? That way he could have established deeper roots for the work, or taken it himself out to the eastern Mediterranean, rather than entrust it to others. In fact he never went to the non-Jews, even though he operated in 'Galilee of the Gentiles', and whenever he encountered them it was always they who came to him.

These were all important and potentially fruitful possibilities, yet Jesus rejected them. Why? Because he was focused. He knew what he was called to do and what he was called to leave untouched. In his ministry profile he had a focused route, not a portfolio of possibilities.

A focusing ring can work in either direction. It can be used to tighten an unfocused image, or to soften one that is too tight. Some evangelists tend more towards obsession than focus, becoming narrowly consumed by thoughts of numbers and of their own success rather than the growth of the kingdom. In contrast, there are many in leadership who are very unfocused, or whose focus excludes evangelism. William Abraham[3] highlights the danger: 'One of the undeniable features of modern theology is the scant attention it has given to the topic of evangelism.' While it concerns those who make the big decisions in dioceses and denominations, he says, 'The focus has shifted to social and political action.'

Evangelists are often very able, gifted and creative people. It is not at all unusual for one of them to launch into an effective and concentrated ministry and soon get 'noticed'. With such attention can come other opportunities, invitations and possible developments. These developments can lead to the evangelist going deeper in a focused way, or they can distort and distract and actually lead to a loss of focus. Something similar often happens with first-time clergy or church leaders. They set out with a very focused desire to grow the church through evangelism rather than transfers from other churches. The focus leads to fruitfulness, but then the success sometimes leads to a softening of that focus.

The most focused evangelist I have ever known is Daniel Cozens. Not only is he an evangelist himself, but he has led many others into the work through his 'Walk of a Thousand Men', his town-wide missions and his schools of evangelism. In his private as well as his public conversations, Daniel continually reverts to a lovely old phrase about 'saving souls'. It is a somewhat dated, and even contentious, expression to use these days (not that this seems to worry him), but it comes out of and returns to reinforce his very focused ministry.

Jesus knew exactly why he was here and what he wanted to achieve, and no one was going to make him lose focus.

---

[3] William Abraham, *The Logic of Evangelism*, Hodder & Stoughton 1989.

2. Godly

> This is my Son, whom I love; with him I am well pleased. (Matthew 3:17)

These are the words heard by Jesus at his baptism. He may literally have heard them, or he may have heard them through an inner experience of the heart. Either way they seem to represent for him a proclaiming and cementing of his relationship with God the Father. This relationship, thirty years in the making, was at the heart of everything he was as a man, and everything he attempted to achieve as an evangelist. Luke gives us a couple of glimpses into the process with the story of the boy Jesus in the temple, and with the comment:

> Jesus grew in wisdom and stature, and in favour with God and men. (Luke 2:52)

This Father-Son relationship was not like fast food, with its shallowness and sameness. It was more like a slowly cooked stew with layers of flavour, where the various elements have become softened and blended into each other. Of course, the problem with this sort of cooking is that it takes time and lots of patient waiting. Jesus and his Father waited and 'cooked' together for three decades, and at his baptism the meal was ready. Well, not quite ready: there was to be one final taste test in the form of the three temptations. Those forty days in the wilderness offered an intensive Father and Son time before the real work began. It was a harsh dedicating and denying time, described graphically by Jim Crace in his novel *Quarantine*:

> No one had said how painful it would be, how first there would be headaches and bad breath, weakness, fainting; or how the coating on the upper surface of his tongue would thicken day by day; or how his tongue would become stuck to the upper part of his mouth, held in place by gluey strings of hunger, so that he would mutter to himself or say his prayers as if his palate had been cleft at birth; or how his gums would bleed and his teeth become as loose as date stones.[4]

Jesus' relationship with his Father was about doing and serving, but deeper than that, it was also about being and knowing. This is so hard to put into words, but phrases such as 'inner fire', 'ground of being' and 'centre of knowing' spring to mind.

The Gospels repeatedly picture Jesus throughout his ministry escaping from the busyness, avoiding people, getting up early in the morning and sending away even his closest followers so that he could find himself again. He found himself in time spent with his Father.

Evangelists are notorious for their inner insecurities. Maybe that is why we try to appear so confident and successful. In our isolation we live with the constant danger of finding our personal value and self-worth in our own effectiveness. The twin demons of failure and rejection are never far away. Jesus the evangelist did not need to prove his value either to himself or anyone else. He found a quiet, deep sense of security in his relationship with his Father. Having said this, however, I am quite sure that he also welcomed and thrived on human encouragement. The two are not mutually exclusive.

Dennis Potter's famous play *Son of Man*[5] opens with Jesus repeatedly asking the question, 'Is it me? Is it me?' This is the

---

[4] Jim Crace, *Quarantine*, Penguin 1998.

[5] Dennis Potter, *Son of Man*, Deutsch 1970.

exact opposite of the Jesus we find in the Gospels, especially John with its seven great signs and 'I am' sayings. There we find a man with a very assured self-knowing, which grew out of his deep and continuous 'God-knowing'.

Not only was Jesus assured and motivated by his relationship with his Father, he seems also to have been routinely guided and equipped by him.

> The Son can do nothing by himself; he can do only what he sees his Father doing, because whatever the Father does the Son also does. (John 5:19)

John Nolland has a lovely way of describing this ongoing working relationship in his commentary on Matthew's Gospel, as he talks about Jesus entering Tyre: 'Here is yet another place for Jesus to take himself, awaiting what God has in store for him there.'[6]

Being an evangelist, then, was for Jesus, and still is for us today, a lonely place. People's huge expectations, the nagging criticism and derision of would-be companions and the evangelist's own extravagant hopes all combine to drain away confidence, enthusiasm and energy. Jesus knew he could not do it alone, depending only on his own resources. His daily relating to his Father was his umbilical cord, his oxygen tube, his food and drink. The problem is that this sort of relationship takes time – itinerancy, familiarity and trust cannot be rushed. Jesus was always short of time, and he must often have felt that he was too busy to maintain that quality of relationship. In effect, however, it was the constant clamouring needs of the people around him

---

[6] John Nolland, *The Gospel of Matthew*, Authentic Media 2005.

and his own weakness that made him realise that he was too busy *not* to maintain it.

3. A people person

Those who have an intense experience of God, and the ones with a very focused sense of purpose and mission, often share a common weakness in coping with people. People can be very demanding. They come in all different types and sizes, make demands at the worst possible times, are frequently confusing, messy and rude, and while some are attractive to look at and fun to be with, many are not. People are just too individualistic to be easily slotted into our prepared holes and projects. Put simply, they create havoc with our elegant spirituality and carefully focused and planned strategies.

Despite his deep spiritual life and rock-like focus, Jesus was a great people person. For example, I sometimes get the impression from the Gospels that every time Jesus got up in the morning and began walking down some long, purposeful road, there was a leper or blind man lurking behind a bush waiting to jump out in front of him at the most inconvenient moment. In these situations Jesus suddenly seems to have time and patience enough to stop his walking and respond. There is a warm, fleshy humanity to his spirituality and focused drivenness. Even when he needs to get away, he can still relate with compassion to demanding, messy people (Matthew 14:14).

Matthew's Gospel gives three instances of the disciples trying to protect a tired and under-pressure Jesus from demanding people: first a hungry, thirsty crowd (14:15), then a bereaved, shrieking mother (15:23), and finally some noisy children (19:13). In each case he rejects the well-meaning protection of the disciples and insists on making contact with these demanding folk.

So much for the 'people person' evangelist in one-off encounters. We can also get glimpses of Jesus in long-term relationships when we look at him with his family, followers and friends.

- The people who seemed to get the worst deal from Jesus were his *family*, which during his adult years probably consisted of his mother, four brothers and an unspecified number of sisters, all younger than him. During the Galilean period they show a caring family attitude of wanting to be close and, where necessary, protective. In contrast, he seems to want to keep his distance. He is a bit harsh to his mother at the wedding in Cana, and cold-shoulders the whole family when they come looking for him.

> Whoever does God's will is my brother and sister and mother. (Mark 3:35)

Perhaps this reflects a frustration that his family was somehow getting in the way, making too many domestic demands on him and not realising what he was all about. By the end, however, it seems that they are among his closest followers. We are left at the cross with a heartbreaking picture of a mother and aunt united in grief, and of a special friend brought in to fill the gap.

> He said to his mother, 'Dear woman, here is your son,' and to the disciple, 'Here is your mother.' (John 19:26)

- For his *followers*, Jesus had a magnetic attraction. He first meets Andrew and Peter, James and John, Philip and Nathaniel. When he beckons, all thought of practicalities and human responsibilities go out of the window as they come to him, like well-trained gun dogs. Even the more worldly-wise and cynical Levi, when invited – or perhaps we should say summoned – to follow Jesus, does just as he is bidden. Boats and nets, families and friends, money and reputation are all left behind. It seems that not only did Jesus like people, but people also liked him. Maybe he just had an 'aura' about him. Or was it that he could see deep into a person's soul and draw them in? Perhaps he was just a compelling and charismatic personality. These followers stuck with him, even when they did not like where he was going, and when they let him down they were still drawn back to following.

- Over years of mixing with evangelists, I have noticed a fairly common phenomenon. Most of them are exceptionally warm and attractive and so have lots of *friends*, but they often have one or two specially trusted intimates on whom they can rely and with whom they can relax. These are usually individuals whom they themselves brought to faith. I wonder if we see something similar in Jesus' life. He was known as the 'friend of sinners' and treated everyone who accepted his commands as a friend (John 15:14). Yet within this great circle of friends, there was the 'disciple he loved', James and Peter, Mary, Martha and Lazarus and Mary Magdalene. Even in the despair of Gethsemane we find Jesus referring to Judas as a 'friend' (Matthew 26:50). How tragically ironic, then, that he greeted him with the ultimate sign of intimacy, a kiss. The whole scene of friends falling asleep on him when he needed them, betraying and eventually denying him brings to mind his earlier words about laying down his life for his friends.

As a faithful and pious Jew, Jesus was an insider, but he loved moving amongst people on the outside. Sinners and sinned against, the unclean and the unwanted, tax-collectors and terrorists, prostitutes and publicans, lepers and liars, the blind and the beggars, adulterers and adulterated – they are all there. Together they form a great big Hieronymus Bosch-style painting of Jesus and the ones who 'heard him gladly', with occasionally a different sort of face in the crowd, a rich woman, an influential man such as Joseph of Arimathea, or even a supportive Pharisee.

The novelist Marianne Fredriksson has written an intriguing story called *According to Mary Magdalene*, in which she offers a possible clue to Jesus' people skills: '"Jesus never judged," whispered Mary. "He judged no one, neither publicans, whores, nor other wretches."'[7]

A friend of mine recently turned up at his local parish church in Leeds to be told by a well-meaning but rather insensitive minister that he could not combine being a Christian with being a member of the BNP (British National Party). Of course we all know what he was getting at, but we also know what Jesus was getting at when he put people before principles.

Jesus was essentially non-judgemental. He accepted people as they were, as the 'birds of the air' (Matthew 13:32). Part of his good news was to say, 'Come to me' (Matthew 11:28). So maybe today we should stop being so judgemental and become more freely welcoming to everyone. Maybe we need to drop our obsessions with sex and with political correctness, and stop looking down on people who smoke and swear and play the horses. It is about simply welcoming everyone, even the ones we

---

[7] Marianne Fredriksson, *According to Mary Magdalene*, Hampton Roads 1999.

do not like; in fact, especially the ones we do not like. While we are at it, we might even relax our ridiculously precious and protective attitudes to our worship and liturgy and simply put people first. (The practice of putting our preferred shape, music and style of worship before people is, of course, common to all traditions and applies as much to recent groupings such as Taizé, Greenbelt and Soul Survivor as it does to more ancient patterns and traditions.)

4. Realist

'Tremendous', 'awesome', 'fantastic', 'great blessing', 'lots of people', 'huge response'. Today's evangelism trade is drunk on its own success stories. Magazine articles, prayer letters and sharing accounts are loaded with superlatives and glossy adjectives. The result is that 'celebrity evangelists' are often made to look far more successful than they actually are, while the 'less exalted' are made to feel somehow not quite as effective.

Expectation, vision, hunger and goals are all essential for evangelists, as they are for anyone who actually wants to achieve something in this life, but 'big' does not necessarily mean 'best'. Faith can easily slip over into fantasy. Our hopes and dreams, aims and objectives should be difficult to attain. They should take us out of our comfort zone and demand everything that we have plus the grace and provision of God, but they should also be realistic. Realistic expectation does not mean reduced expectation, but it does mean living in the real world. Jesus was full of hope and expectancy, he had great aims and objectives, but he was a solid, feet-on-the-ground realist. As the incarnate Son of God, he lived here in the real world rather than on some spiritual fantasy island.

In contrast to many contemporary evangelists, Jesus achieved modest results and was all too familiar with apparent failure. In fact, he seemed to expect most people to walk away and give up on him. The parable of the sower, in which the majority of men and women who are touched by the scattered seed fail to bear lasting fruit, is the utterance of a supreme realist. It is not that he doubted the power of the seed-like word, or his own effectiveness as an evangelist, but rather that he knew what real people are like. Jesus understood, and never underplayed, the shallow fickleness and self-centredness of the human heart. Similarly, when the gospel was thriving and the kingdom was being established like a great field of golden wheat, he anticipated that there would be plenty of weeds growing amongst that wheat. He realised and expected that even with the best of prayerful planning and preparation, some things would go wrong. Jesus was not, in the modern sense of the word, an enthusiastic 'revivalist', but rather an evangelistic realist.

Evangelists love to see large numbers of people. It excites us and gets all our juices running. For us, the crowd is our muse but it can easily become the drug which fuels our 'ministerial trip'. I am convinced that Jesus himself, as a full-blooded male evangelist, must have felt some of this heady cocktail of crowd excitement and ego-burst in the days of his people-pulling Galilean ministry. His reputation as a prophetic preacher, healer and exorcist attracted huge numbers of people, some of whom came from as far away as Jerusalem to the south and Syria to the north. Meetings were held out in the open when houses and synagogues were not big enough. This whole fast-flowing mass movement came to a climax with the huge feedings of first five thousand and then four thousand hungry souls. Yet Jesus never allowed himself to get too carried away by all this. His feet were always firmly planted on solid ground and in the real world; he knew all about thin soils, rising suns and rival interests. He realised that the crowds crying for him to be crowned would one day call for him to be crucified. He provided his own honest assessment of it all with his deep and penetrative questioning of Peter and the Twelve:

> You do not want to leave too, do you? (John 6:67)

On the surface it all looked like a massive revival, but underneath things were quite different.

Realism is not the same as negativity. The parables of the sower and the wheat and tares, which are grouped with the parable of the mustard seed in Matthew and the growing seed in Mark, are essentially stories of triumphant but painful and interrupted growth. There are disappointments and problems, but still there is growth. All of this provides much food for thought for those – and there are many, especially in the historic denominations – who have bought into the 'continuous decline of the church' hypothesis. Jesus' realistic vision for the whole gospel, kingdom and future church enterprise is one of gradual and painfully successful growth.

Jesus' realism meant that he had a fairly low expectancy level from big crowds, but a correspondingly high valuation of individuals. At the heart of Luke's Gospel there are three 'lost and found' parables grouped together (15:3–32). First a sheep, then a coin and finally a son all point to the importance of a 'single sinner who repents'. To Jesus the evangelist, a single follower was supremely important. That was why he put so much energy into holding, developing and nurturing them. 'I have not lost one of those you gave me' (John 18:9).

There is a see-saw here, with individuals on one end and crowds on the other, and the trick is to find the right balance. If we are looking all the time for big number impact, then we tend to lose sight of the individual. However, if we just think of individuals, then we can easily lose the hunger and the opportunities to 'haul in numbers of fish'. Like all good evangelists, Jesus would have had an eye open for the crowd, but a listening ear for the individual searcher. He would have hoped for many, but joyfully accepted fewer.

5. Life-affirmer

I suspect it would be almost impossible to count and categorise the whole of Western art and work out who is the most painted person of all time. If it were possible, then my money would be on Jesus. This leads to a fascinating conundrum, because although no one actually knows what he looked like, his is still the most immediately recognised face in the whole of human history. Despite having all these thousands of faces of Jesus that have been painted, drawn, sculpted and latterly 'PowerPointed', there is still one that is missing. We have lots of baby Jesuses and just as many of him on the cross; we have serious, spiritual and strong Jesuses, Jesus the lover of animals and children, Jesus the healer and the mystic. What we do not have so much of, however, is Jesus at the party, and we certainly do not have a great belly-laughing and joy-exuding Jesus.

Our 'painted' Jesus is good, sinless, loving, holy and self-denying, but he is not exactly a lot of fun to be with. He is not a life-affirmer and celebrator, which is very much what he is in the Gospel accounts. There his first preaching creates a wave of gladness amongst the common people, while his first miracle in John's Gospel turns gallons of water into top-quality wine so that the wedding festivities can go with a real swing. His greatest story, about the 'prodigal son', shows us a father who (in the words of the Authorised Version) 'makes merry' and throws an all-singing, all-dancing party to welcome home his lost child. Still in the feasting mood, his picture of heaven is one of a great banquet or party to which many undeserving people are invited. My own church, the Church of England, has adopted this imagery in much of its liturgical revision in recent years. Now we have 'celebrations' of the Eucharist at which the presiding priest is a 'celebrant'. We have the language, but we are not quite there yet with the mood or the experience – somehow it still does not actually feel like a party.

For the evangelising Jesus, one of his most creative areas of ministry was that of sitting and eating with people, to such an extent that the scribes and Pharisees described him as a glutton and a drunkard (Luke 7:34). For those of us brought up in a post-Victorian, respectable and very English Christianity, this is a shocking picture, and perhaps that is why it is rarely mentioned. Just as shocking is the questioning brought by those who had clearly been impressed by the fasting both of the Pharisees' disciples and those of John the Baptist (Luke 5:33). Why, they asked, did Jesus' own disciples never fast? He answered them by talking about the celebratory mood of an ongoing wedding.

The picture emerges of an evangelist who is keen to be part of ordinary life, who is pure without being puritanical, who is accepting rather than accusing, and who is full, rather than fearful, of life.

I have come that they may have life, and have it to the full. (John 10:10)

Bishop John Finney is one of the clearest thinkers and writers on the contemporary evangelism scene. He has described how the best evangelists are both unusual and special, while also being normal, life-affirming and of this world. If evangelists are just unusual, then they can become too religious and freaky, but if they are simply this-life-affirming, then they have nothing special to offer.

Now here is a very odd thought, but possibly a helpful one. Whenever anyone mentions the word 'evangelist', the first name that comes to mind is that of Billy Graham. Quite right too, for he has been one of the most effective and also one of the most faithful and devout of all mass evangelists. There is much for all of us to learn from and emulate in him. But just think for a moment of another Billy. Think laughter, warmth, humanity, celebration. Think profound thoughts and penetrative analysis of the pain of human living, all expressed in a light and memorable manner. Think humour and pathos mixed together. Think Billy Connolly! Maybe Jesus was somewhere between the two.

Nikos Kazantzakis was a strong and very spiritually minded writer, best known for his novels *Zorba the Greek* and *The Last Temptation.* In his autobiographical *Report to Greco,*[8] he describes his upbringing within what he terms as the permanent Good Friday darkness and winter of Greek Orthodoxy. He needed to break through this constant gloom and discover the colour and warmth of a springtime resurrection faith. This is powerful testimony pointing to a spirituality which is not just peaceful, deep and meaningful, but also large and lively, full and free, life-affirming and life-enhancing. As an evangelist, I find much in Kazantzakis that resonates with the life-affirming Jesus,

[8] Nikos Kazantzakis, *Report to Greco*, Bruno Cassirer 1965.

and it forces me to think about the shape of Christianity that I am both living and trying to share with others.

Traditionally, to become a very committed evangelical convert has meant giving up worldly things. You know the sort of thing: drink, make-up, smoking and cards were all seen as tricks of the devil. What would it look like if, instead of cutting things out, we encouraged converts to put more in – to live bigger, laugh more, have serious bouts of holy raucousness and attend late-night gatherings of combined prayer and partying? Or what about visiting an English cathedral, which feels like some ancient, slightly spiritual library, with hushed voices, medieval music and cold faces? Just suppose there could be a really warm welcome from young as well as old faces, a bustling café in a side aisle rather than tucked away in a distant visitor centre, and suppose there was lively and attractive art and music and children's activities. What if there was a Westernised, incarnational, contemporary and life-affirming icon with a great big smiling golden face?

The word 'joy' is mentioned twenty-three times in the Gospels, and often it is of the leaping variety. In each case the joy comes when people either meet with or receive the words of Jesus, or both. My favourite story is that of the pregnant Mary going to meet the even more pregnant (and soon to be mother of John the Baptist) Elizabeth. When Mary arrives, Elizabeth declares that the child in her womb 'leaped for joy' (Luke 1:44). Throughout his life, this was the sort of impact that Jesus the life-affirming evangelist would have on people.

6. Self-sacrificer

Jesus was a giver. It was not just in his nature, but also part of his nurture, preparation and ministry formation. His commitment to self-sacrifice was part of his self-knowledge and sense of destiny. Continually he chose to overcome his own wilful desires and ego and to renew his decision to give himself to others. As a normal man who denied himself so many of life's normal pleasures, each day must have been a fresh 'giving away'. As a God incarnate in human flesh, every night was surely a small dying.

Ultimately we see the supreme self-sacrifice in his death on the cross. Here Calvary becomes an open-air temple and the cross an altar, a butcher's slab. The whole story was brought visually and barbarically to life in the film *The Passion of the Christ.* There every conceivable part of Jesus' body is beaten and battered, a blood sacrifice on a grand scale. Yet all we really see in the film is the outer wall of his physical sufferings. The centre is missing. The Palm Sunday rejection by his own people, the falling asleep of his closest friends, Judas's kiss and Peter's denial all lead us down an interior passageway. Only when we hear the despairing cry, 'My God, my God, why have you forsaken me?' are we truly at the central heart of the cross. There Jesus is totally alone and plunging into a black hole of nothingness. Even here, however, we see Jesus having a caring concern for the women of Jerusalem and their children, and for the two thieves (Luke 23:28, 43).

Jesus had known about the cross long before he actually got to it, as if it cast a shadow not behind, but in front of itself. He had plenty of time to prepare for it, but also to learn to fear it. On three occasions he tried to share it with his disciples, but they never understood. His was to be a very lone sacrifice. The whole thing is beautifully and symbolically captured in 'The Bound Lamb', a seventeenth-century painting by Francisco de Zurbaran. The lamb is Jesus, the Agnus Dei, lying as a warm, alive and vulnerable creature on a cold grey slab of stone. The lamb's eyes express both knowing and acceptance, its horns are turned down, there is no resistance. The surrounding darkness emphasises its pure white isolation as it awaits the knife.

We who are full-time evangelists have to be careful and honest with ourselves when it comes to this concept of self-sacrifice. We start out with a huge sense of sacrificial living, but we grow older and more comfortable. We pick up some finance and possessions along the way and establish ourselves in a middle-class lifestyle. We get used to people treating us as a minor spiritual celebrity – in fact, we quite enjoy it. We are experts at talking about the cross, but struggle to walk our own talk. We use it to stir a deep emotional response in others, but can develop quite a careless familiarity with it ourselves. We grow accustomed to others giving their money to our work, running around doing the less glamorous tasks and putting in lengthy and demanding hours. The calling for evangelists is not just to talk about the cross, but to attempt to live it as well. In terms of sacrifice, Jesus was the real deal. It touched every part of his life, every day of his life. His self-offering was not just a proclamation, but an incarnation and finally an incineration.

7. Intolerant

The words 'intolerant' and 'Jesus' do not fit well together – unsurprisingly, because he was one of the most accepting, inclusive, understanding and tolerant of people. There was one major exception, however. Like a great reforming prophet, he was intolerant of the hardness, double standards and central emptiness of the religious establishment of his day. He ruthlessly exposed its shortcomings and predicted judgement and destruction if it did not change.

Matthew's Gospel in particular shows us a Jesus whose first missionary intention was to evangelise, or re-evangelise, the Jews, God's special people. Thus when he sends out the Twelve, he tells them to ignore the Gentiles and Samaritans and go only to 'the lost sheep of Israel' (Matthew 10:5–6). When a non-Jewish Canaanite woman asks him to heal her daughter, he responds with the words, 'It is not right to take the children's bread and toss it to their dogs' (Matthew 15:26). He clearly avoids the Gentile cities of the Galilee and works all the time in the Jewish towns and villages, feels deep frustration at their failure to respond, and picks out Chorazin, Bethsaida and Capernaum as particularly disappointing situations (Matthew 11:20). The entire religious institution is condemned as being fruitless in his cursing of the fig-tree (Matthew 21:19), and is summed up as being so much old wine and old wineskins (Matthew 9:17).

Jesus' prophetic evangelising zeal and the unresponsive toughness that it came up against settled around three key issues, which gradually emerged as battlefields.

- The first of these surrounded the endlessly detailed laws and by-laws of Judaism, and especially those involving food, hygiene and the Sabbath. It was not so much that Jesus rejected these regulations, but rather that he was operating on a different level. He was more interested in purifying the heart than protecting it from impure foods; he wanted to wash a person inside rather than outside; and he saw the Sabbath as a time for healing and helping.
- The second area of confrontation surrounded the key personnel of the scribes and Pharisees. The conflict began as a simmer and gradually built up to boiling point when he

denounced them as hypocrites, snakes, white-washed tombs, blind guides and impersonal proselytisers. This was intolerance let rip; there could be no turning back.

- The third and climactic battleground was the city of Jerusalem, 'you who kill the prophets' (Matthew 23:37), and its great temple. Together they formed the political, economic and religious powerhouse at the centre of Judea as a province and Judaism as a religion. It was Jerusalem, with its politicians and priests, that kept the top people on top and the poor at the bottom. Jesus' Palm Sunday entrance, his cleansing of the temple and his prediction of its destruction all put him onto a high-velocity collision course with this nest of power cliques.

At the heart of all this conflict there was the passion of Jesus the evangelist, a passion for the transformation of individual lives and for a religion that should have put God and people first and itself second. The more passionate you are, the more frustrated you get. The bigger your vision, the smaller your tolerance level for petty religious formalities. The more you want it, the less willing you are to go on putting up with everything that prevents it.

Intolerance of organised religion runs like a red thread through the history of Western civilisation, from Dante to Trollope, from Luther to Voltaire. Today's great 'intolerant of all things religious' is arguably Philip Pullman. The *His Dark Materials* trilogy seems to want to blame the Christian church for everything that is wrong in the world. It is clear from this and from his numerous interviews that he just does not like the church and many of its people. There are, however, two main differences between his and Jesus' intolerance. Firstly, Jesus was far more outspoken, unrelenting and provocative in his comments. Secondly, Jesus was a dedicated insider. He loved the Pharisees and sighed deeply for them (Mark 8:11); he had enjoyed his times ministering in the local village synagogues; he made sure that the disciples paid their temple tax. He loved the whole of Jerusalem with its temple and priests so much that he had wanted to gather them in a motherly way, but they had refused him.

> How often I have longed to gather your children together, as a hen gathers her chicks under her wings, but you were not willing. (Matthew 23:37)

It was because he was a dedicated insider that it hurt him so much.

Churches, traditions and religious institutions are easy targets, and it is too simplistic to equate them with the Judaism of Jesus' time. Today the historic denominations and the new churches, which are remarkably like them, are struggling valiantly to be Jesus-friendly rather than Jesus-resistant. They are praying, working and giving to extend his kingdom, not to oppose it. Nevertheless, they can and do become too formal and rule-bound; too obsessed with buildings and bureaucracy; too in love with the external instead of the internal. Their liturgies, culture and language can easily become an in-house style that outsiders have to fit into, rather than an outgoing and welcoming way of life.

Evangelism people are often frustrated and intolerant. Much of this discomfort is something we share with Jesus, but some of it is all our own. Standing as we do on the edge between church and world, we regularly see things that are wrong, yet they are usually not as wrong as we think they are. The church needs its evangelists' eyes, and evangelists also need the church. Jesus never allowed himself to become bitter and cynical. His was the intolerance of a committed and loving insider.

There it is: seven splashes of paint, one face. I could add more, but seven is a good number. I realise, of course, that there is a lot missing, simply left unsaid. There is nothing about Jesus' nobility of spirit, nor about his naïve generosity, nothing about his loneliness, patience, long-suffering and sheer dogged inner toughness. I was tempted to write about him as a northerner attacking the north-south divide, but then I thought that as a Yorkshireman I might be pushing my luck. So there is plenty of bare canvas for others to fill in the gaps. Some of my paint marks have a very modern feel to them. I suspect that in Jesus' day people did not talk much about focus, realism or tolerance, but then I am trying to do it his way in my world. My portrait is very impressionistic, even angular – not so much a Rembrandt, more a Picasso. It probably says as much about the one holding the brush as it does about the one who is the subject of it, but that is one of the important things about painting.

We evangelists love words, presentations, projects and plans, and for all the right reasons. We do need to keep remembering, however, that the gospel is first and foremost not a message that is declared, nor a strategy that is launched, but a life that is lived.

So let us
Behold this focused man
Be inspired by his Godliness
Befriend the people person
Become as realistic as him

Breathe in that life affirmation
Begin to live his self-sacrifice
Bear allegiance to the intolerance
And
Be in love with
Jesus the Evangelist.

CHAPTER TWO

Believe the Message

Words, holy and sacred
Coming from a begotten voice
        from behind the horizon
        from before our time
        from beyond our place

Quiet, then loud then quiet again,
Still, then rushed then still once more.

A message, that I hear because I need it,
A story, that I listen to and believe in
A hope, that I turn towards and welcome into my guarded inner self.

And now it is me being quiet, then loud then quiet,
Me being still then rushing then still again,
My lips, his voice
My sounds, his words
My talk, his gospel.

Jesus was a word person. Matthew, Mark and Luke talk about his first appearance on the Galilee stage, proclaiming and teaching, while John's Gospel actually labels him as 'the Word'. He was also, of course, a healer and exorcist, a listener and people worker, but essentially and foundationally he was a message communicator using words as his raw material.

> I must preach the good news of the kingdom of God to the other towns also, because that was why I was sent. (Luke 4:43)

Evangelists are first and foremost verbalisers. We are the broadcasters of the good news. For most of us, the easiest and most efficient way to receive and understand the news is through word-based media. We find diagrams, symbols, pictures and events all helpful as illustrations of that which is most clearly and precisely communicated in words.

So why is everyone in the church so against words these days? Are we embarrassed by our words? Have we lost confidence in them? Are we less sure of their exclusive and special truthfulness? Do we think they are probably not that powerful after all? Or are we simply frightened of boring people to death, rather than bringing them to life? The 'word-based' ministry has been internally and massively undermined in the church in recent years.

'Mere words' are almost despised as being of little practical help. Worship songs, rituals and extensive liturgies dominate. Pictures are deemed to say far more, when in fact they do not say anything – that is the point of them, they picture things. This is not to say that we do not want pictures. I suspect all of us sometimes reach a point where we would agree with Alice:

'And what is the use of a book, without pictures or conversations?'[1] So by all means let's have pictures – to accompany words, not replace them. Today proclamation has become presentation. Preaching is turned into mere talking. Sermons are shrunk into homilies.

I was recently told at a gathering of clergy, theologians and grant-making bodies that in inner-city areas community projects run by the church are gospel proclamations. Now, of course hands-on work in poor and deprived areas is a vital part of the gospel work of Jesus, and opens channels through which love, justice and healing can flow, but such work is not a proclamation. Works of love supplement words of love, but they do not substitute for them. Gospel actions do not make gospel announcements redundant, they make them redoubtable.

Michael Frayn is part of a loose grouping of atheistic writers including Richard Dawkins and Christopher Hitchens who are clearly determined to attack the idea of faith, the God of faith and the people who have faith in him. Frayn is dismissive of modern-day Christians and their 'word shyness':

> But it is embarrassing to the religious as well. They tend to maintain a decent discretion about their beliefs, as people do (or did) about their sexual feelings, which makes it possible for us all to get along socially. If they are obliged to talk about them they find it difficult to look you in the eye. Or if they do it's with a special fixity and determination which is intended to conceal their unease.[2]

---

1 Lewis Carroll, *Alice's Adventures in Wonderland.*

2 Michael Frayn, *The Human Touch*, Faber & Faber 2007, page 264.

John's Gospel establishes 'the Word' as the beginning, foundation and spinal cord of the Jesus experience.

> In the beginning was the Word, and the Word was with God, and the Word was God. (John 1:1)

In his classic text *Faust*, Goethe questions this high concept of 'the Word':

> Tis writ, 'In the beginning was the Word.'
> I pause, to wonder what is here inferred.
> The Word I cannot set supremely high:
> A new translation I will try.

Faust's rejection of 'the Word' would certainly meet with much approval today, but was he right? In his 'new translation' he replaces 'the Word' first with 'the Thought', then with 'the Power', and finally he tries 'the Deed'. None of these seem to work, however. None of them are big enough. John's vision of 'the Word' encompasses all three but includes an extra element. The evangelising words of Jesus were in effect thought, power and deed plus communication, the divine voice speaking into our human ears.

All the words that Jesus ever used came within a great big envelope. On the outside of the envelope, written in big block capitals, it said simply GOOD NEWS. But this was not the domesticated version of the 'good news' that we have often produced, a sort of 'Have a nice life and cuddle up to Jesus'. No, the 'good news' of Jesus was the world-changing 'gospel'. Pope Benedict sees the proclamation of 'gospel' as being characteristic of the whole of Jesus' early ministry and traces the concept back to the announcements made by Roman emperors:

> What the emperors, who pretend to be gods, illegitimately claim, really occurs here – a message endowed with plenary authority, a message that is not just talk, but reality. In the vocabulary of contemporary linguistic theory, we should say that the *euangelium*, the Gospel, is not just informative speech, but performative speech – not just the imparting of information, but action, efficacious power that enters into the world to save and transform.[3]

'Preach the gospel, use words if you have to.' This statement, attributed to St Francis, is regularly thrown at me, usually by those who are searching for some kind of get-out clause. So you can imagine how surprised I was on visiting Assisi to discover that there Francis is remembered and revered first and foremost as a preacher and proclaimer, as a coiner and broadcaster of words. Evangelists and Christian leaders and workers who do not like words are in the wrong job. They are like dentists who have fallen out of love with teeth, or vegetarian butchers.

Of course we all know how words can be misused to manipulate and exploit. We have experienced them being turned into over-long, tedious, boring and soul-numbing sermons. But non-use is not the answer to wrong use.

Wonderful, alive and inspiring words were at the heart of the apostolic mission to the Mediterranean world. They were the banners of the great Celtic and Saxon crusades, the pearls in the revivalist movements of the friars and monks, the Puritans and Baptists, the Methodists and Ranters. They were used to end the slave trade, bring the children out of the mines and spread a new kind of caring socialist politics. Gospel words are full of hope and excitement. They are pregnant with life and longing to give

3 Joseph Ratzinger (Pope Benedict XVI), *Jesus of Nazareth*, Doubleday 2007, page 47.

birth, they are explosive seed pods bursting with potential and organic fertility. Jesus' words were characterised as 'good news'. The people who heard them recognised powerful authority and were filled with joy.

Given, then, that Jesus the evangelist was a word person, are there ways in which those involved in evangelism today can emulate or even reproduce both the content and the manner of his messaging?

My first exploits as a practising evangelist happened when I was still a new Christian. I had joined a group of young, enthusiastic and naïve believers. Together we ran a sort of evangelistic coffee-bar-cum-youth-club every Saturday night in the Yorkshire city of Bradford. Week by week, a crowd of teenagers would turn up and fill our simple two-roomed church hall. They were a pretty intimidating bunch, made up largely of the leather jacket brigade and skinheads. My job was to stand in the doorway between the two rooms when the music was turned off for five minutes and attempt to belt out some sort of meaningful gospel talk. I was unschooled and fairly unsuccessful, but we all have to begin somewhere.

Several years later, as a young curate, I was called upon to give my first proper set-piece evangelistic talk on a Christian youth holiday. This was a much grander affair than my earlier exploits. I was expected to deliver a forty-minute address, at the end of which there had to be an invitation for people to become Christians. So how was I to frame my message? Sadly the thought of attempting to model myself on Jesus the evangelist never entered my head. Instead I tried to reproduce the sort of evangelistic talk that I myself had heard on numerous occasions. Without realising it at the time, I was in effect following a sort of standard formula, which ran something like this:

- Tell everyone that they are sinners.
- Point out that sin is not just a big thing like murder, but includes everyday incidents such as stealing apples.
- Show that all sinners are judged guilty by God and die.
- Make it clear that doing good things such as helping old ladies across the road or going to church never makes up for our sins. (It never occurred to me at the time that I had never actually helped a single old lady across a road; nor, for that matter, had I ever stolen any apples.)
- Talk about Jesus as the only sinless person.
- Carefully explain how Jesus' death on the cross substitutes for our death and can take away our sin. This would usually involve the use of a diagram of a rift valley, with Jesus appearing as a little stick man and building a cross-like bridge from one side to the other.
- Call upon anyone who has not already done so to repent, believe and ask Jesus into their heart.

In one respect, this is not such a bad or misleading presentation. It contains much of the vital Christian understanding which can be gleaned from reading the New Testament, and it has certainly been a great help to me, and millions like me. It has been about two hundred and fifty years in the making. It started with the eighteenth-century evangelists such as George Whitefield and the Wesleys, was honed by Victorian evangelical reformers of the William Booth variety, refined by the great North American evangelistic combination of Moody and Sankey, and is still used by the likes of Billy Graham, Luis Palau and a thousand others. It is, however, rather formulaic and narrow, and often does not begin from where most people feel themselves to be or relate to their life experience. Most surprising of all, as I discovered later, it is not a formula or message that Jesus himself ever seems to have used. He did not harangue people about their own personal sin and guilt, but preferred to talk about their needs and illnesses. Neither do we read of him giving lengthy and theoretical explanations of how the cross works for sinners. Instead he seems to emphasise his coming and finding of the lost.

Every generation stands on the shoulders of the previous ones. I do not want to dispose of the work and traditions of my evangelising forefathers, but in recent years I have tried in my evangelistic preaching to go right back to the first evangelist.

So far so good: who can argue with the intention of trying to copy Jesus? The big problem is that the Gospels do not record word for word any of the evangelistic-type talks that Jesus gave. They give us partial patterns and summaries: 'Jesus went throughout Galilee, teaching in their synagogues, preaching the good news of the kingdom' (Matthew 4:23). They provide us with a few key words or terms: 'good news', 'kingdom', 'repent', and 'follow'. Somehow we need to pull together all these pieces and model our contemporary message accordingly. First, however, we must try to grasp an overview of the entirety of Jesus' ministry of the word.

Jesus' ministry of the word

The ministry of Jesus can be separated chronologically into three phases:

- *The 'Galilean springtime'.* This is his early period, during which he wanders around from town to village amongst the Jews who live in the Galilee. There are occasional journeys out to Tyre, Caesarea Philippi and the towns of the Decapolis, etc. His ministry combines preaching with healing and exorcism, and the crowds roll up.

- *The transitional middle period.* Jesus leaves the Galilee, and 'resolutely set[s] out for Jerusalem'. The festival mood is left behind, he is increasingly conscious of the cross, and the tensions mount. Mark devotes just one chapter to this middle phase, and Matthew two. In contrast, it forms a major section in Luke, running from chapters 9 to 19.
- *Jerusalem, and the third and final phase.* A fast-moving week leading up to the crucifixion, during which Jesus lives in a safe house just outside the city and travels in daily. He first cleanses and then occupies the temple for his great final week of teachings and prophetic oracles. After the resurrection he seems to have been active and very mobile, but, for understandable reasons, it is a bit difficult to pin him down.

John's Gospel has a different shape and timescale from the other three. He describes Jesus as making a series of visits, perhaps as many as five, to Jerusalem, at different points in his ministry.

This chronological division into three periods is a well-trodden path. Less familiar perhaps is the suggestion that if we look at all of Jesus' public verbal utterances, first in the Synoptics and then in John's Gospel, we can classify them into three main types or categories, i.e. proclamation, teaching and disputation. These are certainly not watertight compartments. Sometimes Jesus would slip from one to the other: for example, a dispute with the Pharisees and scribes became an opportunity to teach the crowds (Matthew 15:1–20). Similarly, the distinction between proclamation and teaching should be seen as a very open frontier.

Nevertheless, I think this classification is valid and can help us to understand both the content and the process of Jesus' public 'word' ministry.

Proclamation

Matthew and Mark both picture Jesus' mission as breaking into the Galilee like an egg into the pan, with a bright yellow yoke of proclamation. 'After John was put in prison, Jesus went into Galilee, proclaiming the good news of God' (Mark 1:14). Luke, in contrast, has a less dramatic description of Jesus teaching in the synagogues (Luke 4:15). The Gospels use three different words to describe this 'ice-breaking' aspect of Jesus' initial impact: *euangelizesthai* means 'to preach good tidings'; *katangellein* means 'to declare or announce'; and *kerussein* is all about proclaiming something as a herald. The central and common idea behind all three is that good news is being announced to people who have never heard it before. This concept of proclaiming, calling out, announcing and declaring is repeatedly used to describe or characterise Jesus' wandering ministry in its earliest phase. It marks the beginning of a subtle distinction, which continues right through the New Testament, between proclaiming or preaching the gospel message (*kerygma*) and teaching the gospel lifestyle (*didache*).

Not only do we see Jesus proclaiming, but we also see him recruiting and sending out the Twelve, the Seventy-two, and even the Gadarene demoniac, to do likewise. Sometimes the proclaiming is linked to teaching (Matthew 4:23), but often it stands alone. Typically it happens alongside healings and exorcisms, but it looks very much as if the proclaiming is the key part of the triangle.

There is a remarkably clear pattern to the use of the word 'proclamation' in the Synoptic Gospels. It occurs seventeen times during the Galilean phase and four times right at the end of the story, as Jesus looks ahead to the post-resurrection period of the apostolic church. Once Jesus left the Galilee behind, the proclaiming was increasingly replaced by teaching and disputation.

There is something piercingly dramatic, fresh and incisive in the trumpet call of the proclamation. We shall return to it later, for here is the very kernel of Jesus' evangelism.

Teaching

Jesus taught in the synagogues, in private homes, out in the fields, by the lakeside, up mountains, on the road and ultimately in the temple, the most important and politically powerful space or platform anywhere in Judea or within Judaism. Sometimes he taught the crowd and at other times he was keen to give extra and deeper teachings to the disciples. The interesting thing about these extra sessions is that even when the disciples do not quite understand, they still make an effort to remember, as if they realise the importance and weight of Jesus' words (Matthew 13:36).

According to Luke, Jesus began his teaching and learning career (the two go well together) as a young boy in the temple, and continued it right through to beyond his resurrection: 'They asked each other, "Were not our hearts burning within us while he talked with us on the road and opened the Scriptures to us?"' (Luke 24:32) The image of teaching which 'sets hearts on fire' is an elusive yet tantalising idea for a generation bored with words.

If proclamation was the first incisive cutting edge, then Jesus' teaching, beginning in Galilee and building up towards Jerusalem, can be seen as the great midfield area of Jesus' 'word' ministry. The line between the two is, of course, blurred, but sometimes we see clearly the heralding proclaimer, and at others the deeply learned teacher.

> There are, no doubt, many different lenses through which we can usefully view Jesus, and it is always good to be reminded of those which have been forgotten. I therefore welcome with enthusiasm the recent emphasis on Jesus as a sage, a teacher of wisdom.[4]

In his teaching Jesus used parables (although interestingly they do not appear until nearly halfway through the Gospels), and single enigmatic statements such as 'You have heard . . . but I say to you. . .', and combinations of the two. It is clear that the Gospels sometimes group together different elements, perhaps favourite anecdotes, themes and oft-repeated figures of speech. In Matthew there are five of these teaching compilations which are traditionally seen as the new Torah or five great law books. At the heart of all the teaching material there are two great set-piece occasions. The first is the 'Sermon on the Mount', with Jesus styled as a messianic Moses, offering a new and deeper way of living for and with God. The second is set in the temple in the final week. This is described by all three Synoptics and shows Jesus the prophet explaining to the Jews their failed history, predicting their future doom and telling them why he is there in their midst.

---

[4] N.T. Wright, *Jesus and the Victory of God*, SPCK 1996.

Disputation

Mark's Gospel, the oldest of the four, has twelve disputation accounts. They begin with emissaries sent down from Jerusalem to check out the Jesus phenomenon, and end, almost symmetrically, with him going up to Jerusalem to clear out the temple. The scribes and Pharisees, Saduccees, Herodians and priests all come with their own issues. Gradually it becomes clear that the real problem is Jesus himself. There are a few members of the establishment such as Jairus, Nicodemus and Joseph of Arimathea who respond positively to him, but for most he is a threat.

Religious leaders are often uncomfortable with enthusiastic and godly members who want to do things differently, ask awkward questions or challenge standard practice. They get used to their autocratic powers and the subservience of their followers. As a reforming prophet, Jesus was never going to be a peaceful and compliant part of the system. Conflict was inevitable. The whole thing is captured particularly well in Lloyd Douglas's novel of the life and death of Jesus, *The Robe.* There the scribes, Pharisees and priests are not just religious leaders, they are also the holders of political and financial power in Jerusalem. Behind them there are the Romans, brutal and in total control, reaching from the local legionaries to the distant emperor. These men – and they are all men – are never going to submit to the reforming 'peace teachings' of Jesus. But neither is Jesus going to kneel before them. The disputations and their painful results are not limited to Jesus. They spill over, just as they did in real life, and suck in his followers, be they Galilean or Roman.

Who is disputing with the evangelists today? Basically anyone who resents the sort of influence we have on people's lives. Outside the church there is a broad range, from the lazy cliché-coining media to popular novelists such as Nick Hornby, Jonathan Coe and Mark Haddon, for whom we are such an easy and comical target, to the likes of the increasingly hysterical Richard Dawkins. As with Jesus, there are also plenty on the inside who want to write us off as intellectually lightweight and spiritually shallow manipulative number-crunchers. The best response is to follow Jesus' example: live an open, inclusive and loving life, offer a straightforward answer, refuse to get sucked in, and concentrate on the people who want to hear.

It is possible to take these three categories of proclamation, teaching and disputation and to set them alongside the three phases of Jesus' ministry. We can then see a developing pattern.

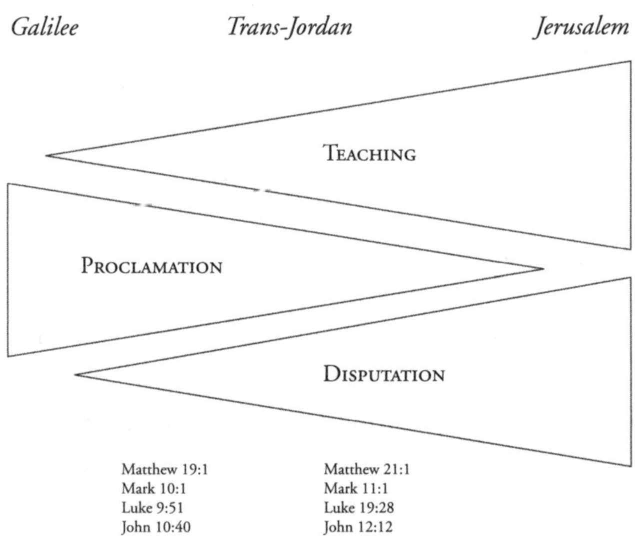

Reality, however, is always messier than a diagram: the dividing lines in this particular one are all very fuzzy and the separate boxes are never watertight. For example, we see Jesus in the Galilee giving deep teaching to the Twelve and other close followers concerning the meaning of the parable of the sower (Mark 4:10). Likewise, there are still large crowds at the beginning of the southward journey (Matthew 19:2), and as Jesus approaches Jerusalem he shifts his focus from the road to ten lepers in what looks like a Galilean-type moment (Luke 17:11). Nevertheless the pattern, although liquid and overlapping, is fairly clear. Jesus spent most of his time in the Galilee in what we would call 'evangelism mode'. As he travelled south, he invested more time and energy in teaching his followers and preparing the future leaders. In Jerusalem it is increasingly about disputation arising out of his final prophetic teaching.

Private conversations

Finally, there is a fourth but very different category within Jesus' 'word' ministry. This is not about public proclamation or teaching, but private conversation. Here we see Jesus the personal evangelist. Sometimes the conversations have been remembered and recorded, such as the ones with Mary and Martha, the rich young man, Nicodemus and the woman at the well, but others have remained hidden. Although such conversations are of a very different order from his public utterances, nevertheless they still provide material which I think we can use in a supplementary way to understand the evangelising message of Jesus.

The purpose here is not to produce an extensive, in-depth survey on the content and theology of all Jesus' public utterances, but to focus in on Jesus the evangelist. So, while making use of the teaching, disputation and conversational passages in the Gospels, we shall concentrate again on his proclaiming. This represents the strategically important, initial ice-breaking impact of his whole messaging, from which all the teaching, disputing and talking flow.

Matthew, Mark and Luke all describe the beginning of Jesus' proclaiming in Galilee:

- 'From that time on Jesus began to preach, "Repent, for the kingdom of heaven is near" ' (Matthew 4:17).
- 'Jesus went throughout Galilee, teaching in their synagogues, preaching the good news of the kingdom, and healing every disease and sickness among the people' (Matthew 4:23).
- 'After John was put in prison, Jesus went into Galilee, proclaiming the good news of God. "The time has come," he said. "The kingdom of God is near. Repent and believe the good news!" ' (Mark 1:14–15)
- 'I must preach the good news of the kingdom of God to the other towns also, because that was why I was sent' (Luke 4:43).

Frustratingly, as we have already noted, we do not possess any straight proclamation-type sermons or stories to study and copy. What we do have is not so much detailed content as banner headlines:

- 'Good News!'
- 'The Kingdom of God is Here!'
- 'Repent and Believe!'

Clearly, this is a briefer, more direct and much sharper approach than the standard sort of presentation that I have earlier described as being used by many of today's evangelists. It is a bit like comparing the *Independent* or *The Times* to the *Sun* or the *Mirror*. Furthermore, these three topics do not arrange themselves into a neat formula or sequence; instead they should be seen much more as a sort of fluid zone in which Jesus the Proclaimer moved around. Our task, then, is to flesh out these big brassy trumpet blasts and see how they can become the basis for our evangelistic message today.

As a little aside, we ought to note that Jesus' basic proclamation has a different feel in John's Gospel. There the idea of the kingdom is replaced by that of 'eternal life', while believing the good news and repenting are merged together into believing in (as opposed to plain believing) Jesus. He is 'the way, the truth and the life', 'the good shepherd', 'the light' and the 'bread of life'. The classic text that flows through the whole is that of John 3:16:

> For God so loved the world that he gave his one and only Son, that whoever believes in him shall not perish but have eternal life.

Good news

The scholars are right in saying that we should view Jesus as an extension of the line of Old Testament prophets, but there is one massively significant way in which he is their exact opposite. They began with the bad news: the people were very sinful, God was angry, judgement was nigh. In contrast, the great opening movement to Jesus' symphony was good news: the people were very needful, God was aware, help was here. Far from announcing death and destruction, he was offering life and salvation.

We can gain more detailed access to the content of the good news by looking at three 'capsules', or summing up passages.

In Luke 4:18–19, Jesus reads the words of Isaiah 61:1–2. Here the prophet had looked into a distant future and predicted that one day there would be good news for the poor, release for captives, sight for the blind and freedom for the oppressed. There is only one phrase which Jesus omits from Isaiah, the one which speaks of the coming day of the vengeance of God; in other words, Jesus' message here is all about promise and not judgement. He emphasises the good and actually deletes the bad news. He finishes reading by calmly sitting down and saying, 'Today this scripture is fulfilled.'

The second passage, Matthew 11:2–6, has a similar feel. The disciples of John the Baptist come to ask Jesus if he truly is the one they are expecting. Jesus says nothing directly about himself, but points to what is happening. 'The blind receive sight, the lame walk, those who have leprosy are cured, the deaf hear, the dead are raised, and the good news is preached to the poor.'

From these first two capsules, then, we can say three things about the good news:

- It was a wonderful transforming of broken human lives. This transforming was happening then and there, not in some hoped-for future, and it was all a result of what Jesus was doing. He was not just the announcer of good news, he actually was the good news – the proclaimer became the proclamation.
- Proclamation, healing and exorcism came together like three intermingling streams in the forming of one great river. It was a combination described simply and succinctly by A.M. Hunter as 'the work and words of Jesus'.
- There is no mention of the recipients being spiritually pure and deserving. God is responding not to their 'good deeds'

> but to their 'great needs'. For a people brought up on the Old Testament concept of covenant, whereby God helps Israel if and when they are faithful to him, this would have been shockingly revolutionary.

I sometimes wonder if we have been a bit too heavy on issues of sin, guilt and judgement and too light on grace, welcome and forgiveness. The Roman Catholic evangelist in James Joyce's *A Portrait of the Artist as a Young Man* frightens his schoolboy listeners into faith with lurid visions of hell and their own sinfulness. A similar note is struck by the reforming vicar in *A Clockwork Orange* written by Anthony Burgess, another one in the long line of English Catholic writers trying to escape from an upbringing in Christian guilt.

This is not just a Catholic issue. The liturgies of the Anglican *Book of Common Prayer* are soaked far more in our sin than in the utter joy of our forgiveness. Meanwhile, evangelical preachers continue to berate their listeners about lack of total commitment, the dark corners of life that have never really been repented of, and continual backslidings. All of this has a place, but not the most prominent – because that belongs to the announcement of grace. Of course our sin needs to be dealt with and our lifestyles need to be changed, but it is all about balance. Jesus clearly put his emphasis on the 'good news' of forgiveness and new beginnings.

The third capsule passage is even more poignant, and laden with both pathos and hope. It is the Beatitudes from Luke 6:20–21. While Matthew 5 recorded nine of these 'blesseds', here Luke presents only four. The scholars point to the first three of these as the essential and historic core of the idea of beatitudes. They are all about 'grace' and 'gift' rather than 'doing' and 'deserving'. These three then resonate strongly with our earlier two passages. They talk about the saddest, most neglected and pathetic of human beings, the ones who have nothing, suddenly getting everything.

> Blessed are you who are poor,
> for yours is the kingdom of God.
> Blessed are you who hunger now,
> for you will be satisfied.
> Blessed are you who weep now,
> for you will laugh.

Unlike the other beatitudes, there is no mention of any of these tragic souls doing anything themselves actually to deserve this blessing. There is no issue of reward, nor even of the need for any sort of moral response. The good news is all about the generosity of God and the compassion of Jesus. As John Nolland says in his commentary, 'The language of poverty is the language of neediness.'[5]

I am constantly trying to become more effective in both my personal evangelism and my evangelistic speaking. So in late 2007 I crossed the Pennines to Sheffield to listen to a brilliant evangelist. That night I learned a lot about style and presentation, but was disturbed by the message. As those of us in the hall were repeatedly told that we were sinful and had broken God's commandments, I tried to recall an example from the Gospels when Jesus had given a message like this. I could not think of one. Jesus the evangelist saw us as sad rather than bad; as having broken God's heart and not just his commandments.

Jesus seems to be a lot more generous with his giving away of the good things of God than are most contemporary evangelists.

---

5 *The Gospel of Matthew*, page 198.

We have a tendency to ration them to those who are suitably aware of their own personal sin and wretchedness. Jesus gives much bigger helpings and to lots more people. He gives more because he loves more.

Our word 'blessed' translates the Greek *makarios.* This 'happiness' word was used by the ancient Greeks to describe the untroubled life of the gods and the carefree living of the rich. The commentators use phrases such as 'good fortune now' (Nolland), 'oh the happiness of' (Floyd Filson), 'blessedness declared, promised and given by Christ' (David Hill) and 'blessing on' (Tom Wright) in an attempt to get across the enormity of the good news.

A final thought before moving on: nothing is more shrouded in solemn and pietistic reverence than the Beatitudes, and there, right at the heart of them, is the word 'laugh'. That word should impact our prayer meetings, our preaching and our liturgies. How and why have we managed to get rid of the concept of laughter in the church? You just cannot do the good news in a straight-faced, joyless and puritanical sort of way – it is just too good for that. There is a huge, all-embracing 'feel good, laugh out loud with disbelief and weep joyfully with amazement' factor to Jesus' good news.

There is something optimistic, hopeful, confident and even naïve about Jesus' belief in the good news. He was utterly sold on the idea that what he was offering was absolutely life-transforming, that it was true and that it really did work. Today we are less sure and optimistic about our message (which is actually his message). We think it might help a certain kind of person to find a spiritual sort of peace, but when it comes to filling the empty, turning tears into laughter and mending broken lives, we feel ourselves to be on thin ice. Before we preach the good news, perhaps we need to re-experience and re-embrace it for ourselves – not the theoretical formula, but the sheer impacting power of it. To rediscover that what we now offer in his name can make people very, very happy.

Jesus' most potent image or metaphor for describing the human condition was that of lostness. People were like lost sheep, they were shepherdless, and when they did have a spiritual guide it was the blind leading the blind. Of course, the most lost of all are those who do not know they are lost. Sometimes the first evangelistic task is not to show people the way home, but to open their eyes to the big dark wood in which they are lost. At the heart of Luke's Gospel there is a group of three parables with a common theme of lost and found (Luke 15): first a sheep, then a coin and finally, most wonderfully of all, a greedy, selfish prig of a son. All three share the same existential reality, that Jesus' evangelism turns lostness into foundness, cold into warmth, wilderness into home, pointlessness into purpose and fear into faith.

Looking at its art, the twentieth century, which for most of us is still 'our time', was a century of lostness. Edvard Munch's iconic 'The Scream'; Picasso's mournful blue and pink periods; his succession of tragic women and great masterpiece 'Guernica'; Chagall's 'floating somewhere Jews'; Lowry's crowds of 'going nowhere' Lancashire mill workers; Edward Hopper's desolately lonely filling station and coffee bars; Dali's melancholic people and landscapes, being eaten away by marauding ants; Francis Bacon's strangely distorted portraits – they all tell the same story. All you need to complete the effect is to listen to The Beatles' 'Eleanor Rigby' while looking at the pictures. Today Britain's most popular artist is Jack Vettriano. We buy his work in prints, as postcards and even stamped on our umbrellas. When he is not painting waiters serving afternoon tea on a windswept beach, he is painting lonely people, usually late at night and trying to find some sort of consolation in drink, tobacco and sleazy sex. All we like sheep have gone astray.

The good news of the coming of Jesus that we ourselves have heard; the gift of blessedness, of living like gods, that we have received: this is our answer to the despair of the artists.

> When he saw the crowds, he had compassion on them, because they were harassed and helpless, like sheep without a shepherd. (Matthew 9:36)

Of course, lostness is not just about the lost. It is just as much about the loser. Anyone who has lost keys, credit cards or a good friend will know exactly what I am talking about. Losing things leaves holes in our heart, and the biggest holes are left by losing children. Holes cause pain. The mission of Jesus the evangelist begins in the holes in the Father's heart. The truest and best of our evangelism is born out of a combination of the pain of losing and the joy of finding.

The kingdom of God

The kingdom of God or heaven is the big idea or major theme which rises in Jesus' proclamation and flows right through the middle of all his teachings. As such it has been massively covered by all the big 'Jesus books' of recent years, so there is no point in me doing poorly what they have all done so well. Here, as an evangelist writing about Jesus the evangelist, I will simply offer a few observations.

- Whatever the Jews were hoping for or expecting, Jesus did not deliver the kingdom as some sort of religious/political revival of the nation of Israel. There was to be no lifting up of Jerusalem as capital city with a magnificent temple cult and reigning earthly king. For him it was all about God being king and ruling in human hearts. The kingdom then becomes a sort of experiential reality when people choose to obey and follow the king.

- The kingdom is made real and present in the work of Jesus. It is no longer a vague and futuristic hope. By breaking into Satan's kingdom and setting people free, Jesus is actually introducing the kingdom to the world and people to the kingdom (Luke 11:20–22). This all happens in the 'now'. As David Bosch describes it, 'Something totally new is happening: the irruption of a new era, of a new order of life. The hope of deliverance is not a distant song about a far-away future. The future has invaded the present.'[6] But there was still a 'not yet'. From the perspective of Jesus' teaching times, his cross, resurrection and final return were all still in the future (Mark 8:31).
- The Sermon on the Mount has been labelled as the new Torah or manifesto for the kingdom. There, as elsewhere, Jesus weaves together morality and spirituality and takes them together to a deeper and more intimate level. A ban on violence and adultery becomes a ban on secret inner anger and lust. Prayer is taken beyond the public domain into the private and personal. Fasting becomes a matter of joy rather than seriousness, while daily trusting in God's provision becomes a new philosophy of life. The kingdom is not a new set of commandments, but a new way of

[6] David Bosch, *Transforming Mission*, Orbis 1992, page 32.

being a person and living life in the fullest, richest and most colourful way.

- To live as part of the kingdom is not so much to be a religious devotee, but more like being a guest at a really good party. Matthew's and Luke's choice of the parable of the banquet strikes a note of celebration and hospitality, where belonging and relationship are part of the believing and obeying. (See Matthew 22:1–14; Luke 14:15.)
- The kingdom is not just a high moral lifestyle based on justice and love; nor is it merely associating with other kingdom people, although it certainly involves both of these. Essentially it is about having a relationship with the king. So evangelism is not about getting people to change their life or opinions, but a sort of divine introduction agency. Before you can serve the king, you first have to meet the king. There are actually those in the church who are very keen to uphold and campaign for kingdom values and justice, but who neglect or patronise this first step of individuals meeting the king. Socialism has always seemed to me to be the nearest thing to kingdom living. The problem is, socialism is centrally empty: there is no transcendent core of individuals meeting with God. No wonder the poet Carol Ann Duffy describes it as 'the tree that never grew, the bird that never flew' (from the poem 'Politico'). Kingdom values and justice without kingdom evangelism is exactly the same.
- Like individual mustard seeds, or whole fields of wheat, the kingdom is a growing thing. It is designed to grow over time in a person's heart and lifestyle. Just as important, it is designed to grow corporately, as more and more people accept God's kingly rule.

> The kingdom of heaven is like a man who sowed good seed in his field. (Matthew 13:24)

In summary, then, we can say that Jesus proclaimed and delivered a new and celebratory way of living and loving with God the king.

The biggest threat to kingdom living is money living. Jesus would have loved Harry Enfield's 'loads-a-money' satirical routines of the 1990s. It was his favourite subject: rich men and poor men, inheritance and earnings, treasure and greed.

- Lust for money chokes out growing belief (Matthew 13:22).
- A rich young man has to choose: money or God? (Mark 10:17)
- Trust in God, worry less about money (Matthew 6:25).
- The fool spends all his life making money, and then dies (Luke 12:16).
- A poor widow gives her money to God (Luke 21:1).
- Greedy tenants kill God's messengers and keep the money (Matthew 21:33).
- Wealthy Lazarus ignores a poor man and ends up in hell (Luke 16:19).

So was Jesus obsessed by money, or did he have a profound understanding of human nature and self-centredness?

Roger Osborne's *Civilization* appeared in 2006, as a major new history of the Western world.[7] He argues that we have now arrived at a point where all but the very rich and the very poor are ruled by an oppressive cash triangle – what Jesus might have termed an alternative kingdom. According to Osborne, typical Westerners

---

[7] Roger Osborne, *Civilization*, Pegasus 2006.

now spend the first part of their adulthood worrying about a mortgage, the middle part struggling to pay for the education of their children, and their final working years desperately trying to put together some sort of pension. It all sounds very true, rather sad and just the sort of situation that Jesus talked about. In his evangelism he kept punching away at the great 'money god' and his kingdom: he knew his enemy. He compared the two kings and called on people to make a conscious choice or decision. He wanted the very best for people. He was bitingly relevant then and still is today.

Repent and believe

Jesus was never content simply to preach the good news of the kingdom, announce the final hymn, serve a cup of tea and then let everyone go home and forget about it. In the words of traditional evangelism, he was 'preaching for a verdict'. He longed for his listeners not just to listen passively, but actually to do something, to hear and then to enter. Yes, he wanted people to listen and reflect, but then he wanted them to repent and believe.

> Everyone who hears these words of mine and puts them into practice is like a wise man. (Matthew 7:24)

To repent (*metanoeo*) is to change our mind, opinions and beliefs and, more importantly, to change the way we live. James Dunn points out that repentance includes a sense of regret and that, in Jesus' use of the term, it goes even deeper than the concept of change to include that of returning.[8]

[8] *Jesus Remembered*, page 498.

Believing (*pisteuete*) should follow repentance, as day follows night. Together they are the 'chip and pin' access to a new way of life with God, with all its attendant riches. Slap in the card and punch in your personal number, turn from the old and believe in the new. Just as repentance is about remorse and regret, so believing is about reformation and rejoicing. The classic 'repent and believe' parable is, of course, the story of the prodigal son. There we find all the key elements of returning, of a father-son relationship, of a great welcome home and of sorrow turned to joy.

Sadly, many in the evangelism trade have become fixated on a Protestant Reformation view of sin and repentance. In our preaching about repentance many of us (and I do include myself) have sometimes come to sound more like John the Baptist than Jesus the Evangelist. For Jesus, 'repent and believe' was not just the turning away from sin and moral failure that we seem to think it is today. He appears to have seen it much more in the Deuteronomic sense, as a turning, or returning, to God, body and soul (Deuteronomy 30:2). For us, repentance has come to mean rooting about in our deep and guilty cellar; for Jesus, it meant throwing open the front door and inviting God in.

For Jesus, repenting and believing were not just individual, private acts. They had a corporate application too, especially for the religious and political leaders of his day. In using this terminology, Jesus was both calling on the individual and also attempting to reform the religious and political attitudes of the whole nation of God.

If the seed was to bear fruit, and if the kingdom was to grow, then there were big decisions to be made. People had to choose which of the two masters they would serve (Matthew 6:24); which gate and road they would follow, the hard or the easy (Matthew 7:13);

and whether they would build their house on a foundation of apathy or obedience (Matthew 7:24).

When giving an evangelistic talk, I sometimes describe life as a constant going round in circles on a rounders pitch with three bases. The bases are called 'Treasure', 'Pleasure' and 'Leisure', which is what these three choosing parables of Jesus are all about. (I have been known to give the same talk to young 'studenty' types using the titles 'Supping', 'Shopping' and 'Shagging' for the bases – it's crude but effective!) The point is to ask the big question about what people really want to get out of life, and then to help them make conscious decisions, rather than just drift, like sheep without a shepherd.

This is the bit that we all find frightening. Frustratingly, it is also the bit where others in the church often accuse us of emotional manipulation. When speakers lead their listeners onto the clear ground of decision-making, they are acting like Jesus and doing them a loving, life-enhancing service. They are honest and caring salespeople, helping someone to buy what they need. They are midwives, saying, 'Push now!' They are 'go-betweens', carrying messages from one lover to another. They are not forcing people into a corner, but freeing them out of one, into a broad and open place.

J. John is one of our brightest, sharpest and most relevant contemporary evangelists. He is also very generous and encouraging in his teaching and mentoring of other, younger evangelists. He has a brilliant phrase when discussing the decision-making process: he talks about the 'So What Factor'. 'You have heard the good news, *so what* are you going to do about it?' 'You have thought about the new type of living with God, *so what* are you going to do with it?'

Most of us shy away from inserting the 'So What Factor', probably as a result of our own insecurity and sense of impending failure. The need for us today is to step up to the plate and, with equal measures of boldness and sensitivity, to re-create a Jesus-style decision moment. Traditionally, the evangelism trade has used the word 'challenge', a strong masculine term. I wonder if Jesus might have viewed his call to 'repent and believe' as a softer and more feminine 'invitation' or 'gift'.

> Come to me, all you who are weary and burdened, and I will give you rest. (Matthew 11:28)

This is an invitation that can be offered with a lightness of touch and a sweetness of intent.

In recent years there has been a major shift from asking the 'big question' at an evangelistic service (crisis) to running some sort of enquirers' group (process). The thinking is that people no longer respond to the traditional 'altar call'. They now want time to think, ask questions, build a few relationships and weigh things up. Process evangelism is about people journeying, a strong contemporary concept. This has been a helpful and positive switch, greatly aided by the appearance of such courses as Alpha, Emmaus and Start. There is a weakness, however, which is that many people take part in such a journeying group without ever making a definite decision about turning to, or turning back to, God (repentance). In fact, sometimes they do not even realise that there is such a decision to be made. Gradual osmosis is not a bad way of spiritual travelling and is suited to certain temperaments and personalities, but even on the most gently drifting of journeys we have to make a few key decisions concerning destination, direction, and so on. I am convinced that there is a helpful way of combining the 'big choice' and 'ongoing process' models; it *is* about making a journey, but one that will involve occasional 'crossroads' decisions.

It is a great shame that inviting people to make 'big decision' responses is out of fashion these days. Rather than pressurising, it actually liberates people from the wall-to-wall materialising pressures of our postmodern world and gives them power over their own life and future. John Finney quite rightly warns, 'Those who evangelise often look for quick results.'[9] This is a serious problem for our profession, but it would be tragic to lose completely that encouraging of individuals to make big and life-changing decisions. In my experience, it is not the decision-making which pressurises people so much as the dulling routine of daily life in which they are robbed of personal freedom.

As a practising evangelist, I feel frightened, lonely and wide open to rejection every time I invite people to respond. Frankly, I wish I did not have to do it, but I do have to do it, because Jesus did it before me. I am always negative beforehand, constantly seeing myself as not very good at my job and fully expecting that nothing will happen. Equally, I am always surprised, because someone always does respond.

The practice of asking responders to 'come forward' – in what is conventionally known as the 'altar call' – was probably first used in the UK by the visiting American evangelists Moody and Sankey. It was taken up and developed by William Booth and his Salvation Army preachers, with the so-called 'penitents' bench', a low form placed at the front of the meeting room so that repenting souls could come and kneel there. Billy Graham became the ultimate

---

9 John Finney, *Finding Faith Today*, page 25.

'come down to the front' evangelist, using huge auditoriums and football stadiums for his mass appeals. I am convinced that, despite what we keep being told by the trend-followers, there is still value in this semi-sacramental act. Furthermore, I am pretty sure that if we had more invitations being offered by more preachers, we would see more people receiving and responding.

Sensitive evangelists will use a whole assortment of variants on the basic model, ranging from the private and easy-to-do response to the more public and demonstrative act:

- 'Come and have a word with me over coffee.'
- 'Take a booklet off me at the church door.'
- 'Light a candle or place a rock at the foot of the cross.'
- 'Raise your hand or stand up in this time of prayer.'
- 'Remain behind at the rail after taking communion, for prayer.'
- 'Come out to the front during the final hymn.'

The suggested outcome of all this inviting and responding might well be that of complete repentance and belief (although I would always advise using the more understandable terminology of 'turning to God', or 'asking God to come into your life'). It might be a bit more cautious: 'Draw a step closer,' or even, 'Why not think about beginning to draw closer?' Hopefully, whatever the terminology, it will be followed by an encouragement to continue the process, perhaps by joining an enquirers' group. In the end it is all about the right invitation for the right people at the right time.

The parables

Jesus' use of parables was clearly one of the unique and most characteristic features of his 'word' ministry. They do not fit neatly into any of our categories, but are so significant that they need a section of their own. Sometimes they are part of the basic gospel announcement; at other times they are used in the teaching of the kingdom, or for the in-depth instruction of the disciples, or even as part of Jesus' disputations with the scribes and Pharisees.

If 'good news', 'kingdom' and 'repent and believe' are the big bold headlines of Jesus' proclamation, then the parables can be seen as forming part of the core of the content. They are stories, and stories are always far more intriguing than blocks of straight information or theory. Most intriguing of all, they are human stories, stories about people just like us living in a world just like ours.

> Jesus generated his parables and images by noticing a wide range of human experiences and activities and reflectively presenting them in the light of the reign of God. He told of things that happened frequently or at least every now and then. There was no gap to close between his parables and everyday life.[10]

- 'There was a man with no money, and one with shedloads of it. . .'
- 'Here is a father with two very different sons. . .'
- 'A man was mugged in a strange town. . .'
- 'So there was this guy who lived in a big posh house and threw a great party. . .'
- 'The office manager was not doing a very good job. . .'
- 'A publicity person sent out thousands of flyers. . .'

The parables first illustrate the message, then they apply it to our ordinary lives, and finally they get us to make a decision. They are

---

[10] Gerald O'Collins SJ, *Jesus: A Portrait*, Darton, Longman & Todd 2008.

like little verbal videos or PowerPoint presentations, except they really do make the point and do it with power. They connect with people, pull them in and hold a mirror up to them.

Jesus used parables because he was desperate for people to get the point. 'Have you understood all these things?' he asks his listeners (Matthew 13:51).

Supremely, we can think of his parables as incarnational stories on the lips of an incarnational Jesus.

We shall return to the theme of parables when we look at Jesus' 'style' later in the chapter.

His proclamation in our world

Our world is obsessed with entering a new kingdom which has drawn close, believing in a new teaching and repenting into a new way of being. Makeovers are everywhere, offering new gardens, homes, holiday destinations and nip-and-tuck bodies. Trinny and Susannah, Alan Titchmarsh and Jamie Oliver are the new evangelists. Their proffered conversion, however, is about putting the old me into something new rather than making me a new person – not so much transformation as transportation. The vast majority of people will always be looking for something better, even if they are looking in the wrong places. That is precisely where Jesus the evangelist began.

Trying to do it his way, I immediately notice three major differences between Jesus' proclamation and the traditional evangelistic talk I outlined earlier in the chapter.

Firstly, Jesus is simpler, sharper and punchier, using just three banner headlines instead of an elaborate seven-point formula. This is just what we want in a postmodern, media-slick culture.

Secondly, his message is not soaked in the wretchedness of personal sin. He is more interested in humanity than morality, and sees people as 'sad and needy' rather than 'bad and guilty'.

Thirdly, and perhaps most difficult for us to come to terms with, he does not include complicated descriptions of the cross and how it works. We shall return to this thought, but first I want to look at Jesus' big three headlines and imagine how they might look and sound for us today.

Good news

- For anyone who is struggling with life, under pressure, stressed out, or feeling isolated. God is here for you.
- For those of us with marriage problems, worrying about work, frightened of dying, or filling up with suppressed anger. God knows all about it.
- For those of us who are in the grip of some sort of addiction, be it gambling, drugs, drink or pornography. God knows about your hidden life and shares all your pain.
- For those who are just lost and do not know which way to turn. God is here to listen and guide.
- And for those lucky souls who find everything in life is just great, but who still think there might be something more. There is, and it has a name: God! This is not the God you think you know all about and can live without. This is our best friend God, the one who is closer than you think, the real God.

Kingdom

Unlike first-century Jews, today's Westerners are not expecting some sort of 'kingdom', but they are hungry for a better life.

- For anyone looking for deep inner peace, acceptance and friendship, you *can* begin a new life.
- If you want something beyond money and work, home and TV, then reach out for a new way of living with God.
- If you want to become a new you, then before thinking about a new house, garden or clothes, think about a new living with God.
- This new kind of life is not so much about having a new religion, but more about having a new relationship.
- It is about being a guest at an eternal and very welcoming party thrown by God.

Repent and believe

The promised gift of God to touch our need and the invitation to live his new life is for everyone.

- It is about turning or returning to God like a long-lost son or daughter coming home again.
- Sometimes in life we are faced with great decisions, or perhaps we should say opportunities, and this is one of them.
- You can respond to this opportunity right now. If you feel interested but still a bit uncertain, or if you just want a chance to think and talk, then why not. . .

Well, this might all seem a bit too loose for some, or it might feel too programmed for others. Do not worry or get uptight at my attempts to put Jesus' proclamation into our world. Just try yourself to take his big three statements and make them work for your audience.

What about the cross and resurrection?

There is a major 'before and after' difference between Jesus' proclamation and our own. He evangelised before the crucifixion and made little explicit reference to it. He discussed it three times in deep conversation with the disciples, though even they never understood it in that 'before time' (Mark 8:31; 9:31; 10:33). He alluded to it in his private conversation with Nicodemus (John 3:14) and in the 'parable of the workers in the vineyard' (Matthew 20:1). In his sharing of bread and wine at the Last Supper he sacramentalised it (Matthew 26:26). Perhaps the only place where we see him actually explaining the cross was when he was trying to show the disciples what servanthood looked like in Mark 10:45:

> For even the Son of Man did not come to be served, but to serve, and to give his life as a ransom for many.

In contrast, we live and proclaim our message in the 'after the cross and resurrection time'. This has an impact on our whole understanding of the good news, the kingdom and the invitation to repent or turn to God, and so, along with the first apostles, we preach 'Christ and him crucified' (1 Corinthians 2:2). This does not mean, however, that we have to stick slavishly to our beloved explanations of how the cross operates or our lengthy pieces of post-Jesus atonement theory. In fact, when the cross is mentioned in the early Acts, there is no attempt to explain it, but it is linked to the resurrection and to the need for repentance and forgiveness (Acts 2:23–24; 3:13; 4:10–12; 5:30–31).

The cross is at the heart of everything, the great watershed. Jesus proclaimed his evangelistic message of good news, kingdom and repentance before it, and the first Christians picked up and ran with these great themes after it. Only in the light of the cross does the message make sense and create a true reality. The cross is like a great prism. Jesus' evangelising ministry is concentrated into it like a single beam of pure light on one side and is refracted into a flood of colour on the post-resurrection side – our side.

In a very beautiful and mysterious way, I have increasingly found that the fact of the cross transcends attempts to explain it. Almost as soon as it is mentioned, it begins to do its own work. A memorably haunting example of this phenomenon is provided by Caradog Prichard in his autobiographical novel of life in a Welsh slate-quarrying village, *One Moonlit Night.*[11] The book, a modern classic, recounts the story of a visiting choir of on-strike coal miners. At an outdoor evening concert, the choir perform various spiritual songs which climax with a solo tenor singing:

> The one who then was crucified
> For a sinful man like me
> Who drained the cup completely
> Himself on Calvary.

The hushed audience respond: 'And without anyone saying a word to them, everyone fell on their knees on the grass, and everyone bowed their heads and closed their eyes. And David Evans' voice was praying.' The story is about people having not an explanation, but an experience of the cross.

---

11 *Un Nos Ola Leuad* 1961, transl. Philip Mitchell *One Moonlit Night,* Penguin 1995.

I sometimes talk about, and display as little stage props, three different crosses. One is the kind of cross that many people wear round their neck, the second is the 'Palm cross' that a surprisingly high number still remember, and the third is a crucifix. I carry examples of all three and can often sense the shared experience as I bring them out of my pockets. The fundamental thing about the cross in an evangelistic context is not so much to get people to understand it, but to help them to reach out and touch it.

If you have seen the film *Spartacus*, you will remember the scene near the end when Spartacus and a handful of survivors from his slave army have been captured by the Romans. The Romans do not actually know the identity of Spartacus, whom they plan to crucify. In a moment of massive loyalty, one by one his followers all claim to be him. They want to spare him the cross and are willing to take his place. It is an inspiring but hopelessly sentimental episode. Everything we know about beaten men tells us that this could not happen, and that they would be much more likely to push Spartacus to the front in the hope of saving themselves. The true story of Jesus' crucifixion is the exact opposite of this scene in *Spartacus*. Jesus is deserted by his followers and left alone to face the pain and loneliness of the cross. No one offers to take his place – in fact, he is taking ours.

For Jesus, the cross was a holistic experience. It destroyed his body, mind and spirit, the exact opposite of his own holistic preaching, healing and driving out of demons. It was his own personalised holocaust. And yet, because he was the Son of Man, it was also a fate that he shared with many men. At his death Jesus plunged into a black hole, a place of nothingness from which no thing, no light, no organic life and certainly no hope can escape.

I have often presented the cross in a two-step process. The first step involves using visuals, music, a few dramatic words and a huge cross or picture to re-create the event. The second step is about inviting people to come out and literally touch the cross, place a candle or kneel and say a prayer at the foot of the cross . . . or is it that the cross itself does the reaching out and touching?

In the story of Jesus, the cross does not stand alone. It is always the middle act in the three-part drama of the life, death and resurrection of the king.

Cross and resurrection belong together like night and day, winter and spring, despair and delight. Although resurrection was not a part of Jesus' evangelistic message, it was very much the climactic part of his evangelistic life.

There are two great 'something out of nothing' moments in the history of the universe. The first was the 'Big Bang', and the second was the 'Big Resurrection'.

Evangelists have traditionally seen the resurrection as a major exercise in apologetics. We have put the newly alive Jesus in the dock and produced the items of evidence such as the empty tomb, the reported appearances, the changed lives and written stories. It has all been focused on convincing unwilling believers. I am now certain that this whole approach shows a failure to understand not only the nature of evangelism, but the nature of faith itself. This is not to say that we should get rid of apologetics entirely, but rather that we should put it on the back-burner once in a while. That way, it is there when we need it while we get on with the main evangelistic task of helping those whose heart and intellect are open and inquisitive as they struggle with the issues of life and death. This is what Jesus did when he turned Mary's tears of grief into tears of joy

(John 20:11), when he turned around the despair of the friends on the road to Emmaus (Luke 24:13), when he bolstered Thomas's doubting heart (John 20:26) and rebuilt the big mess of the big fisherman (John 21:15).

Our task is not to prove the unprovable, but to open the unopened. These days it is impossible to pass through a single UK town or city without seeing at least one roadside shrine marking the tragic death in a car accident of someone's child, husband, parent or wife. There they are, bright in the sunshine and drooping in the rain – bunches of flowers, favourite teddy bears, and brightly coloured football scarves tied to railings and lamp-posts. And there they stay, for weeks on end, sad and universal proclamations of the power of death. It seems that our cool, scientific, grown-up, sophisticated world still struggles with its natural fate.

Dylan Thomas called upon his father, dying not as a young man in a road accident, but simply from old age:

> Do not go gentle into that good night. . .
> Rage, rage against the dying of the light.[12]

Philip Larkin spent years looking ahead and dreading death:

> Waking at four to soundless dark, I stare.
> In time the curtain edges will grow light.
> Till then I see what's really always there:
> Unresting death, a whole day nearer now.[13]

---

[12] 'Do Not Go Gentle Into That Good Night' 1952.
[13] 'Aubade' 1977.

The human heart cries out for that which only the resurrected Jesus the evangelist can provide. He is the unflickering, inextinguishable light in the eternal darkness, the swelling song in the endless silence, the birthing of hope in the place of death.

Over the last ten years or so, I have been using Easter as a special time for evangelism. It is a time when consciousness of the cross and resurrection draws a bit closer, like some visiting comet. The air is thinner between then and now, between the searching Jesus and lost people, even between life and death.

In Manchester we have turned Good Friday into 'God Friday', running many evangelistic events – 'an hour at the cross' – all over the city. These are gentle, fairly quiet, almost always deeply moving invitation services as the preached word is combined with pictures, a bit of poetry, some silence and gentle singing.

In complete contrast, as a way of somehow re-creating that first tomb opening, on Easter Day I play the music of Aaron Copland's 'Fanfare for the Common Man' at great volume. The thunderous drums are like a liberating earthquake. The purity of the trumpets has a clean, piercing truthfulness. Where possible, I accompany the music with appropriate pictures, follow it with a proclamation of the gift of eternal life and offer an invitation to the opened doors of heaven. Resurrection, from the Son of Man to the Common Man.

> They will see the Son of Man coming on the clouds of the sky, with power and great glory. And he will send his angels with a loud trumpet call, and they will gather his elect from the four winds, from one end of the heavens to the other. (Matthew 24:30)

Early in 2007, hearts were all a-flutter in Manchester when it was announced that the city was to be the site of the first national 'super casino'. On Easter Day that year, I found myself preaching at a little inner-city church sited next door to an already established, normal-sized casino. It suddenly occurred to me that Easter was the exact opposite of such a place. In a gambling house there are many losers and just one winner. On the cross, God's casino, there was just one loser, just one who paid so that there might be many winners.

Jesus' style

> Jesus' teachings have the ring of originality. They betray a mind whose processes were swift and direct, hitting the nail on the head without waste of words.[14]

So far we have looked at the content, 'the treasure in the chest', of Jesus' proclamation. Now it is time to offer a few observations (which is all that the limited information we have in the Gospels will allow) about the chest that houses the treasure: his manner or style of delivery.

- Jesus was a powerful, trumpet-like announcer, a sort of newspaper headline-writer and vendor rolled into one. His incisive 'in yer face' style was impossible to ignore and clearly commanded immediate attention. Today we are inclined to talk to people with a more measured, seminar feel, and they are more inclined not to listen.

---

[14] C. H. Dodd, *The Founder of Christianity*, Macmillan 1970.

Jesus was more like a politician on the campaign trail than a schoolmaster; more like a composer than a violin teacher. He was a herald, the bringer of an urgent message that could not wait, could not become the stuff of academic debate.[15]

- You only make a first impression once. Jesus made an immediate impression that was positive, bright, optimistic and authoritative. To put it bluntly, he believed in his product.
- 'See the birds of the air.' He was a very visual speaker, seeing and using pictures everywhere, in fields, villages and cities. Pictures open mental doors, go deep and leave lasting memories, and there is more to it than the blanket use of PowerPoint tools. So if you haven't got a computer, don't worry, and if you have one, turn it off sometimes and be a bit more imaginative. For a CD-buying, iPod-wearing age, songs and tunes are often our pictures. In the late 1980s I began working with my colleague Neil Short on a series of gospel presentations based on rock music. These started out, in those pre-PowerPoint days, as slide presentations alongside single songs. They were so successful that they quickly grew into full theatrical events involving visuals, dance and mime, audience participation, live music and the preached word. *The Gospel According to Queen* was soon followed by *The Beatles Bible* and later by *Oasis at the Cross.* They were of the culture and of the moment, and created a great response.
- As we have already seen, Jesus was a great story-teller. 'There was once a king / a poor man / a bunch of bridesmaids. . .'

---

[15] N.T. Wright, *Jesus and the Victory of God.*

Note that these are all stories about people. I am hooked already. There is an ongoing debate about the actual purpose of Jesus' use of stories or parables. Some see them as a deliberate strategy to somehow disguise or hide the truth from the wrong sort of people, based not least on statements like that of Jesus in Mark 4:11–12. But if Jesus is all about letting light shine, opening gateways and leading people into the way and truth of all things, it is just about impossible to imagine why he would want to put a cover over the message (Matthew 5:15). Mark 4 can be read not so much as Jesus describing his cloaking device as him reflecting back on people's blindness and lack of curiosity. This leaves us open to learn from and model the conventional understanding of parables, which is that they are the creations of a master story-teller who wants his listeners to get the point. They are tales, illustrations, metaphors. They are devices that make it easy to remember. They are fun. They remind us that most normal people are not at home in the lecture room or sanctuary, but in the seven days a week, non-precious wraparound world.

Jesus spoke all these things to the crowd in parables; he did not say anything to them without using a parable. (Matthew 13:34)

- Not only was Jesus incarnate, he was also incarnational. He had the common touch. He had the feel of ordinary life and of the ordinary people who lived it. He knew and talked about village life, jobs, money, relationships and children. These days, I find myself listening to many very good, but very religious talks. They have references to spirituality and church, and quote well-known Christians or medieval saints, long passages from the Bible or famous hymns. I am convinced that if Jesus was with us now, he would be quoting from *EastEnders* and *Match of the Day*. Many years ago, I worked with a team to organise a series of evangelistic family services. In effect it was an early 'Fresh Expression', entitled 'Bart Simpson Meets Jesus'. This gave us a rich, deep vein of colour, fun, stories and relevance to work with. We were being trendy, gimmicky and incarnational, and it worked. How often do we see the church with the 'common touch' today? Where do we see 'the common people hearing us gladly'? What is our gospel for young, single, 'living it big' adults? And, most shocking of all, when will the working classes have the good news brought to them?

- Jesus was both inclusive and exclusive. He was inclusive in his appeal to every man and woman – communicating with both *Sun* and *Telegraph* readers, if you like. He was exclusive in that his proclamation had a definite end product. He did not finish with a helpful thought, but with a strong invitation to jump in or jump out. In many of our churches today, deep and passionate experience of the good news is a bit like Frances Burnett's *The Secret Garden*. The walls are high, the door is covered in ivy, and the key has been all but lost through non-use. We need more robins on spades showing the children how to get in.

When the people first heard Jesus, they were gobsmacked. It must have been a bit like the first 'talkies' or colour television: they had seen that sort of thing before, but never like this. They were amazed and thought it something completely new (Mark 1:27).

He was praised by everyone (Luke 4:15) and his fame spread far and wide (Matthew 4:24). The big word in all of this is 'authority'. Clearly Jesus had masses of it.

Jesus' authority was manifest in three ways. Firstly, while other rabbis taught and repeatedly quoted from the past teachings of other, earlier rabbis, he was much more direct and self-confident: 'You have heard that it was said . . . but I say to you. . .' Jesus was his own man, offering his own opinions, making his own pronouncements. In other words, he was either very arrogant or very special. His listeners got the point (Matthew 7:29). Secondly, his words were accompanied by acts of healing and the driving out of unclean spirits (Mark 1:27). Thirdly, Jesus did not just talk about forgiveness, he declared and delivered it (Mark 2:10). This is a powerful, indeed authoritative, combination: the word of truth, the touch of compassion and the promise of forgiveness.

As with so much of his own mission, Jesus passed his authority on to his disciples (Mark 6:7). This same authority is lent to us today when we do it his way in our world, and it still carries a massive self-authenticating impact. When we are listening both to the words of our God and the needs of our neighbours, just as Jesus did, then we are suddenly different from all the other scribes and Pharisees.

The preaching of the good news of the kingdom and the encouragement to repent and believe has been a 'restricted practice' in the church for far too long.

- It has become restricted largely, though not entirely, to evangelicals. It is the responsibility and privilege of all traditions. We can all do it in our own way and using our own language.

- It has become restricted to a few strange extroverts called 'evangelists'. In fact, just about everyone should have a go: preachers, Sunday school teachers, youth leaders, etc.
- It has become largely restricted to men. No wonder the whole enterprise has got a tough, hard-edged and often intimidating feel to it! We need more women evangelists.
- Finally, and most tragically of all, it has become restricted to a few occasions and a few places. How many more, both inside and outside the church, would accept the invitation if they actually received it?

In making these comments about Jesus' proclamation in our world, I have tried to demonstrate something that is broad and inclusive; something that is very true to the gospel, while being flexible enough to be used by Catholic, evangelical, charismatic and liberal evangelisers; something that is people-friendly and incarnational.

The fundamental truth is that of grace. Grace is about unconditional, transparent, all-giving and vulnerable love. The word 'grace' is a Pauline term and never actually appears on the lips of Jesus, but Paul did not invent grace – he found it in Jesus. He found it tattooed into every one of his actions and woven deep into his proclamation. No wonder the writer of John describes Jesus' appearance and life by saying:

> We have seen his glory, the glory of the One and Only, who came from the Father, full of grace and truth. (John 1:14)

Evangelists, who are supposed to be the announcers and givers-away of his grace, have often had a problem with its sheer scale of generosity. We have felt inclined to add the odd qualifier, trim its theological broadness, and ask people to respond in a way that involves them paying a little bit for something that is free. It is the joyful vocation of everyone who is a member of the grace community to help proclaim that the all-giving-to-all-people love of God comes rushing towards us and offers us everything.

Your words. . .

Call me to listen
Dawn a sense of hope
Prick me to tears
Push me to laughter
Open my inner door
Stir up my mud
Disturb my sleep
Incline me to hide
Help me to decide
Make me want to believe

Are suddenly silent
You have stopped speaking
You are listening to me
Waiting for me to reply. . .

CHAPTER THREE

Plan Like He Did

> When he humbled himself to come among us as a man he fulfilled the plan you formed long ago. (Eucharistic prayer for Advent 1, from the Roman Missal)

Having looked afresh at Jesus the man, and considered again the content and style of his message, I now want to focus on his evangelistic methods. This will involve looking at his people skills, healing ministry, discipleship and community-building strategies.

First, however, we look at the way he operated a free and flexible yet carefully planned mission.

'Could you just give me a rough outline or overview of Jesus' ministry, so that I can sort of get a handle on it?' It was a reasonable enough question, and who better to ask than an evangelist who is supposed to be emulating Jesus? No one had ever asked me this question before, however, and I had never asked it of myself. My brain went into a kind of search-cum-spin mode, while my mouth moved into automatic pilot as I desperately tried to give the impression that I knew what I was talking about. Thinking it over afterwards, I realised that I did not have such an overview. I had no big picture and certainly no detailed sense of shape or progression. I had a vague, unformed jigsaw picture of Jesus whizzing around the Galilee like a bumblebee in a jam jar. There were lots of boats, crowds of people, loaves of bread, lepers and villages, endless activity but no real pattern. Then there were other jigsaw pieces that were set in Jerusalem – Palm Sunday, tables, temples and trials, then the cross, then the resurrection, full stop. After years of reading about and preaching on individual stories, I had all the best pieces, but they were not exactly connected. So I set out on a different kind of reading and thinking process, in order to assemble the picture.

What emerged was not so much a string of incidents, but a narrative, a story with a beginning, a middle and an end. In many respects it is the familiar story of a hero who is sent out from the safety of the king's castle to a strange land on a rescue mission.

Jesus was an evangelising missioner sent out on a mission by his missionary Father. What interests me now in the big overview jigsaw story of Jesus the evangelist is the *pattern*. Was there a plan? If there was, can we work it out? And can we adopt it and use it in our world?

Planned evangelism

Looking at the careful details of timing and location around both Jesus' birth and his launch into mission thirty years on, seeing his singleness of vision and direction to the cross through the different phases of the journey, noting the way he recruited and trained his key followers, I am now convinced that there is a basic mission plan behind Jesus' ministry. In fact, when I think it through, I would be amazed if there was not such a plan. This is not quite the same as saying that he set out with a detailed blueprint and followed every detail on some sort of Ordnance Survey route march to messiahship. I do, however, assume that there was some sort of rough plan of action leading to the accomplishment of his God-given task. Reflecting back on what he had witnessed, Peter seems to have come to the same conclusion: 'this man, handed over to you according to the definite plan and foreknowledge of God. . .' (Acts 2:23 NRSV). Matthew's Gospel is particularly keen to see the various events in Jesus' life as fulfilling Old Testament prophecies, so I think we can say that here also there is the notion of preparation and anticipation. There are three building blocks or aspects in the plan, which I am going to label as the 'geographical', the 'organisational' and the 'vocational'.

Geographical

Actually, this could just as easily be described as the 'developmental' or 'journeying' part of the plan, but calling it 'geographical' gives it some nice local colour. It begins in the Galilee (Luke 4:14). This was an area that had been recolonised by the Jews a hundred years earlier. The Greeks and Romans administered the area from their cities such as Sepphoris and Tiberias. Jesus clearly avoided such Gentile centres and devoted his attentions to travelling between the smaller Jewish towns and villages (Matthew 9:35). Josephus, a first-century Jewish historian, tells us there were two hundred and forty of these. Jesus seems to have concentrated most of his attention in the north-west, around Bethsaida, Gennesaret, Chorazin and Capernaum, where he had his base. Galilee was the land he knew best. Here he felt confident and on the people's wavelength. It was also the area that was furthest away from the Jerusalem-based power elites.

This Galilee period was a time of proclamation, healing and exorcism. The crowds were sucked in from north and south in a continually evangelising, recruiting and growing festival of the kingdom.

The Galilee was not a huge area, perhaps the size of a couple of English counties. Most of the places Jesus visited would have been within a two-day walk of his base at Capernaum, so it looks as if he had a semi-itinerant, semi-localised, Pied Piper sort of mission.

Opposition arrived in the form of Pharisees sent down from Jerusalem, but it all looks very much as if Jesus was in control. Occasionally he travelled further afield, to Tyre in the north and the ten towns of the Decapolis to the south-east, perhaps to escape the crowds, perhaps to test out the waters, but he always returned to the Galilee. Late in this time phase he sent out the disciples on their own mission, 'from village to village'.

At the heart of it all are the great nature and feeding miracles. The calming of the storm and Jesus' walking on the water both stress his power to command the forces of nature and the disciples' failure to understand him: 'Their hearts were hardened' (Mark 6:52). If the nature miracles are about Jesus' power, then the feeding of the five thousand and then the four thousand are probably best viewed as being all about his providing for the needs of the hungry and the poor. In effect, they are a bit like massive, all-inclusive eucharists. Some commentators take them to be a duplication, two versions of the same story. Others, however, note the differences and see two separate occasions. Since the time of Augustine, there has been a tradition of seeing the feeding of the five thousand – which happens in the Galilee, with the people sitting on grass and twelve basketfuls of leftovers being collected – as symbolic of Jesus' mission to Israel. In contrast, the feeding of the four thousand occurs outside Jewish territory in the desert. Here, in place of the twelve final basketfuls (symbolic of the twelve tribes), there are seven, this significant number being all about Jesus' sufficiency to feed the Gentiles.

His visit to Caesarea Philippi and the episode known as the 'transfiguration' are recorded by all three of the Synoptic Gospels and clearly form a turning point. In the first, Peter leads the disciples in their awakening to who Jesus really is (Matthew 16:16), while in the second event it is Jesus' Father who vocally recognises and encourages him (Matthew 17:5). For the first time, Jesus talks about his destined death and soon after that, 'he left Galilee and went into the region of Judea to the other side of the Jordan' (Matthew 19:1). From this point on, he is no longer 'zig-zagging' around the villages. He is on a purposeful road towards Jerusalem, passing down through the communities of the Jordan valley.

Matthew and Mark tell a similar story of crowds still following him, growing opposition and deep teaching of the disciples. The feel is always that of a focused progression. There are asides along the way, but the destination is clear.

> They were on their way up to Jerusalem, with Jesus leading the way, and the disciples were astonished, while those who followed were afraid. (Mark 10:32)

Luke follows the same course, but adds much more information. He tells of Jesus' rejection by the Samaritans, the sending out of the Seventy-two, and adds more teaching, parables and healings.

The third and final phase of this geographically planned mission happened in Jerusalem. It opened with the King of Peace coming to reclaim his capital city, and continued with him purifying the temple and making it into a great teaching theatre. Each night Jesus returned to his 'safe house' in Bethany after an increasingly threatening day in the city. We see him falling deeper into his enemies' hands, but he seemed to anticipate and prepare for this. Movements and venues were carefully planned in advance as Jesus and the disciples moved through the now familiar steps of the Passover, then his betrayal, trial, crucifixion and resurrection. This whole geographical movement looks very much like a planned campaign. Jesus was all the time taking the initiative, deciding time and place. He was the one holding the map.

How might we emulate some aspects of Jesus' tripartite plan? When it comes to drawing up a geographical plan for evangelism, a church or Christian agency needs to think about its surrounding neighbourhood with all its community features, schools, gathering points and types of inhabitants. Added to this are the human networks of its own members and the organisations, children's groups, drop-ins and social care projects that it runs itself or with which it engages. In this way, 'local' or 'rooted church' is combined with the relational spread of what Pete Ward calls 'liquid church'.

It is great fun and very motivational to put all of this, along with numerical 'guesstimates', onto a big diagram or mission map. In effect, this is the local Jesus-type evangelisers plotting out their own 'Galilee' and preparing for a localised itinerant work. I have done this exercise with literally hundreds of churches – small rural and inner-city as well as large suburban ones – and have always been touched by their excitement as they realise that they are not the isolated 'Johnny No Mates' groups that they thought they were. By doing this simple mapping activity, the average local church discovers that it has anything from a hundred and fifty to five hundred close contacts, and that its fields really are ripe for harvest. Furthermore, I have learnt myself that we cannot simply divide our society up into two big boxes marked 'unchurched or de-churched', with a smaller 'churchgoers' box alongside. There is another huge category which spills over into the others and is constantly receiving new members. I think we should call this organic swirling mass something like 'in contact with but not yet churched', or 'I have recently been touched by their love and am open to know more about the church'.

Organisational

The planned mission did not just involve Jesus – it included a whole people movement which gathered around him and had to be carefully organised if it was to hold together. The key twelve disciples were recruited in the early days in Galilee (Mark 3:13–14). They were taught, sometimes as part of a wider crowd, but more often, as time went on, as a select group. They witnessed the healings and exorcisms, sometimes helping out as apprentices, and were themselves sent out in pairs on mission (Matthew 10:1–4). Of these twelve, Peter, James and John were developed as a sort of inner core and Jesus was hardly ever seen without them. It seems that, unlike many of today's evangelists, he never worked alone and he did not want his disciples to work in a vulnerable and isolated way either.

This is a great organisational model for any church, mission team or agency to follow. A visionary leader works with a small inner group who both learn from and offer support to the leader. Then there is a slightly larger – though still small enough to be actively involved – leadership group. Finally, there is a third and larger grouping, who are not so much passive members, but rather active followers. For any would-be pioneer, newly appointed leader or creator of such a grouping, Jesus offers a great pattern to follow in the way that he recruits, envisions, spends quality time with, trains, delegates and finally hands over responsibility to his team.

The Twelve were not the only ones. Luke introduces a group of women who had been cured of evil spirits and infirmities, who travelled with Jesus and were there at the end, and he also refers to 'many others' who provided for Jesus and his team out of their own resources (Luke 8:1–3). There was a second sending out of missioners, numbering seventy-two (Luke 10:1), and a band of about a hundred and twenty companions who were still together in Jerusalem after the ascension (Acts 1:15). Various individuals are mentioned such as Mary, Martha and Lazarus, Mary Magdalene, Jesus' mother Mary and her sister, along with his brothers and sisters, Nicodemus, Joseph of Arimathea, Justus and Matthias and the two friends walking back to Emmaus, all of whom were to some extent part of the movement.

Bringing and holding this group, or series of groups, together, and keeping communications, preparations and relationships good and operational must have called for plans that were well thought through and executed. We gain a restricted glimpse of a small part of the organisational task with Matthew's mention of the gathering in Galilee before the march to the south (17:22).

Good organisational plans are all about vision, broken down into ultimate goals and medium-term objectives. As with Jesus, two to three years is probably the best time frame for most of us to work with. Having a clear vision will help us to establish the priorities that shape our use and deployment of people and resources. Organising what we are going to do also involves recognising what we are *not* going to do. Attempting to do too much in a hopeful but unfocused way is, of course, the great 'woodworm' that eats away at our effectiveness. 'Never forget that it is not what you do yourself as much as what you get others to do that will be the making of the Army.' So wrote General Booth, the founder of the Salvation Army, to his subordinate in America.[1]

When it comes to organising, we all want more people, more money and better buildings. We all want more because we want to do more, hence our frustration. I have often found the parable of the talents to be a great guide in these matters. If we are only given two or three talents or people resources, then that is all we are expected to work with. We invest time and energy according to our means. The scale of our initial resourcing and resulting interest or impact are all God's affair.

Vocational

Jesus' geographical and organisational plans were the practical and logistical outworkings of his deep-down vocational plan. A person's vocational plan begins to form when he or she asks God, 'What is it that you want me to do with my life? What is the mission that you have for me?' According to James Dunn, this is the one 'overarching question concerning Jesus' life'.[2] Of course, we in the evangelism trade already know the answer to this one. Quoting John 3:16, we sing out in unison that Jesus came to save all who place their belief in him – but maybe there was more to it than that.

Jesus' first vocational intention, or focused goal, was to bring some sort of renewal or reformation, not to the world, but to the people of Israel. In this mission he was continuing the work of the

---

[1] Quoted in Roy Hattersley, *Blood and Fire*, Little, Brown 1999, page 249.

[2] *Jesus Remembered*, page 489.

Old Testament prophets and John the Baptist, but he was doing it in a bigger way:

> Something has happened between the mission of John and that of Jesus, something which has lifted possibilities onto a new plane . . . John represented the period of preparation, Jesus the period of fulfilment.[3]

Matthew locates the beginning of Jesus' ministry in 'the area of Zebulun and Naphtali' (4:13–15), the land of the Gentiles, but shows his vocation or calling as concentrated entirely towards the Jews. He has Jesus going to Jewish settlements and teaching in synagogues. In calling twelve men to be his closest followers, he mirrored the twelve tribal patriarchs. His preaching of good news, kingdom and repentance should probably be seen first and foremost as a calling on Israel to return to its covenant God. His use of the shepherd and sheep, vineyard and fig-tree metaphors all have particular allusions to Israel. His sense of commissioning was to Israel, for he could not give their food to dogs (Matthew 15:26), and it was this that he passed on to his disciples:

> These twelve Jesus sent out with the following instructions: 'Do not go among the Gentiles or enter any town of the Samaritans. Go rather to the lost sheep of Israel. (Matthew 10:5)

His movement towards Jerusalem and planned reclaiming of the temple and crucifixion should be seen first and foremost as the zenith of his mission to restore Israel.

---

[3] James Dunn, *Jesus Remembered*, page 452.

The problem was that it became increasingly clear to Jesus from early on that the plan was not working. Chorazin, Bethsaida and Capernaum all failed to repent and perhaps he began to wonder whether he should have gone instead to Tyre and Sidon (Matthew 11:20).

Not only did the Jews fail to acknowledge him, but the exact opposite happened with the non-Jewish Canaanite woman and the Roman centurion. There are two occasions in the Gospels where Jesus is 'amazed' or 'astonished'. The first occurs in Mark's account of his rejection by his own people at Nazareth: 'he was amazed at their lack of faith' (6:6). On the second occasion he is struck by the amount of faith displayed by the centurion: 'When Jesus heard this, he was astonished' (Matthew 8:10).

Amazement is a very powerful sensation, much stronger than mere surprise. It is about expectations being confounded and plans being altered accordingly. It was here, in this at first negative, then positive, amazing and – one might say – fuzzy central period of his mission, where success was diluted with failure, that he seems to have changed his thinking. Or perhaps we should think of it as an evolution, from the renewal of Israel to something much bigger. Certainly Jesus would have known from his earliest days that the Old Testament kingdom restoration prophecies of Isaiah, Zechariah and Micah were not for Israel alone but that Israel should become a light for all the nations (Isaiah 42:6). He reminded the Jews of how God had blessed such Gentiles as Naaman the Syrian and the widow of Zarephath (Luke 4:26), and this wider vision comes through in his picture of the birds of the air (coded language for Gentiles) resting in the branches of the mustard tree (Matthew 13:32).

At the end of Matthew's Gospel, Jesus again sends the disciples out on a vocational evangelistic mission. This time they are sent not just to Israel, but to the whole world (28:19). Similarly, at the end of Luke, he makes it clear that the message must go out to 'all nations' (24:47). I would argue, then, that we can see a worldwide vocational plan emerging out of the plan to restore Israel.

In our world, vocations come in all shapes and sizes. They are wrapped around with all the buzzwords – spirituality, communications, administration, teaching, theological education, liturgy, political activism, community care, music and the arts, etc. However, having seen that Jesus' own vocation, and the one that he passed to his disciples, was about sharing the gospel, perhaps we should ask whether Christian vocation should always at least include an element of doing it in his evangelistic way.

At what point did the cross become part of the plan? (We know it was God's plan, but it is another thing to say that Jesus clearly saw it coming from day one.) Did it gradually occur to him as he saw Israel's leaders refuse his ministry and harden their opposition? Or perhaps it formed out of all the swirling clouds of his early proclamations and healings as he realised that something far bigger was required. The gradual appearance of the cross as the ultimate and climactic part of the mission begins in the latter stages of the Galilean period. Once Jesus had 'resolutely set out for Jerusalem', there are three reported moments when he talked about his coming crucifixion with the disciples alone (Matthew 16:21; 17:22; 20:18). Reading the Gospels, there is a strengthening impression of the cross – you might call it his muse, or a siren's voice singing him onto the rocks, calling him to his sacrificial and magnetic destiny.

> Just as Moses lifted up the snake in the desert, so the Son of Man must be lifted up, that everyone who believes in him may have eternal life. (John 3:14–15)

Here we have Jesus the reforming Mosaic prophet, Jesus the Lamb and Jesus the evangelist together as one.

Is it possible for us to take Jesus' methodology of a planned evangelistic mission and apply it to our own situation?

Evangelists are well known for always having an answer. Some years ago, I discovered that a question was much more revealing. Answers fill people up, while questions open them up. So here are two big vocational questions to open us up:

1. To what extent are we an evangelising church today?

- Am I an 'evangelism person'?
- Is the local church to which I belong a missionary church?
- Where do I put my time and money?
- Do we have a passionate vocational sense of what we want to achieve?

2. Is ours a planned mission?

- Is prayer, passion and activity enough?
- Do we have a plan with a goal?
- Do we all know and believe in the plan?
- Is the plan working?

Total evangelism

Jesus was not a conventional religious leader who did the odd spot of evangelism from time to time. Such a thought automatically shrinks and tames him; suddenly we see a wild tiger caged up and made safe in a zoo. His kingdom evangelism was not so much something that he did, but more something that he was. He was a total evangelist, sent out by an all-missionary God, and part of his mission was to create a totally missionary movement.

In giving birth to a people movement, Jesus was not creating a group where everyone was always on the move in a geographical sense, like a travelling circus, but one where movement and following could happen within a stable lifestyle in the village as much as on the road. As we have seen, he operated as a sort of semi-itinerant, semi-localised missioner. Sometimes he was journeying with a band of followers; at other times he was based in one place, probably developing a more rooted kind of presence.

> The evidence points, I suggest, towards Jesus intending to establish, and indeed succeeding in establishing, what we might call cells of followers, mostly continuing to live in their towns and villages, who by their adoption of his praxis, his way of being Israel, would be distinctive within their local communities.[4]

His was a movement in that it was moving in its evangelistic vocation. It was 'apostolic' (Matthew 10:2). There are two modes to being apostolic: the first is about spending time with and learning from Jesus, and the second is about being sent out by him (Acts 1:21). Obviously, there must have been plenty of followers who did not share in this apostolic character. Then as now, there must have been many who were content to attend meetings, receive his ministry, make a small donation and then go home for dinner – the 'turn up, fill up and shut up brigade'. There is nothing to be gained in having an over-rosy view of the past. People are always people. Nevertheless, we cannot avoid the conclusion that in the main this

---

[4] N.T. Wright, *Jesus and the Victory of God.*

was a radical and total missionary movement. Total mission or evangelism is by definition an absolute, and there has never been a single church or individual other than Jesus who has achieved it. It is still a meaningful ideal to work towards, however. It is a bit like the Dutch concept of 'total football', where every player is expected to be totally committed, and where pure football can happen in every part of the pitch and throughout the entire game. The Dutch never actually achieved total football, but in reaching for it they created a newly beautiful and powerful game.

Total planned evangelism today

If we could develop a hunger to save the lost and grow the kingdom which was normative rather than exceptional in the church, then we would have a new kind of beautiful, total Christianity. In his inclusive totality, Jesus never seems to have set aside a few individuals called 'evangelists'. There is no mention of a specific gift or anointing and certainly no committees or groupings for those who were interested in the subject. His was a bigger vision, that the whole of his followers would at some point be involved in the adventure. At the end of Matthew the charge was given to the remaining Eleven, but they were representatives of the full tribes of the new Israel (28:19). In Luke the sending out is linked to the empowering of the Holy Spirit and is extended to 'all' of them (Acts 1:6–8), the 'Eleven and those with them' (Luke 24:33).

> You are witnesses of these things. I am going to send you what my Father has promised. (Luke 24:48–49)

Our church of today had its genesis in Jesus' own people movement. We share their DNA. Yet somehow we have mutated over the years into a rheumatic and insecure institution, less concerned with saving lives than with preserving our own. The flame of evangelism has not gone out, however. In fact, it is probably burning more brightly than it has done for quite a while and looks like getting even brighter in the future. In 2004 the Church of England published a mould-breaking report, entitled *Mission-Shaped Church*. This was born out of a growing belief in and practise of mission and evangelism that had been swelling over the previous twenty-five years or so. The report has birthed a pan-Anglican and Methodist movement. Today the church is pushing forward, both to plant 'Fresh Expressions' and to 'refresh' traditional expressions of church.

For the church to shift back from institution to movement and to aim for total mission does not mean that we suddenly curtail all activity apart from evangelism. To do mission you do not have to drop maintenance. In fact, as I wander around different churches, I almost always find that the ones who do the best maintenance are the mission churches. However, it probably would mean for most of us that we close down some of our busyness and replace it with some more specific missionary work as we rebalance the books. In the main, the reorientation is about a change of spirit rather than a change of shape. The vocation to evangelism has first to infiltrate our attitudes before it can affect our activities. So it may well mean that we do less teaching and more proclaiming, spend less time and money on ourselves and more on others, employ less introspection and more outward vision, do less chasing of academia and more chasing of lost sheep, and certainly produce less committee and more compassion. It will also mean that every funeral, wedding, uniformed group, social event, school involvement and community project that we continue to undertake will have a 'Jesus the evangelist' edge to it, proclaiming the good news.

In an attempt to be good stewards, leaders of large churches, organisations, denominations and dioceses can easily slip into management mode. Here the agenda soon becomes that of the 'three Bs' – buildings, budgets and bureaucracy (moving people around). The mission is then in danger of concentrating on the question 'How do we keep running?' rather than 'How do we keep growing?' Good management, buildings and finance are all important, but they take on a different perspective when we go from maintenance to mission, from institution to movement. Callum Brown is over-pessimistic when he talks of the churches as 'in seemingly endless decay' and British Christian culture as being 'in its death throes'.[5] He dismisses our attempts to halt this decline as so many management reshuffles. A major rediscovery of our evangelistic vocation, however, would be far more than a management makeover. It would be a return to our roots, and we could become again the Jesus church doing it his way in our world. Such a renaissance could actually be the 'destiny-changing turning point' that Brown says we so desperately need.[6]

David Bosch and Richard Fletcher have both produced major surveys of the rise and fall of the historic churches as evangelising missionary movements. Bosch has covered the entire history of the church (in *Transforming Mission*), while Fletcher has worked in greater depth on the Dark Ages and the medieval period (in *The Conversion of Europe*). Both make the same point, that it is not that sometimes mission works and sometimes it does not, but that sometimes the church engages in mission and at other times it fails to do so.

---

5 *The Death of Christian Britain*, page 196.
6 *Ibid.* page 7.

> It is observable that in the course of Christian history churchmen have been now more, now less concerned with spreading the faith. Why did Pope Gregory I decide to send a mission to convert the English to Christianity? What was it that took Patrick to Ireland, or Boniface to Germany, or Anskar to Sweden, or Cyril and Methodius to Moravia?[7]

Perhaps the question facing us is this: 'What is stopping today's church being sent afresh to today's world?' Is it theological confusion in the library, fear in the vestry, apathy in the pews, lack of money in the treasury, or institutionalism in the headquarters?

I recently attended the national conference of the Church of England Liturgical Commission. It was advertised as being about liturgy and mission, but when I got there it actually seemed to be about liturgy and liturgy. It was a bit like spending a few days in a national park, where the messy, struggling, contemporary world is kept at a distance, and where Cranmer's *Book of Common Prayer*'s commitment to the general public, the use of the vernacular and local relevance are all quietly dropped. Even in the 'protected zones' of spirituality and liturgy, which have developed a life of their own in recent years, there has to be an awakening to the idea of evangelism. We are not the liturgical wing of the National Trust with a mission to preserve all that is best from the past. We are the Jesus movement with a mission to serve and to save in the present. Perhaps there is a question here about how much we value our insider traditions compared to our outsider fellow human beings.

Evangelists and evangelistically minded church leaders have been increasingly aware in recent years of the large number of people

---

[7] Richard Fletcher, *The Conversion of Europe*, page 6.

who come to faith, perhaps during a mission or enquirers' course, but who cannot find a way into worship. Many of them find the worshipping community to be unwelcoming and the event itself to be lengthy, remote from their culture, wordy and boring.

Grace Davie's thesis[8] on the shift from a culture of obligation to a culture of choice should be required reading for all those of us who are involved in the creation and leading of worship. She argues that in a culture of obligation people attend meetings and church services purely out of a sense of loyalty and commitment: they come because they feel obliged to. In contrast, people who live in a choice culture attend things that attract, meet their expectations and satisfy them. In a richly varied world, there are now many different things that they can do with their Sunday mornings, and they will choose to do what pleases them the most.

The danger is that the church is still operating in a 'culture of obligation' mode, but we have a mission to a world that is operating in a culture of choice and that has moved on from us in recent decades. We are creating our type of worship, be it traditional, charismatic or alternative, and expecting the outsiders to come in and appreciate it. We have moved from incarnationalism to institutionalism. We are not doing it 'his way in our world', but 'our way in his church'.

It is not just clergy, worship directors and church leaders who slip back from the sharp edge of total mission. Evangelists, too, can lapse into 'maintenance mode'. Ian Knox is one of the most experienced and respected English full-time evangelists. I asked him what key factors sometimes lessened the flame of evangelists. He gave me three answers:

---

[8] Grace Davie, *Europe: The Exceptional Case*, Darton, Longman & Todd 2002, page 148.

- As evangelists become well known, they pick up more and more invitations to speak at Christian events and conferences, to teach rather than to do. 'Frankly, it is easier to gain the plaudits from Christians, rather than non-Christians.'
- Gradual aging means it takes longer to recover and bounce back from tiring and difficult missions. Evangelism can be a rough old game.
- Evangelists are often very insecure and negative about themselves, their work and their level of impact. They are easily hurt and injured. It is easier in this situation to pull back to do training, organising and writing.

Of course speaking at conferences is important, while writing and training are vital, but every evangelist will understand Ian's honest words.

Currently in the Church of England there are two major areas of unrest threatening to dominate and disrupt the enterprise. The Anglo-Catholics are very consumed by the issue of women bishops, while the evangelicals are all in a lather about homosexuality. Interestingly, although these issues dominated the run-up to and the agenda of the 2008 Lambeth Conference, they were both described by John Sentamu, the Archbishop of York, as being of lesser importance than the primary matter of mission. He is surely right. Leaving aside the rights and wrongs of each topic, what unites them is that they are both secondary and both disuniting. Jesus' vocation to evangelistic mission is the big and primary subject. (It might also be the one single issue that could unite us afresh.) He was concerned for human destiny, not just doctrinal purity. If we are to be his church, made in his image and following his mission, then we need to return to our true roots. We need to do it his way in our world – in effect to be less in love with ourselves and more in love with his world (John 3:16).

- Evangelicals need to read afresh the real Bible story of Jesus the evangelist.
- Catholics should be reminded that a truly catholic church is also an apostolic one.
- Liberals must be open enough to realise that the only way you can get an inclusive church is by going out and inviting everyone in.
- Charismatics have to be encouraged to thirst not just for church renewal, but for a spirit of total church vocational mission.

Planning his evangelistic mission in our world

Jesus had a huge sense of empowering vocation and it looks very much as if he channelled that energy into a carefully thought-through plan or series of evolving plans. In fact, he also had a plan for the apostolic church, to be put into operation after his ascension and the coming of the Holy Spirit:

> You will be my witnesses in Jerusalem, and in all Judea and Samaria, and to the ends of the earth. (Acts 1:8)

Having a plan enabled Jesus to know what he had to do and, by implication, what he could leave alone or at least put on the back-burner:

> Let us go somewhere else – to the nearby villages – so that I can preach there also. That is why I have come. (Mark 1:38)

His planning was proactive, enabling him to achieve his specific goals rather than being sidetracked by lesser ones.

I was recently asked to meet with a group of ministers who were all in their first year of leading their first church. Theoretically they were all keen on evangelism, but somehow they had lost it in the unfocused, hamster-wheel life of weekly services, funerals, routine and paperwork. There was one exception: John, a young Anglo-Catholic vicar. He knew that first and foremost he was there to help people find God. This sharp awareness was central to all the other 'vicar stuff' that he was doing.

Malcolm is a brand-new evangelist who comes and talks to me. He is enthusiastic, passionate and very capable. So it is not very surprising that people keep asking him to do things. His ministry has become barnacle-encrusted with pastoral visiting, teaching, children's work and youth work. Fortunately he has seen this and has begun to rediscover what it was that he was 'called out to do'.

Jesus' sense of vision led to his proactive planning, which created a structured time and space, which in turn allowed him to be reactive, responding to individuals and situations along the way without losing focus or direction. It was strategically thought and prayed through in advance, while also being subjective and intuitive in its daily execution. In our psychological make-up, most of us tend to be either strongly proactive and strategic, or reactive and intuitive. The key is to restrain our stronger side and strengthen our weaker side, and so to balance the two. In effect, this means that planning and strategising people like me must focus less on projects and allow more space for other people, while those who are great at always being there for others will need to get away from daily demands, find a bit of time and space and do some serious planning. Having a firm yet flexible plan which we follow in a disciplined way, while allowing for reflection and ongoing evaluation, is an effective and Jesus way of working.

Jesus the Planning Evangelist

Proactive	---------	Reactive
Strategic	---------	Intuitive
Objective	---------	Subjective
Projects	---------	People

Proactive, careful, visionary planning is not an alternative to reactive, spontaneous leadership, but an aid which brings clarity and direction to it. As well as planned events, there will always be crises, happenings, people and occasional unplanned-for opportunities.

Planning and reacting are not opposites, but siblings. I was recently involved with a 'Fresh Expressions' church plant where the relationships, skills, commitment, prayer and personalities that had all been built up around the launch were superb. But there was no plan – no strategy, no goals, no support mechanisms, no thought for a possible Plan B if things did not go too well. There was a big sense of vision, of where they wanted to get to, but no road map. Doing a bit of preparatory planning would not have gone against all the rich elements in the project; it would have helped to bring out their full potential.

The elements of a good plan are grouped around three questions:

- Where are we now?
- How do we get there?
- Where do we want to be in three years?

We can see these three questions in each of the three strands of Jesus' master mission plan. Geographically, he started out in Galilee and travelled to Jerusalem. Organisationally, he began as a lone individual and assembled a cohesive missional community. Vocationally, he had a vision of what he wanted to achieve and went out and did it. He began with a calling and ended with a Calvary.

In my home diocese of Manchester, we launched a project in 2003 called 'Plan for Growth'. We were concerned to stimulate and assist all of our churches towards mission and evangelism. The essence of the scheme was to provide advice, resources and a planning template to help the local church draw up and then put into operation a three-year development plan. Reflecting on the scheme now, I have two main observations. Firstly, and sadly, the majority of our churches have declined to take part. Natural church conservatism and a reluctance to change are big obstacles to the kingdom. Secondly, the majority of the seventy or so churches that have participated so far have clearly found that it has worked really well and has helped them to move forward into growth.

Working with and to a plan seems to be a difficult idea for many of us involved in Christian ministry. To some it appears a bit like wearing a straitjacket, or perhaps the setting of goals is seen as another opportunity to fail. To others it looks like a secular way of operating that somehow limits the visionary freedom of the Spirit, or does not take account of the unique nature of our vocation. Maybe it is just too radical for those of us who have built a comfort zone out of our traditional way of operating.

We all know that 'where there is no vision, the people perish' (Proverbs 29:18 AV). Well, the opposite is equally true: where there is a vision, the people flourish.

- Vision, dream, goal – all create a sense of direction and destiny, enthusiasm and energy. Vision is about imagining our future history rather than just letting it happen to us. It is so vital that God called the prophet Habakkuk to write down his vision (2:2). He clearly wanted it to be understood and not forgotten.
- Planning is the act of putting the vision down on paper, working out what help and resources are needed, and spacing it out into manageable units.
- Envisioning happens when we start to share the plan with others, listen to their response, and see their commitment levels rise.

Careful planning is an important part of the journey. Jesus once told the story of a bunch of women who went to a wedding without bothering to plan or prepare. He called them the 'foolish virgins' (Matthew 25:1).

In 2007, English football reached a new low when the national team failed to qualify for the European Nations Cup after defeat at the hands of Croatia. The more perceptive in the football world realised that it was not enough just to change the manager if the 'kingdom of football' was to pull out of decline and into growth. Speaking on one of the more intelligent of the endless discussion programmes, Howard Wilkinson said that three things were needed:

- A plan for a complete rebuild.
- Not a plan that was on the agenda, but one that was top of the agenda.
- A plan that would stay at the top of the agenda for ten years.

Who has ever written a great book, set up an effective charity, made a lengthy journey, conducted a successful political campaign, built a magnificent cathedral, organised a big fun barbeque, or decorated the back bedroom without some sort of plan? So why do we assume that the creating, journeying and building that are involved in the Christian mission can manage without one?

> Suppose one of you wants to build a tower. Will he not first sit down and estimate the cost. . .? (Luke 14:28)

It was Graham Gooch, the cricketer, who made famous the helpful little aphorism, 'If you fail to plan, then plan to fail.'

This is not to say that we should progress in a rigidly prescribed manner. The best plans are organic, and the best creations incorporate plenty of spontaneity and improvisation. Nonetheless, enthusiasm, commitment and hopeful prayer are not enough: they need some sort of architectural vision if their full potential is to be realised. It is possible for vocation, vision, strategic planning, the energising of the Spirit and last-minute, desperate prayer meetings all to work together. It looks like that was how it was for Jesus and how it can be for us.

If we want to learn from Jesus' evangelistic methodology, then I suggest that the first place to start is in the area of planning. For those involved in 'Galilean-style' itinerant evangelism, the planning process will be different from that needed for those working in a more locally rooted 'parable of the sower' context. Despite this, there are similarities and overlaps. There is not the space here to present two fully developed planning schemes, but we can pick out a few salient features.

Itinerant evangelism

- Establish strong links with local churches and maintain good ongoing communications. If cracks are opened, things will fall down them.
- Decide to whom the mission or event is directed. Is it to the congregation, based on the 'Jesus to Israel' model? Is it to the fringe, with a 'come in deeper and closer' feel? Or is it out to the local community, in a pioneering 'building bridges and getting to know you' initiative, rather like Jesus sending out the Seventy-two? Making this decision and then sticking with it is the most important step in your planning.
- Organise events with a style and feel to fit with the people, not the other way around.
- Work out a strategy for how you are going to contact and invite the people with whom you want to engage.
- Plan in advance with the local church how best to conduct follow-up.

Local church

- Foster the desire for growth in the hearts of the congregation. Here you are adopting the Jesus agenda or vocation as that of your church. Of course you will never get everybody to run with it, but once you have about a third of the people thinking in terms of mission and evangelism, you are motoring.
- Set up a few realistic growth targets. Remember: many seeds, a few good plants, much fruit.
- Obtain the necessary teaching, training and consultancy for the leaders and members. Jesus put a lot of deep time into equipping his closest followers.

- Put in place an effective evangelism strategy. I work most of the time with a plan called 'The Four Ps': Presence, Proclamation and Persuasion all wrapped up in Prayer. (For more on this see Chapter 7.) Laurence Singlehurst has a similar system, which he describes in his very helpful little book *Sowing, Reaping, Keeping*.
- Alter your styles of worship to make them more user-friendly, welcoming and colourful.
- Jesus sent his disciples out in twos. Do not become isolated. It can be a great help for a leader or leadership team to find one or two other groups or churches on a similar journey and then spend quality time together, perhaps two or three times a year. Thus the church, or church leader, has a learning companion, a 'study-buddy'.

This sort of in-depth looking and planning ahead takes time, space and prayer, all of which are the exact opposite of frenetic activity. Luke tells us that Jesus was thirty years in the waiting, preparing and planning (3:23). That is a lot of time to grow 'in wisdom and stature, and in favour with God and men' (2:52).

Whatever, whenever and wherever we are planning something, there is a very common mistake that many of us make. We over-expect what can be achieved in one year and under-expect what can be established in three. We need to break out of the short-termism of planning days, weeks or just months ahead and set ourselves some serious and meaty long-term goals. As you work at this, you might find this four-step approach helpful:

Sense the vocation – Be strengthened.
See the vision – Be clear.

Share the plan – be talkative.
Stick to the road – be persistent.

Sticking to the road does not mean that the plan is unalterable. As we saw with Jesus, things change as you go along; life is messy; we are building with real live people, not Lego bricks. The best plans are made of bendy rubber, not brittle cast iron. What it does mean, however, is that we keep going and complete the task. How many half-finished initiatives are there in your attic? On the cross Jesus said, 'It is finished.' He had sensed his vocation from the beginning, and had seen how it could take shape in a particular vision. As he went about the task, he shared the plan with his followers and stuck to the road despite opposition and distractions.

As the Messiah, Jesus' evangelising mission was actually a part of the Father's plan. This is the big plan, beginning with creation, journeying on with the cosmic history of the universe, the creation of life, the birth of human beings, the emergence of Israel and the reclaiming work of the prophets. Jesus' mission was the opening out and climaxing of the whole eternal enterprise.

So, if working in a carefully planned and visionary sort of way is good enough for the Father, became the pattern for Jesus, was passed on to the apostolic church and is meant to coincide with the workings of the Holy Spirit, is it too much to ask that local churches, evangelists, organisations and even whole dioceses and denominations work in this way, planning to use their time, energy, finance and people in a way that leads them out of decline and into growth?

> This is what the kingdom of God is like. A man scatters seed on the ground. Night and day, whether he sleeps or gets up, the seed sprouts and grows, though he does not know how. (Mark 4:26)

Now, after all the pushing and groaning of the last few pages, perhaps I can end this chapter with a personal reflection that will bring encouragement, an impression that I pick up as I wander around many churches today. Something is happening concerning evangelism, and it is not just happening in the usual 'evangelism friendly' corners, but all over the place. It is a bit like the beginning of Kenneth Grahame's *The Wind in the Willows*:

> Spring was moving in the air above and in the earth below and around him, penetrating even his dark and lowly little house with its spirit of divine discontent and longing.[9]

From the very heart of divine loving and seeing
There is a creating, evolving and flowing

The Father's planning and sending
The Son's preparing and missioning
The Spirit's baptising and empowering
The Church's going and planting
The World's receiving and becoming
    and ultimately returning
To the very heart of the divine loving

---

[9] Kenneth Grahame, *The Wind in the Willows*, 1908, Methuen paperback 1961, page 7.

CHAPTER FOUR

The Healing Evangelist

The evangelising Jesus broke like a great wave of music over the hills and villages of the Galilee. His high-impact arrival established widespread interest, a developing reputation and a crowd-pulling, magnetic attraction. Everyone came, everyone heard, everyone wanted.

There were three campaign elements in his great wave:

- The proclamation of the good news.
- The healing of the sick.
- The driving out of demons.

These three actions were the strings, brass and woodwind sections of his orchestra, the three primary colours on his palette. They were three separate ropes woven together to form the strongest cord. They were the load-bearing angles in the pyramid, toughest of all building shapes. They were three streams coming together to form a young river full of bubble, burst and brightness. Jesus was breaking into the lostness and brokenness of people's minds and bodies. He was redeeming their spiritual communities.

He was bringing God's kingdom into their world, and he was doing it in three integrated ways.

Jesus the proclaiming evangelist was the supreme 'wordsmith'. When Matthew, Mark and Luke describe his initial bursting onto the scene, they all emphasise his proclaiming of the good news.

> Let us go somewhere else – to the nearby villages – so that I can preach there also. That is why I have come. (Mark 1:38)

Clearly this proclaiming of the good news was the central of the three chords, the base of the equilateral triangle, the direction-setter of the three streams, the first of his three primary colours. But he was never content to use words alone.

> Jesus was not just a teacher or a preacher in purely intellectual terms, not just part of the history of ideas. He not only discussed the kingdom of God; he enacted it. (John Dominic Crossan, *Jesus: A Revolutionary Biography*, p. 93)

He wanted to bring the good news to the whole person, not just the person's mind. His was a holistic, 'body, mind and spirit' salvation experience.

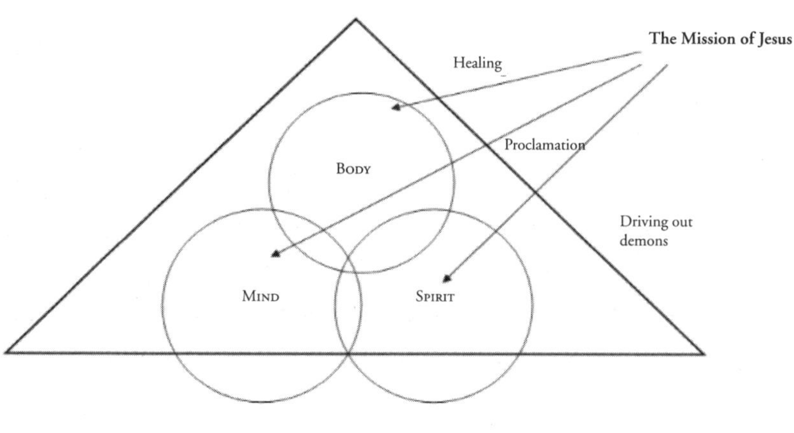

There is something here about the wholeness of being a full human being – the wholeness of health and healing and the opposite wholeness of bad health and illness. Carl Jung was one of the earliest great minds of the twentieth century to recognise this wholeness of integrated body, mind and spirit:

> Meaninglessness inhibits fullness of life and is therefore equivalent to illness. Meaning makes a great many things endurable – perhaps everything.[1]

No wonder he could describe himself as a 'doctor of the soul'. However, it is the wholeness of Jesus' impact which makes him the ultimate doctor and Saviour, not just of the soul, but of the entire person.

The Gospels contain twenty-six different stories of Jesus healing individuals, sometimes in pairs and on one occasion in a group of ten. In addition, there are ten crowd scenes of what can only be termed mass healings, and these happen in town centres, by the lakeside, on mountains and in synagogues. And it was not just Jesus himself. He sent out first the Twelve to proclaim the good news, drive out demons and heal the sick (Matthew 10:8), and then the Seventy-two to cure the sick and tell them of the kingdom's nearness (Luke 10:1–8).

Finally, we should note the inclusive capsule-type statements, where Jesus is wanting to sum up everything that he is about. The first of these is in the form of his reading from Isaiah at Nazareth (Luke 4:18), and the second comes in his words to John the Baptist's disciples:

---

[1] C.G. Jung, *Memories, Dreams, Reflections*, Collins 1963, page 373.

> The blind receive sight, the lame walk, those who have leprosy are cured, the deaf hear, the dead are raised, and the good news is preached to the poor. (Matthew 11:5)

In these six emphatic and unqualified statements, Jesus combines his words and works as a single way of saying, 'Yes, I am the one, and now is the time.' This is all about the arrival of the long-expected Messiah, with the disabled being made able, the unclean outsiders being included, and the least valued being the first to receive the most valuable of messages.

If we look at the incidence of healing stories and crowd scenes, we see a pattern very similar to the proclamation/teaching one that we noted in Chapter 2.

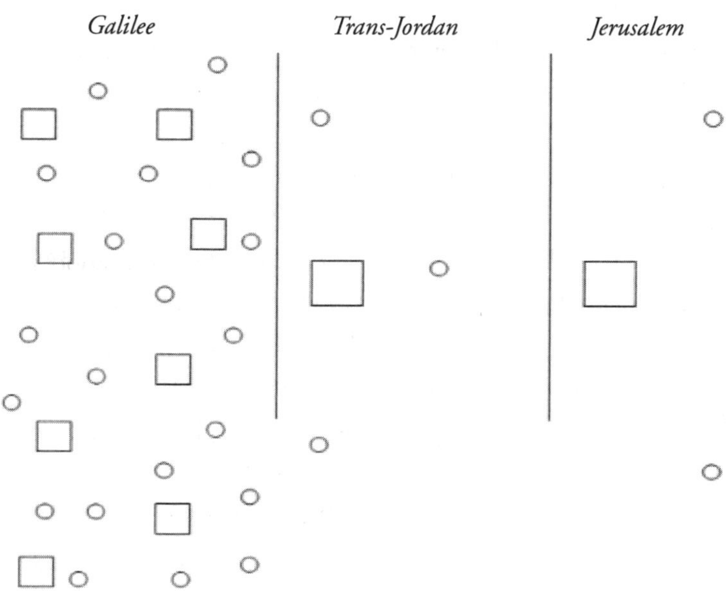

Key:
Healing stories – ○
Crowd healings – □

Of the twenty-six healing stories, twenty-one occur during the Galilean period, three occur while Jesus is travelling through Judea, and two come in the final week in Jerusalem. In addition, we note that eight of these twenty-six healings include some form of exorcism or driving out of evil spirits, all of which fall into the Galilee phase. Similarly, of the ten crowd scenes, only one is set on the Judean journey (Matthew 19:2) and one in Jerusalem (Matthew 21:14), while eight take place in the Galilee. Commenting on Mark's account of the healings at Gennesaret as being typical of such passages, Morris Maddocks says:

> The truth which they encapsulate to an even greater degree than the miracle stories, is that Jesus not only healed, but spent a substantial amount of time and energy in healing. To ignore this fact is to diminish the gospel deposit and to proclaim less than the good news of God's reign.[2]

Jesus' healings and exorcisms were largely, though not exclusively, limited to the initial 'trumpet-blasting Galilean springtime'. I suspect that many of us have a vague picture of Jesus wandering in a roundabout way towards Jerusalem, scattering healings and exorcisms as he went. In fact, the real picture is far more interesting. It is a picture of an evangelist healing and driving out demons, establishing an immense presence and following in a strictly localised itinerant ministry. Only when this phase is finished does the evangelist move on, both in terms of location and *modus operandi*, into a deeper teaching, discipling and preparing type of ministry.

---

2 *The Christian Healing Ministry*, SPCK 3rd ed. 1995, page 42.

John Wimber writes of these miracles, saying:

> Jesus' signs and wonders were his calling card, proof that the kingdom of God had come . . . Jesus' miracles have another purpose: to show us what the kingdom of God is like, to reveal glimpses of God's love, peace and joy.[3]

Jesus' healings

The cast members of the healing stories were a motley and tragic bunch of blind beggars, maimed lepers, deaf mutes, epileptics, paralytics, the possessed, bleeding women, withered men and sickly children. In three cases the patient had actually died and required not resuscitating, but resurrecting. Each one was a unique individual, with only one chance at life.

Jairus was an important man in the community, a leader of the synagogue, with prestige and reputation. He also had a twelve-year-old daughter, and when she fell ill he was a desperate man – desperate enough to fall on his knees in the dust in front of a large crowd and implore Jesus to come and help (Luke 8:41). I can identify quite a bit with Jairus, although I have spent my time leading churches, not synagogues. Like him, I have a desperately needy daughter. Zoe, my little girl, is now a big girl and has never been healed by Jesus, despite being constantly prayed for and living a life built around his presence. So I think I can smell something of Jairus's desperation in this story.

Lazarus was one of Jesus' special friends. Or perhaps he was more the brother of Mary and Martha, who were the special friends,

---

3 *Power Evangelism*, Hodder & Stoughton 1985, page 97.

providing that essential feminine support that a single male leader needed. When Jesus arrived too late and discovered that Lazarus was already dead and smelling, he began to cry (John 11:35).

The woman who had been bleeding continuously for twelve years was an unclean and thus excluded person. The bleeding had emptied her of life and energy, the doctors had emptied her of money, the unfairness of life had emptied her of hope. Hiding in the crowd, she anonymously reached out to touch Jesus. This was her last chance to live, and it worked (Mark 5:25). The incredible thing about this story is that, more than any other, it shows Jesus' sensitivity towards women. Most evangelists are men, and men are embarrassed and simply cannot cope with what we rather dismissively term 'women's problems', especially ones that involve bleeding. So how utterly wonderful is Jesus, who is completely unfazed by this poor woman and searches her out and blesses her with peace.

So it goes on, person after person, crowd after crowd. There is a powerful and disturbing scene in the film version of *Jesus Christ Superstar*, where Jesus is almost swamped by a great mob of demanding lepers. The film has brilliantly captured the insatiable hunger of the gospel crowds, but it has dismally failed in its portrayal of the gospel man. It never shows us the deep love that Jesus felt for every individual leper, and the power that he held in these situations. He was never in danger of being swept away by a tidal wave of sickness; he was actually rising above the wave and pulling people out of it. These, then, were the poor and wretched creatures who were drawn in their thousands to Jesus.

When we look carefully at the stories, we notice a particularly moving detail. It seems that many of the sick did not come in their own strength, but were actually brought to Jesus by friends and family. The bringing of the paralytic by his friends is the most well-known example (Matthew 9:2) and is typical of many others. These bringers of the sick were often filled with faith, hope and a desperate compassion for their loved ones. The office of carer is an ancient and noble one.

> When the men of that place recognised Jesus, they sent word to all the surrounding country. People brought all their sick to him. (Matthew 14:35)

Undergirding this exhilarating stream of ministry, Jesus was doing seven things:

1. He was introducing the kingdom in words and works, by articulating and putting into action the good news. 'But if I drive out demons by the Spirit of God, then the kingdom of God has come upon you' (Matthew 12:28).
2. He was overcoming the satanic powers with a greater power. 'Or again, how can anyone enter a strong man's house and carry off his possessions unless he first ties up the strong man?' (Matthew 12:29)
3. He was putting right the confused mess between illness, sin and impurity. He simply cut through the tangled knot of thinking by breathtakingly forgiving people's sins and cleansing the unclean. 'I am willing . . . Be clean!' (Matthew 8:3)
4. As a caring evangelist, he was generously administering compassion. 'When he saw the crowds, he had compassion on them, because they were harassed and helpless, like sheep without a shepherd' (Matthew 9:36).
5. He was exercising his own faith and responding to the faith of others. 'Go! It will be done just as you believed it would' (Matthew 8:13). This, of course, is the exact opposite of how

many of us in the evangelism trade operate today. Our thinking is often that 'healings will lead to faith'. Jesus, by contrast, believed that 'faith will lead to healings'.

6. He was demonstrating an authority that none of the other religious leaders possessed. 'They were all filled with awe and praised God. "A great prophet has appeared among us," they said' (Luke 7:16).
7. He was reaching out and touching people in their most immediate and pressing needs (Mark 3:5).

Over the last couple of centuries or so, the Western mind has grown increasingly uncomfortable with Jesus the healer. We love him as a teacher and great prophetic radical, but find his supposedly miraculous powers impossible to fit into our modernist mindset. Part of the problem is our 'Enlightenment' concept of a miracle as something that breaks the 'scientifically sacred laws of nature'. Interestingly, the Gospels do not label any of Jesus' acts as miracles, but as 'deeds of power' or 'signs', and Josephus, the Jewish historian, never calls Jesus a miracle-worker, but a doer of 'extraordinary deeds'. The healings and exorcisms should be viewed, then, not so much as 'divine, supernatural magic', but as God's love breaking into an already broken world. Even in John's Gospel, where the 'deeds' are labelled as 'signs', they are seen more as clues than as the sort of scientific authentication for which we crave.

> A sign is not the same thing as a proof; a sign is merely a marker for someone who is looking in the right direction.[4]

---

[4] Philip Yancey, *The Jesus I Never Knew*, Zondervan 2002, page 178.

Interestingly, our nineteenth-century-type liberal theological thinking has still not caught up with contemporary scientific thought. Einstein's work on relativity, the birth of quantum physics, the uncertainty principle and the development of chaos theory mean that we no longer see the world as being permanently controlled like a Swiss clock by rules of nature which never lose a single nanosecond. Today we believe that there is much more elasticity and randomness in how things operate. Sometimes it is more about where you are looking from than what you are looking at. Perhaps we should view his healings and exorcisms then, and their occasional reappearances now, as part of the mysterious, unexplained and maddeningly confusing way of nature, as one more feature of relative and random chaos. Except that it is not so much the way of 'nature' (a modern and fairly secular concept), but rather 'creation' (something much more ancient and sacred).

Jesus was never going to fit comfortably into some Newtonian universe controlled by natural law. He was always going to be far too unpredictable for that. T.S. Eliot pictured him as a wild tiger, not some sedate tabby cat. He was filled with untameable love, raw, passionate concern, explosive authority and a hunger to heal.

> Jesus' healings are not supernatural miracles in a natural world. They are the only truly natural thing in a world that is unnatural.[5]

If the healing stories are seen as being untrue, invented or developed in an exaggerated way from tiny beginnings, then that raises the problem of how they were inserted into the Jesus tradition. In a culture of careful oral preservation, and with the memories of Jesus

---

[5] Jürgen Moltmann, *The Way of Jesus Christ*, SCM Press 1990, page 99.

still fresh in people's minds, how could this major theme have been created and then slotted into the story without anyone noticing and objecting? James Dunn is one of a growing group of scholars who argue that it makes more sense to see these stories as part of the original authentic oral and written traditions about Jesus, than to imagine that they were somehow produced at a later date.

> Whatever we now may think of the events which might have occasioned these stories, the most obvious conclusion to draw is that there were various incidents during Jesus' mission which were experienced/witnessed as miracles, understood as healings brought about by divine power flowing through Jesus.[6]

Jesus driving out demons

The intellectual struggles we have with Jesus' healings are modest compared to the problems we have with his exorcisms, the driving out of demons. The story of Jesus overcoming and driving out demonic creatures from human beings is a common feature in all the Synoptic Gospels, although it is completely absent from John's. It is told in a particularly forceful way in Mark, which is almost certainly the earliest of the three Synoptics. Sometimes the healing stories contain a demonic element, at others there are straight exorcism accounts with no mention of physical illness. About half of the healing crowd scenes refer to demons or the possessed.

Exorcism feels like too strong and definite a feature of Jesus' ministry simply to be written off as a pre-modern description of psychological illness. Certainly some of the people described

---

[6] James Dunn, *Jesus Remembered*, page 683.

would probably be diagnosed in this category today, but we would still be left with the dark and frightening idea that it is possible to be overpowered and somehow taken prisoner by dark forces.

One of the most convincing pictures of 'possession' I have come across is provided by Ursula Le Guin in her *Earthsea* novels. There a young wizard's ego, pride and hate release a darkness which she calls a 'power of unlife'. This destructive force then threatens to take over his body, mind and spirit and turn him into a *gebbeth*, a puppet.

Again, this type of image may well grate with our Enlightenment, modernistic mindset, but it continues to resonate with an enormous number of people. These are bright, thinking science-accepters who are often convinced that they themselves, an elderly parent, a young child, or even the house where they live are in some way possessed or oppressed by an unwelcome and sinister presence. As always, today's postmodern society is happy to live in a contradiction of its own making. We mutely accept the concept of demons and possession in films, television dramas and 'Harry Potter' land, but reject it when reading the Bible.

In Matthew's account of the Beelzebub dispute, Jesus cures a blind and mute demoniac. He then describes this as an overpowering of Satan and a plundering or setting free of his captives (Matthew 12:22). Elsewhere he uses the imagery of casting out, or cleaning the dirt from the house, and warns against allowing what has been got rid of to return in a more virulent form (Luke 11:24–26). Interestingly, this is very close to the way in which certain returning viruses are described as operating today. Jesus' victory over the demons was a clear demonstration of his authority, and it was this same superior power that he gave to the Twelve and the Seventy-two when he sent them out on mission, so that when they returned they could report a similarly successful power-encounter.

> The seventy-two returned with joy and said, 'Lord, even the demons submit to us in your name.' (Luke 10:17)

Today we live among a population which is crawling with phobias, addictions, bad memories, guilt and fears. In a typical year in the UK, the National Health Service dispenses 32 million prescriptions for anti-depressants. It may be that all of this can be explained away rationally, but who is to say that there are *not* malignant forces beyond our understanding lurking in the shadows, causing at least a part of all this suffering? Some will conceive of such a force in personal devil and demon terms, while others will prefer to depersonalise it. However we view it, the point is that there are many people with bad stuff inside them and in desperate need of inner peace. Like Ursula Le Guin's 'power of unlife' our modern spectral spirits of stress, guilt, fear, anxiety and addiction have no physicality in themselves. They need a host body, an open mind and a vulnerable heart, so they can come in and lay their eggs. They are like devouring tape worms or choking ivy; they are the Japanese knotweed of the human garden. They often find their way into us when we are at our weakest, perhaps in a time of physical or emotional ill-health, or through a childhood trauma.

Of course, it is one thing to explain the darkness away and quite another to drive it away. There is always a danger of covering the ministry of exorcism or deliverance in a sort of Gothic shroud, with moonlight and garlic fumes, turning the whole thing into a major Hammer House of Horror production, a sort of 'John Wimber meets Christopher Lee' combination. The integrity of the church's exorcism ministry has sometimes not been helped by the often weirdly intense characters who have been attracted to this strange world. Nevertheless, there has always been a recognition in the church that demon possession, or something which looks very much like it, is a reality, and that dealing with it is as much a spiritual issue as it is one of mental health.

The united testimony of those who operate in this field is twofold: firstly, that there is still a tremendous need, and secondly, that the authority Jesus gave to his evangelising followers is still available today.

My own cautious and rather insecure experience in this field is that exorcism, the driving out of demons – or, as I prefer to think of it, the instilling of peace – should still be seen as part of the good news mission. For some involved in this work, their key tool is the word of command, such as, 'In the name of Jesus, I command you to leave.' In contrast, my own first and most effective tool is that of simple listening. Actually, listening is not at all a simple business – it is exhausting and rare, demanding real patience, a holding back from giving advice and a very attentive attitude. Listening gives a person space and time. It offers them someone they can trust. Listening involves asking the right sort of personal question. In asking someone what is going on inside them, we are inviting them to open up and empty it out. When the disquiet, pain, bad memory, guilt or inner haunting is emptied out, we can then assist the person to replace it with the peace and sense of well-being that comes from God. In Mark's Gospel there are sixty-seven reported occasions of Jesus asking a direct and personal question. I think it is fair to assume that each time he asked such a question, he listened carefully to the answer. The key question he asks is, 'What do you want me to do for you?' (Mark 10:36, 51)

Of these two tools, one is very masculine and the other is rather more feminine, which is not at all the same as saying that one is used by men and the other by women. I think we all need to have access to both tools; Jesus certainly did. In practice, then, this ministry ranges from a tough 'driving out of demons' to a softer 'praying for inner peace'. At both ends of this spectrum, however, lies a recognition that there is something dark which damages the human spirit.

In a two-stage process, this darkness has first to be driven out, and then the inner deep human space, the 'me' chamber, can be filled with the breathing in of God's peace. This is peace in the Hebrew sense of *shalom*, meaning wholeness or completeness. This is the *shalom* that could be used on a building site to mean 'the building is finished', and in the realm of relationships to mean 'now we are friends again'. More importantly, it is used of people to say 'now they have peace, they are whole'. This is the peace which is of the kingdom and part of the proclaimed 'good news' that the disciples recognised in the words and works of Jesus the evangelist (Luke 19:38). It is the peace of Jesus, which 'passes all understanding'.

John's Gospel shows us the resurrected Jesus driving out the darkness of the disciples' inner fear and replacing it with peace, as he breathes the Holy Spirit onto them (20:21–22). In the same way that light is much more than non-darkness, or heat is not just the ending of cold, so this sort of peace is far more than the absence of conflict or pain. It is a positive something in its own right; it is security, a sense of being safe, a knowledge of joy and salvation in all its fullness.

Clearly there are thousands of disturbed people who need a far more specialised medical care than we can provide. Yet there are many others who will be grateful. Michael is an affluent but vulnerable man in his late twenties who turned up for the Sunday morning

Eucharist at Manchester Cathedral. After the service he was clearly agitated and asked to talk to me. We sat for half an hour together over coffee and he told me of strange disturbances in his flat at night and his feeling of having somehow upset God. All I was able to do was to listen, pray and, in as few words as possible, reassure him of God's love. I was amazed at how much this seemed to help him. At the very least, some of the darkness had left him and some of God's love had visited him.

Being involved in this evangelistic driving out of demons and ushering in of peace is actually a much more matter-of-fact ministry than many imagine. Sometimes there is a definite experience which can be seen in a person's face or in their tears, and sometimes nothing much seems to happen. Annie was coming to the end of a long and faithful Christian life and was disturbed by the experience of seeing occasional apparitions at the foot of her bed. These may have been entirely imagined or absolutely real – the point is, they were real to her. I visited her several times, listened carefully as she talked through her disturbance, and prayed for her. Unfortunately, the apparitions never went away, but the talking, listening and praying still seemed to bring peace to her. I have this very strong feeling that whenever people are frightened of something they do not understand, they are always relieved and comforted to have someone alongside, and that 'being alongside' may at some point involve the joyful sharing of the good news message which ultimately sheds the biggest single light of all.

Our three-stringed cord

Jesus' strategy of combining proclamation, healing and exorcism has had a huge impact on the church over the years. We see it straight away in Acts 3, when Peter and John first heal a crippled beggar, and then preach an evangelistic sermon to the assembled crowd in the temple. Paul also combined a word ministry with times of healing and exorcism. His stay in Ephesus is perhaps the best example of him speaking out boldly in the synagogue for three months, while healing the sick (Acts 19:8–11). Such healings, however, look much more like exceptional events in the early church, when in the earlier Galilean period of Jesus' work they had a more daily and typical flavour.

The church has kept returning to Jesus' holistic concept of evangelistic caring mission. The first Christian merchants, settlers and missionaries took the faith beyond the limits of the Roman Empire into the Black Sea area of the Danube Basin and the Scottish and Irish fringes of the north-west. They were talkers, translators and preachers and they were also carers, exorcists and healers. The evangelising, wandering Celtic saints, pushing down into England and Wales and then across the Channel to the Saxon homelands, were story-telling proclaimers and doers of great deeds. Richard Fletcher's great work, *The Conversion of Europe,* tells the story. In the Middle Ages the monasteries taught the faith and cared for the poor, opened doors for lepers, set up hospitals and established schools. And so the heroic tale continues, with an evangelising mission that both brought children out of the mills and gave them Sunday schools to attend, and which sent missionaries and clergy of all theological backgrounds to live the 'works and the words' of Jesus in newly discovered continents and in the hell-holes of the newly industrialised cities. This broad view of mission has led Christians to be involved in the reform of prisons, the establishing of political parties, the setting up of such organisations as Barnardo's, Christian Aid, Cafod, Shelter, Alcoholics Anonymous,

Amnesty, TearFund and the hospice movement. All this effort has been inspired by the body, mind and spirit, triangular good news of Jesus the evangelist.

Sadly, over the last hundred years or so, the three-stringed cord or three-stream river has been pulled around quite a bit, to the extent that at times it looks a bit more like three separate strings, or three separate theological streams.

- *The liberal/Christian presence stream.* With a biblical foundation that combines the healing stories of Jesus with the parable of the sheep and the goats (Matthew 25:31), the Beatitudes, the Magnificat and Jesus' quoting of Isaiah in the Nazareth synagogue (Luke 4:18), the liberals have established a community welfare, educational and political shape of mission. They are committed both to caring for the victims of society's ills, and to trying to correct the inequalities that make it such a sick society. They have taken their caring into the poorest and most difficult parts of our cities and the developing world and are still there today, caring for the AIDS sufferers and the addicts, the asylum seekers and the deprived families. The problem is that in embracing the healing and social caring side of Jesus' ministry, they have often lost sight of his proclaiming of the good news. They are often scornful of traditional concepts of evangelism and see the act of caring as in itself the full work of the kingdom. Liberals have a massive impact on the outlook and mission strategising of the historic denominations. They occupy a lot of key positions, control big resources and are in place to make major decisions. The 'Faith in the City' movement, which began in the early

1980s and is still running, is the ultimate example of a truly glorious 'kingdom of God', community-transforming piece of work, but it was nevertheless very one-sided, placing a reduced emphasis and precious little money on evangelism. It continues as a wonderful but one-dimensional practice to this day. It is the weaker for it.

However, having worked for several years in Manchester with a loose grouping of clergy under the banner of 'Liberals and Evangelism', I think I see a new trend. A growing number of younger liberals are realising that to do some of the works of Jesus we do need strong and active congregations. They are turning afresh and with a new theological openness to the work of evangelism and the insights of the church growth movement.

- *The evangelical/evangelising stream.* While the liberals see a world where God is already present and waiting for us to join him in mission, the evangelicals tend to see one lost in darkness, into which he sends us as missionaries. Both are right, of course, but neither is fully correct. With their emphasis on the proclaimed word and the individual's need for salvation, the evangelicals have been the exact opposite of the liberals. In recent decades they have maintained the emphasis on evangelism and have continually worked at devising newer and better schemes. Evangelical churches are now seen to be growing, while the liberals and Catholics are still in the grip of decline. This is one reason why a new generation of liberal and Catholic clergy and leaders are interested in learning from them. Historically, evangelism has not always been seen as an evangelical thing – but sadly it has sort of shrivelled into that position through neglect over recent decades. It is often claimed that traditional evangelicals have abandoned the tougher urban areas and concentrated on the middle-class leafy suburbs. If this was ever true in the past, it is certainly not the case today. A whole new generation of evangelicals has headed into the inner cities and housing estates, practising a combination of community care and personal healing alongside the proclaiming of the good news.

- *The charismatic/Catholic healing stream.* This third movement has emerged strongly over the last forty years or so. It draws both on Pentecostal and traditional Catholic roots and is largely peopled by a combination of charismatic evangelicals and renewal Catholics. It has both grown out of and been responsible for the major revival of the healing ministries in the last third of the twentieth century. Smith Wigglesworth, J. Cameron Peddie, David Watson, Francis MacNutt, John Wimber and Bishop Morris Maddocks have all been influential leaders in their time. 'Although I was the first Roman Catholic priest to attend one of these Schools of Pastoral Care, I saw immediately that the basic teachings on healing were very much in line with Scripture and with my own religious tradition.'[7] This third stream or cord puts great emphasis on the healing and exorcism stories in the Gospels and Acts, and attempts to model them for today. However, much of this renewed healing ministry has happened inside the church, rather than outside in the world. There has been a tendency to focus on the needs of the individual and to be fascinated by the 'unusual'.

[7] Francis MacNutt, *Healing*, Ave Maria Press 1977, 1999, page 17.

Community-care and faith-sharing evangelism have sometimes been elbowed out, but things are changing. The organisation 'New Wine', which is probably the largest single grouping of healing charismatics in England, now contains a number of traditional evangelisers and many younger clergy involved in community ministry in deprived areas. Meanwhile, Walsingham, the spiritual home of Anglo-Catholicism, has started running courses in church growth and evangelism.

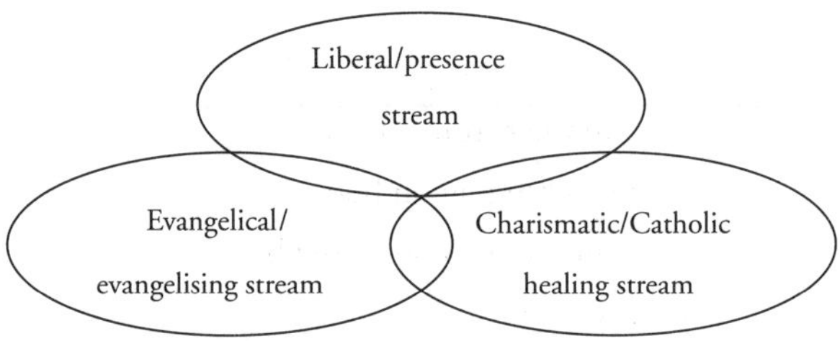

Of course, as soon as we see the three groupings set out in a neat and orderly fashion, we realise that nothing is that straightforward. The edges are always fluid, there have always been many crossover people who have lived in all three camps and, as the contemporary scene warms up, there is more dynamic movement than ever before. Nevertheless, the three groups do exist and I suspect that, as you have been reading this, you have been automatically identifying and allocating people you know into one or the other; perhaps you have also recognised yourself.

Each of these three traditions have brought into our world something authentic from Jesus the healing evangelist, but they have also each left something behind, hanging up in the Galilean wardrobe. Community building and transformation is not of itself evangelism; proclamation which is just word based is not the Jesus way; and healing which operates most of the time in church services and buildings should be outside, on the edge. A true Jesus-type mission can only happen when the three streams or cords are brought together, when the triangle is rebuilt, when the model of Jesus the evangelist is truly embraced and emulated.

Doing it his way in our world

There were ten lepers

One was suffering from AIDS
And another from allergies
One was binging on booze
And another was possessed by porn
One was completely stressed out
And another was a complete outsider
One was racially abused
And the other one was abusing him
One was overweight
And another one was undervalued
Not one of them knew where to find help.

And then there was Jesus.

Our world is not that different from his: there are still millions of people in a mess and all wanting to get better. That is why the National Health Service is continually at the centre of the political debate, and because we are never satisfied with what it can deliver, we have more alternative health practitioners than GPs in the UK today.

In our postmodern, post-religious, affluent, educated and scientifically aware society, we are up to our eyes in sickness. As individuals we are sick in body, mind and spirit. Our communities are diseased and disrupted. Families, marriages and friendships are dysfunctional. Schools, workplaces and even hospitals are increasingly tense, under pressure, dirty and stressful. People are looking for help.

The mood was brilliantly captured by David Lodge, one of our best modern novelists, in his book entitled *Therapy*. His central character, Laurence 'Tubby' Passmore, is suffering from a strangely painful knee and an aching, meaningless life. Having been recommended many solutions by his equally aching friends and colleagues, he realises that people are 'game for every kind of therapy except chemotherapy'. Tubby gradually comes to understand that, as well as looking for physical healing, he is also on a spiritual journey, and he is desperate for the warmth of first human and then divine love.

In a lonely and hurting world, there are three doorways at which people are queuing up to find help. One of the doorways is labelled 'healing', the second is all about the search for the spiritual or sacred, while the third one is for those who are desperate for human acceptance, friendship and love. Although the queuing masses do not realise it, each doorway is a 'Narnian' wardrobe leading from a world of lostness to one of foundness, from the confines of this world to the kingdom of God.

The church is a great and ancient alternative healing agency which goes all the way back to Jesus himself. We do healing, the sacred and human warmth better than anyone else. We have both modern and ancient mysterious resources and experience. We can open all three doors. We have, however, allowed others to pinch our clothes and muscle us out of the marketplace. It is time, once again, for us to do it his way.

Of course, doing it his way is a lot easier said than done. I have spent years believing in and searching for a healing dimension to my evangelism. I have read books, attended seminars and events and joined with others at major conferences. Sometimes I have pressed forward in the Jesus-shaped healing ministry. At other times I have performed an embarrassed body swerve around and away from it. The prospect of failure has often been too strong for my human pride to cope with. I have let it gather dust in my mental attic. Occasionally I have imagined that I was near some sort of 'breakthrough', but most of the time it feels like something at which I ought to work harder. Despite the fear of failure and times of neglect, the fundamentally important Gospel stories have kept pulling me back to the roots of Jesus the evangelist. In recent years the pull has become much stronger and more compelling.

One of the keys to doing it 'his way' is to realise that I will never do it 'his way'. That is to say, I will never see the amazing number of healings that Jesus did. After years of bouncing around on the edge of the charismatic movement, that simple lesson has taken quite a lot of learning, due to the thorough schooling I have had in the expectation that Jesus' ministry is there to be reproduced by his followers. In this respect, John 14:12, with its words about those who believe in Jesus doing greater works than him, is surely one of the most overworked verses in the New Testament.

The single most helpful experience of the healing ministry for me came when I got involved in the 'Wimber movement' of the mid-1980s. More than anything else, this put healing evangelism on my agenda, and on that of St Augustine's, the church where I was serving at the time as vicar. Wimber and his team taught me, equipped me and inspired me. Unfortunately, they also loaded me with a burden of unrealistic expectation, for they seemed to suggest that I and many others like me could all reproduce the signs and wonders of Jesus in our own ministries. This is a common theme or aspiration in the charismatic healing movement: it is attempting to encourage, but actually goes too far. There is a huge difference between modelling ourselves on Jesus' healings and exorcisms and imagining that we can recreate their full scale and impact.

It is clear in the New Testament that the disciples during Jesus' time, and the apostolic church afterwards, never reproduced the sheer power, authority and massive scale of his healing evangelism. At its crudest, we can say that the healing quota drops dramatically from the Gospels to the Acts. The disciples and the early church did perform exorcisms, healings and signs and wonders, but not of the quality and quantity that Jesus had. Why should they have? They were not the messianic kingdom bringers, but the disciples, the learners, the followers of the one and only Jesus. Of course, I may well be the only one struggling with this sort of unrealistic 'Jesus reproduced' type of expectation, but I suspect not. In recent years I have realised that before I can begin 'doing it his way' in terms of healing and evangelism, I first need to shed the burden of inflated expectancy. Doing it his way does not mean that we somehow clone or replicate his historically one-off impact. It means that we make him our mentor and guide and embrace his values of compassion, faith and authority. It means that we try to see others through his eyes, try to touch them with his hands, and try to breathe on them not with our own personality, but with his Holy Spirit. Occasionally it all works wonderfully and at other times it all works out woefully, but in almost all cases something works a bit.

In following Jesus into healing, there are a few footprints in which we can place our own, but there are no techniques that we can copy. Jesus had 'different strokes for different folks'. Sometimes he did it with a word, at other times he did it with a touch. Sometimes it was gradual and at other times it was immediate. Often he healed in public, but sometimes he took the sick into a quiet and private place, 'away from the crowd' (Mark 7:33). Sometimes it was all about the recipient's faith or their carer's faith, and sometimes it was all about the faith of the healer. 'Then the disciples came to Jesus in private and asked, "Why couldn't we drive it out?" He replied, 'Because you have so little faith' (Matthew 17:19–20).

There may not be techniques to follow, but there are two vital guidelines. The first is all about love, mercy, compassion and caring. The second is simply about getting on and doing it: doing it not because we have a particular gifting or anointing (these seem to be concepts developed later in the life of the New Testament church as it worked to establish a structure and order to its ministry and leadership), but doing it out of love for people and obedience to him. I have noticed in my own life that the more I push my boat out of the harbour and into the wide seas of healing, driving out of demons and evangelism, the more I see happening – although I never see quite as much as I would like to. The more I leave my boat tied up in the harbour, the more secure and unthreatened I feel, the less seems to happen.

To steer our little craft out of the safety of our cosy harbour and launch out into an evangelising healing mission is to begin an amazing adventure. It is one which goes beyond our comfort zone, into waters which are deeply mysterious and which defy our attempts at control or prediction, where the threat of failure and ridicule is never far away. It is a journey which takes us into places where we never imagined ourselves being, and where lives really are regularly touched and sometimes transformed by the finger of God. If the mission is to be modelled on Jesus, then it will need to address the whole person, body, mind and spirit, combining evangelism with healing and the driving out of troubling spirits, and it will have to happen in the 'synagogue', outside in the community, in our own church buildings, in community centres and in people's own homes.

I want now to tackle this adventure first as an individual, one-to-one mission, then as a corporate, shared church enterprise.

The individual healing and evangelism mission

The great thing about beginning a personal mission is that anyone can try it. There is no one there to check up on us, or even to know that we are launching out. We do not need to have some sort of special gift, or even to be good at it. What we do need is plenty of love, for that is where the vocation comes from, and the help of the Holy Spirit, because that is where the power comes from. We all know many sick and worried people, so we can all begin today. Literally today: why not make a list of five needy people whom you know, make sure that some of the names are those of non-Christians, and then make a start?

As someone who is a bit of a coward when it comes to the healing ministry, perhaps I can offer a series of 'steps for getting started' for other diffident people. The first steps are quite manageable. They become increasingly tension-inducing, but more powerful, as we move deeper in:

- Pray for each of the people on your list every day for a week.
- Visit each of them, being kind and attentive, perhaps taking a small gift.

- Offer to pray for them at your church, or in your own daily prayers.
- Ask them if they would like you to pray with them. If they say 'yes', then do not make it too cringy with lots of words and physical contact. If you want to lay hands on them, ask their permission first. Remember, Jesus often took individuals into a quiet place away from the crowd before ministering to them.

In all of this it is important to follow one or two basic guidelines, such as keeping a door open in private places and respecting gender differences and the sensitivities of partners at all times.

Each of these actions represents an initiative of grace on your part, a work of the kingdom. The keynote has to be sensitivity, not evangelistic pushiness. We want to respect and love people, not to pressure them.

Stand back after this initial piece of ministry and ask yourself three questions:

- How do I feel about it?
- How do I think they feel about it?
- Has anything happened?

All of us are obsessed by the 'Has anything happened?' question. We are desperate for a 'yes' and fearful of a 'no'. A 'yes' might mean that someone on your list is feeling much better and there has been a healing. It might mean that someone has felt deeply loved and cared for. It may involve someone still having their ailment or worry, but being able to face it with a greater sense of inner peace. Or it may be that someone has felt God, or one of God's people, drawing close. At this stage, it might be a good thing to talk the whole thing through with someone else, and think about where you want to go next in this ministry.

Some years ago, I heard that an old friend of mine had had a baby, who was being kept in intensive care while its young life hung in the balance. So I went along to the hospital and prayed over the child. The next day, the mother, to whom I had not spoken for years, rang me up to say how moved she felt by my visit. It seemed as if this small initiative of grace had brought some healing both to the baby and to the mother.

Operating in this field, as what can only be described as an insecure and not very effective healing evangelist, I have learned three things about myself:

- I am very concerned with the 'me' in all of this – my ego, reputation and sensitivity. Jesus was always consumed by the 'other'. He looked out (not in) and saw them, and was moved by compassion for them, not by self-absorption (Matthew 9:36).
- My engagement with my own human fear and negativity makes me want to do less. Jesus' engagement with needy people drove him to do more. His healings before the feeding of the five thousand were a good example of this characteristic (Matthew 14:14).
- There is almost always a positive response to my attempts at ministry: even when nothing much seems to happen, the vast majority really seem to appreciate it and find it helpful at some level or other. Furthermore, as in the case of Jesus, they can recognise love and goodness (Luke 13:17). I regularly visit a large office where a friend works and have got to know some of the staff, one of whom suffers from a recurring

muscle complaint. The first time I discovered this, I asked her, in good charismatic style, if she would like me to pray with her there and then. As a normal person, she clearly considered this a bit weird and quickly declined my offer. The second time around, I spent a bit of quality time listening to her and then simply said that I would remember her in my daily prayers. This felt very different and was a much more sensitive approach – and she was clearly moved by the whole experience.

Does anything happen, yes or no? In terms of this question, I have one abiding conviction, which is that the more I go out on my initiatives and attempt things, the more things happen. It is all a bit messy and insecure, like learning to ride a bike, but there comes a time when we all have to take the stabilisers off. As John Wimber used to say, 'Faith is spelt R-I-S-K.'

A corporate approach to healing evangelism

There are lots of things that a Christian body such as a church, school or agency can do to initiate or go further with a healing evangelism mission. Here are six suggestions drawn from my own experience of working in an inner-city area, not very original, but potentially fruitful if done carefully.

- Talk about healing evangelism in the pulpit, in the Mothers' Union, in house or cell groups, in your PCC or elders' meetings. The more a thing is talked about, the more it becomes part of that corporate body's own culture, and the more things start to happen.

- During my time as vicar of St Augustine's Church in Bradford, we began to launch out into this adventure. We started holding a healing service once a quarter. A team of suitable people were recruited and prepared, to share the ministry with the clergy. At these events the songs, readings, testimony interviews and prayers were all connected to the preaching theme, which was always about healing. These became very special times in the life of our church. And that was the problem: they were inside the church, rather than being inside the life of our local community. Church members would occasionally bring a needy friend as a guest, but we never really learned how to invite the world in. They were beautiful healing services, but they were not Jesus-style healing evangelistic ones. We should have advertised widely; drawn up a list of fifty sick or struggling people we knew as a church, and given each one a personal invitation; encouraged each church member to launch out and invite one person; laid on great refreshments to make it a very special gathering . . . but we did not. Such is the wisdom of hindsight – which is why I am practising it now.
- In the 1990s we organised a series of city-wide evangelistic missions in Bradford, and I noticed something very significant. The movement began with just a handful of local churches running a week-long marquee event in our local park, and we called it, not surprisingly, 'God in the Park'. Our missioner was Daniel Cozens, and he brought with him a large and very capable team. 'God in the Park' was a stunning success and was followed by 'God in the Parks', when we did four such missions in different quarters of the city. 'God in the City' came after that, this time held

in the city's main concert hall, and a similar pattern was used for 'God in the Millennium'. At each of these events we built a special healing night into the programme. This was at the suggestion of Daniel, who was experimenting with healing evangelism at the time. I had strong doubts about this, but he had stronger faith and a greater courage to go for things.

On every occasion these healing nights became one of the most memorable of all the things that happened in the missions. Lots of people came, lots of Christians invited lots of people who were prayed for, and finally lots of people made some sort of faith step forward.

As a result, I have now tried to incorporate healing into my own missions. One particular event sticks out and became a bit of a template. We had booked the doctor's surgery in the town of Haworth, but quickly had to find somewhere bigger when we realised how many were planning on coming. For the first part of the evening the audience were able to put their questions to a panel of Christian doctors and nurses. We then had a refreshment break before I shared the 'good news' and invited people to receive prayer for healing and to draw closer to the healing God. The response was the largest we had at any of our gatherings for the whole week. It felt as if we had opened a door and people were keen to enter in.

- St Augustine's was a very busy church with a very busy vicar: he and they were very programme orientated. Something changed, however, when Ken, Hillary and Brenda went on a 'Christian Listeners' course. I had no problem with them going on the course, but it was another thing altogether when they wanted to introduce it to an already project-stuffed church. Nonetheless, they persevered, and persuaded me to let our staff team do the course. It had an immediate impact and, speaking for myself, it completely changed the way in which I related to people. Suddenly we were slowing down, getting alongside people in an intimate way and touching deep issues. In a very English, undemonstrative sort of way, I think we had started driving bad things out of possessed people and ushering in the peace of Jesus.

- Neil Short, who was our curate at the time, introduced to us the idea of holding remembrance services for departed loved ones. These were gracious and moving events held at All Souls time (early November). Neil and his team worked meticulously in their planning and inviting. The response was huge as crowds of people turned up, so many in fact that I think we were taken by surprise at first and were not ready with sufficient follow-up preparations. As the leader in the church, it took me a long time to see the hugely transforming 'word and work' potential in what was in effect both a remembrance and a healing service. Perhaps more than any other single act of healing, this event took us outside the church and into the world.
- As a church we ran a whole range of community care projects such as a café, clothing store, credit union and endless kids clubs. This brought us into contact with many people who were genuinely grateful to us and our God. Looking back, however, I have often thought that we could have done more to proclaim the good news to more of these people. We were often offering them the works of Jesus without the words. This is something we must always keep in mind.

Mark Haddon has written a very touching novel called *The Curious Incident of the Dog in the Night-Time.*[8] The central character is Christopher, who has Asperger's Syndrome, and who is cared for faithfully by his father. I know from my own experience that caring for someone like Christopher is both a very demanding and also a very lonely business. Christopher's dad is doing a great job of looking after him – until he snaps. Three times in the course of one evening he blasts at Christopher that 'God only knows' how hard his life is. The tragic irony is that earlier in the book we have discovered that Christopher and his dad do not 'do' God. What he is actually saying is, 'No one knows how hard my life is.' But there is someone who knows. Christopher and his dad are not alone: there is a healing, helping God, and there are supposed to be plenty of God's healing and evangelising people out in the real world making the connections.

Throughout the history of the church, there has been a continuing story of often strange individuals, groups and movements who have sought to reproduce something of the healing ministry of Jesus in their own time and place. In *God Inside Out,*[9] Simon Ponsonby has rendered us all a great service by tracing out some of the key players in this long and continuing story. The thread which began with the first apostles led on to Ignatius of Antioch, Justin Martyr and Irenaeus; to Clement of Alexandria, Origen and Novatian; to Cyril of Jerusalem, Gregory of Nazianzus and Augustine. In medieval times the story was continued by Bernard of Clairvaux and Hildegard, by St Francis and Catherine of Siena. On then to the Reformation with Luther, and the Scottish Puritans, all involved in

8 Mark Haddon, *The Curious Incident of the Dog in the Night-Time,* Vintage 2004.
9 Simon Ponsonby, *God Inside Out,* Kingsway 2007.

the healing ministry. In the eighteenth and nineteenth centuries John Wesley, Charles Spurgeon and Edward Irving kept the flame burning. (These are only the edited highlights, and I do not know who some of them are either, but it all looks very exciting!) In more recent times we are familiar with the name of Smith Wigglesworth, a Bradford-born working-class Pentecostal operating in the early years of the twentieth century, who developed a worldwide healing evangelistic work. Another was J. Cameron Peddie, a Glasgow minister who in 1942 lay in his hospital bed and desperately prayed for the man in the next bed to be healed. This led him into an amazing lifelong work which had an impact on the poorer areas of Glasgow, on the Iona community and on the lives of over a hundred Scottish ministers who followed him into doing it Jesus' way in their world. Then came the Christ-like and compassionate Mother Teresa, and Morris Maddocks, who set up the Acorn Healing Trust, and Francis MacNutt, David Watson, John Wimber . . . the list goes on and on. These, of course, are just the well-known ones. I have not mentioned my friend Ken, a Baptist minister no one has ever heard of, or an old Sunday school teacher I once knew. None of them were ever as effective as they would have liked to have been, yet all had *some* effect and all held together the three-streamed river of healing evangelism.

Most of us are much more matter of fact and unexceptional. We want to try and be like Jesus, but are frightened of failure. In the field of child psychiatry, Donald Winnicott has introduced the notion of the 'Good Enough Parent'. Few of us are great parents and many of us are on a permanent guilt trip, but maybe there are actually many of us who just get on and do it and are much more able than we give ourselves credit for. I just wonder, then, if what we need in the healing evangelism field is not so much a handful of amazingly gifted men and women, but thousands of 'Good Enough' healing evangelists.

> Great crowds came to him, bringing the lame, the blind, the crippled, the mute and many others, and laid them at his feet; and he healed them. (Matthew 15:30)

Dear Sweet Jesus
evangelist, healer and deliverer
proclaim words to my searching mind
breathe peace into my disturbed inner place
touch my hurting body.
Then
touch my hurting mind
proclaim words into my searching inner place
breathe peace into my disturbed body
And finally
breathe peace into my disturbed mind
touch my hurting inner place
proclaim words to my searching body.
My Lord and Saviour. Amen.

CHAPTER FIVE

The People's Evangelist

> Come to me, all you who are weary and burdened, and I will give you rest. (Matthew 11:28)

And they did,
in their masses.
And he did,
To each one of them.

Evangelists are like circus ringmasters. We love the crowds, packed in and expectant. We get excited by a full marquee, church, theatre or pub, with ourselves at the centre and in the spotlight. This is our world, our very own Galilee.

Jesus was the ultimate crowd-pulling and crowd-working evangelist. So about ten years ago, when my own 'crowd evangelism' was not going very well, I set out to read again the stories of Jesus, and to model myself on him. As I read and re-read, I saw something that I had not seen before.

He was indeed a great 'crowd-puller'. Sometimes he went looking for the crowds in towns and villages. More often they came looking for him. By the lakeside, up the mountain or in the market square, Jesus really did the business with these crowds. He healed the sick, proclaimed the 'good news', drove out demons and taught the people about the kingdom. But then, very often, he walked away from them and concentrated on a lone individual.

Thus we see him sailing away from the crowd at the lakeside and delving into deep spiritual one-to-one conversation with Peter (Luke 5:4). In the midst of a pressing crowd, he suddenly feels a desperate woman reach out and touch him and all his attention goes to her (Matthew 9:20). In the packed town centre of Jericho, he leaves the throng behind to go and spend quality time with Zacchaeus (Luke 19:1).

In my reading and reflecting, I came to the conclusion that this pattern of public ministry to the crowd followed by intensive, time-consuming work with individuals was Jesus' characteristic and preferred way of operating. In fact, not only did he move away from crowds, but he seems to have had a very low expectancy of them. In John's Gospel, soon after the pinnacle of his crowd ministry in the feeding of the five thousand, and at a time when his popular appeal was at its hottest, we find him talking to the Twelve about giving up on him (6:66–67). When he healed ten lepers (quite a crowd), only one came back to say 'thank you' (Luke 17:11). And, most negative of all, the Palm Sunday crowd became the Good Friday mob shouting for Barabbas (Luke 23:18).

The parable of the sower (Matthew 13:1–9), a disarmingly subtle analysis of how people responded to the words of Jesus, comes at a critical point in the story. It is located towards the end of the Galilean mass evangelism period. It looks very much like Jesus' own assessment of the depth of impact of this phase of his ministry. Here he arrives at the conclusion that the majority fall away, while a small minority make a deep and fruitful response. The story fits perfectly with his pattern of public crowd event followed by private, small-scale, in-depth engagement.

For me, as I came to terms with these features, this was a new way of looking at Jesus the evangelist, and it caused me to change the shape or emphasis of my own work. I did not want to walk away from the possibilities of large numbers and crowds – in fact, I wanted to do that part of the work even better. But the crowd or the event ceased to be the main thing for me. It became the shoal out of which I wanted to catch a few individual fish, the mountain from which I could dig out a few nuggets of gold.

So let us look in more detail at the Jesus crowd, the great seething mass of human tadpoles out of which some came through to faith. We have already thought about 'Jesus the people person' and the amazing range of individuals he met, spent time with, listened and talked to. Here I want to try to gather this crazy 'Sergeant Pepper's Lonely Hearts Club Band' of needy men and women into two camps. The first camp holds the large tribe of what we could call 'outsiders'. The second emerges out of this huge outsider camp, as a smaller but significant group of 'seekers' or 'searchers'.

It is here, in this 'on the edge' human environment, that we see Jesus, like some great Pied Piper, playing his compelling tunes of hope and joy, leading those who are seeking into a new land. He is a prototypical 'Oskar Schindler' figure, gathering handfuls of followers and guiding them safely through to a new life. Schindler saved his followers from the death camps of Nazi Germany. Jesus saved his from the jaws of poverty, illness, religious neglect and Roman brutality.

The outsiders

In Jesus' world, most people were outsiders. The Pharisees had built an insider religious zone of rules-obsessed, whiter-than-white legalism. Jerusalem, with its great temple and cabals of priests and Sadducees, was the throne of power at the heart of this insider zone. Here religious, political and financial power all wound together in an impenetrable knot. You did not have to do anything particularly bad to be an outsider, you just had to fail to be one of the insiders.

The Poor	– Always with him, And he is always with them.
Tax-gatherers	– Corrupt and cold-shouldered. He launched a specialist mission to them.
Women	– Abused by men, Honoured by Jesus. Last at the cross, first at the tomb.
Fishermen and farmers	– Caught in his net.
Sinners	– Let us eat, drink and be friends.
Samaritans	– No longer the 'looked down upon'. Now the 'lifted up'.
Unclean	– Touched, embraced, accepted and forgiven.

These were Jesus' people,
More to the point, he was their Jesus.
Their teacher, their prophet,
Their doctor and priest,
Their friend and evangelist.

Robert Graves's novel *King Jesus* has a completely fictitious, yet hauntingly moving picture of the boy Jesus. It is set during the time of the family exile in Egypt, with Joseph, Mary and Jesus living in a small Jewish colony. While they live their respectable lives, Jesus secretly develops the practice of slipping out beyond the town to the 'Camp of Lost Souls', a place of thieves, beggars, maniacs and worn-out prostitutes, where the poorest of the Jews are driven to eat crows, rats and lizards. The boy Jesus goes to the camp 'to persuade the lost souls that they can still be found by the Lord's mercy'. This is fictional truth about Jesus then and now, poetic and prophetic.

The poor are 'non-persons', 'subhuman', 'dehumanised', 'human fodder'.[1] It is difficult for us to realise just how rejected some of the familiar Gospel characters were. To us, the beggars and prostitutes are like old friends from Sunday school days, but in reality they were lonely and lost, hard-worked and poorly paid, living bleak lives behind grown-old faces. I have never seen a picture in a Children's Bible which attempted to re-create the filth, smelliness and utter despair of their lives.

Here are three scenes from the story:

- A woman (always a potential problem for a single and male religious leader) comes to Jesus in a Pharisee's house (Luke 7:37). The woman makes physical contact, washing his feet with her tears, drying them with her hair and kissing them as she anoints them with ointment. She is described as a sinner, and the whole picture points to sex and pain. Perhaps Jesus is the only one to see her not as a

[1] Jürgen Moltmann, *The Way of the Jesus Christ*, page 99.

temptress of men, but as someone who is abused by them. The incident is a typical example of Jesus' awareness of women and sensitivity in engaging with their issues. However we explain the story, the inevitable conclusion is that Jesus is a long way outside the safety of the 'Holy City' comfort zone.

Some years ago, I began the practice of always including a 'girls' night out' on week-long missions. Everyone gets dressed up for food and drink, music and atmosphere in a local hotel or smart pub. During the evening a couple of female team members will run a fun women's quiz and then interview one or two of the guests about their faith. I give a talk about Jesus as the one man in a woman's life who will never take from her, hurt, forget or abuse her. The presentation ends with a rendering of Roberta Flack's 'Killing Me Softly With His Song', while pictures of Jesus are flashed up on a big screen. The evening has an air of welcome and fun, but also a deep sense of Jesus touching the pain and hopes of women.

- Tax-gatherers handled the money of the despised Greeks and Romans. In effect they were semi-employed or contracted by them and made money, a lot of money, out of their own Jewish kindred. No one liked or socialised with them, and if they wanted to party they had to do it with other tax-gatherers. In going to Levi's house and joining in the gathering, Jesus was crossing sides, becoming a spiritual and class traitor (Luke 5:29). Not only did he make an evangelistic beeline for Levi, but he used him as a launching point from which to begin a mission to tax-gatherers.
- Who really cares about beggars? The most they do is to stir our sensitivity a little, especially if others are watching. In the

Gospel story the beggars are poor, vulnerable and marginalised. They have no land or capital and no one to stand by them offering security or protection; they will not be missed when they die. It was not just that Bartimaeus was blind, but that everybody was blind to Bartimaeus (Mark 10:46). In stopping his whole entourage to attend to a tiny part of the human dross of poverty, Jesus was doing something that very few important people on an important mission ever bother to do. No wonder Bartimaeus became such a joyful member of the rag-tag Jesus army.

Why is it that we all look down on beggars? On the odd occasion that we actually give them something or buy a *Big Issue* magazine, we have an inner glow of bountifulness, but we are essentially condescending. We treat them as less than ourselves, not quite equal. When the church does something for them it is usually some sort of community care work; hardly ever do we take seriously the thought of sharing the gospel message with them. We look down on them rather than lifting them up: how different we are from Jesus.

The question for us is this: 'Who are our spiritual and social outcasts?'

Eloi, Eloi, lama sabachthani?
My God, my God, why have you forsaken me?
Racists and wrongdoers
Hen parties, HIV positives and the homeless
Gays, Goths and gamblers,
Swearers, smokers and skateboarders,
Sex industry workers and small-time drug-pushers,

Depressed, debt-ridden and drink-sodden,
Fox hunters, fur wearers and child fondlers,
Alzheimer sufferers and all-aloners. . .
The 'God forsaken'?
Or just the 'church forgotten'?
Maybe the 'for whom I came'
The 'for whom I myself became
the forsaken by God'.

These, then, are the residents of our contemporary and wealthy post-Christian, postmodern 'Camp of Lost Souls'. It looks as if we are not quite as welcoming and inclusive as we thought we were. The list reads like a running order from *Little Britain.* Perhaps it should be renamed as 'Lost Britain'.

In addition to the contemporary forsaken, there are three huge categories of people who appear to be increasingly outside the world of the church and the gospel.

Those 'below the middle class'

The church is certainly Christ-like in its social care and concern for the working classes and the poor (no longer the same thing), especially in their more desperate extremes of sickness and need. What we are less good at is sharing the good news with them and building churches amongst and with them.

I was recently working with a group of senior church leaders who served a largely working-class northern area. It suddenly occurred to me that all but one were speaking in well-educated, south-east, upper-middle-class accents. Where was the incarnational Jesus the evangelist 'man of the people' in this group? Where was the opportunity for local 'non-club members' to rise up to be power-holding leaders? Jürgen Moltmann commented, 'The Jesus movement in Galilee was a movement of the poor' (*The Way of Jesus Christ*, p. 100).

Twenty-five years ago I was taught the importance of small Christian basics groups. I was working out my second curacy at the time at St Paul's Church in York. The vicar, Dereck Wooldridge, was a brilliant example of a local parish mission priest. St Paul's was what every local church should be, a worshipping, welcoming, caring, pastoral community with a huge commitment to evangelism. These were pre-Alpha days, when Dereck and a small network of like-minded clergy from across the country were developing a new type of tool. When I became a vicar in inner-city Bradford, I applied what I had been taught and found that it worked well in a northern urban context. The problem, which became gradually more apparent, was that all the materials, booklets and courses were being churned out by a largely southern-based, middle-class evangelising movement (which in those days was also predominantly evangelical).

The model of a 'basics group' worked well for us, but the material never fitted our people. It was as if they were borrowing, or accepting as second-hand gifts, someone else's clothes. Eventually we followed the incarnational path of Jesus the evangelist and produced our own stuff (this was eventually published by CPAS as the *Start Course*).

In the last thirty years, the working classes have prospered to such an extent that the term now seems out of date. They have bought and extended their own homes, discovered foreign holidays and sent their children off to university. Yet there is still a culture there which forms the minds and lives of millions, and which is still 'outside the city wall' of the middle-class, white-dominated, north-south-divided church. As for the poor, in the 1980s and 1990s we used the dreadful term 'the under-class'. Today they are so under, they are almost forgotten. After years of Tory tight-fistedness and New Labour largesse, the gap between rich and poor is as wide as ever. The Church of England's *Faithful Cities* report, published in 2006, reminded us all that the poor may be hidden, but they are still with us. Their futures are a repetition of their pasts, their neighbourhoods are threatening and violent, while their children are either too big or too small (obesity and physical underdevelopment make strange bedfellows). What *Faithful Cities* failed to do, however (and in this failure it mirrored the earlier *Faith in the City*), was to talk about the need for both a proclaiming and a healing kingdom work. It is almost as if the poor are below the evangelism line.

The church is still there in the poorest areas and providing essential spiritual and civic capital, but it needs money, people and resources to come from the richer end of Christendom. It also needs to rediscover the work of Jesus the evangelist. Let us be honest: if Jesus were here with us today, we all know which part of the city he would be living in. We who occupy the middle-class experience that we call Christianity can hardly imagine how our poor neighbours live. They are the Grundys from *The Archers*, the Royle family, and the Shameless crowd.

At the heart of it all, there is a painful dichotomy for the poor. The Christians who care most for them, generally speaking, are the liberals, but they do not care that much for evangelism. Those who do care most for evangelism are the evangelicals, but they do not care that much for the state of the poor. When we run caring projects for them but do not share the words of the gospel, we patronise the poor. When we preach at them but do not get involved, we pontificate.

Young adults

If there is one thing we have learned from Jesus, it is surely that of letting our children come to him, or positively guiding them to do so. The resources, time and sheer people power that we put into children's work is extraordinary – to such an extent that it actually goes beyond Jesus' own way of working. Our problems arise as the children get older and turn from bright little keenies into bored teenagers and post-church young adults. There seems to be a sort of 'anti-Jesus Pied Piper' playing his tunes to our emerging adults, while the rest of us are busy looking after the next generation of children. The result is that as young people reach their most demanding time of life and need more from Jesus the evangelist, they actually receive less.

There is a tragic irony in the realisation that if we draw up an age profile membership graph for the church as a whole, or for most individual churches, we end up with something that looks remarkably like a chalice or Communion cup. And who are those who are hardly ever there to taste the blood of Jesus?

If Jesus were here today, he might be saying to his disciples: 'Suffer these bright young adults to come to me, stop ignoring

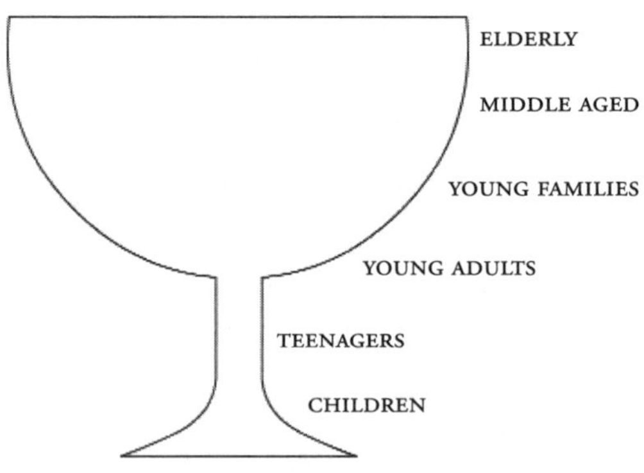

them, don't just use them as people to help out in the youth group, give them teaching, worship and a challenge which excites all their young blood. Take notice of the fact that they are slipping away from my church.'

It may well be that young adults, i.e. those aged between eighteen and the late thirties, are the least spiritually interested age group in our society. This certainly seems to be the conclusion of *Making Sense of Generation Y*, a research-based book by Sara Savage, Sylvia Collins-Mayo, Bob Mayo and Graham Cray:

> Neither did we find much evidence among our young people of beliefs in other spiritual or supernatural realms beyond the here and now . . . There appears to be an absence of young people being involved in explicit spiritual seeking.[2]

Having worked as an evangelist with young adults for the last ten years, first in Bradford and then in Manchester, I agree with the cold realism of such assessments, but I do not think it stops there. Running weekends away, missions, pub nights and worship events specifically for Gen-Yers, I have found that even in the midst of their easy, materialistic, non-commitment lifestyles there are still inner places that can be reached. Build a relationship with a young adult (not nearly as difficult as many imagine), ask one or two probing spiritual questions, invite them to an attractive and relevant gathering and some of them will respond just like any other group of human beings.

---

[2] Savage, Collins-Mayo, Mayo and Cray, *Making Sense of Generation Y*, Church House Publishing 2006, pages 37, 51.

Some years ago, I found myself joining with other church leaders in Bradford to stage an outdoor evangelistic event in the city centre on the Saturday of the Easter weekend. Halfway through, as I stood on the top of a stepladder with arms outstretched, squeezing oranges to represent Christ bleeding on the cross, I looked down and wondered where all the young adults were. They were not just missing from the assembled church members, but from the passing crowd as well. I realised afterwards that they were all in bed, sleeping off their Friday night out on the town.

I was working at the time with my great friend Dave Banbury. Together we had set up a group for the eighteens to thirties called Eternity. We decided to chase the crowd. What followed was a series of short, open-air Communion services at 10.00 p.m. on Friday nights in the middle of club and pub land. We used big-screen images, live music, lots of atmospheric smoke and light and brief punchy preaching, but the most electric part was the sacrament itself. On a raised platform we set up a large, snowy white, candle-festooned table with five robed priests in attendance. At the key moment we went amongst the crowd tearing chunks of bread off the consecrated loaves and offering them to any who wanted. This, of course, broke all the rules of the Anglican Church, and the accepted orthodoxy about people coming to faith before coming to Communion. It was our hope, however, to somehow bring Jesus out of the church box and to the people.

It is impossible to quantify this sort of event and the strange, presence-full silence that came over the crowd. At its heart, it was an attempt to reach out to an outcast and neglected group of people (many of whom are not as far away as we and the gurus of postmodern mission imagine). Looking back, I have both a positive and a negative reflection to offer. The positive is that something of Jesus really happened, and the negative is that we gave up too soon. We lacked the full courage of Christ to push on, many of the assembled crowd were more tuned in than we realised, we had a spiritual authority, but I think our nerve ran out. When I use the words 'we' and 'our' in this context, I should really be saying 'I' and 'my'.

I live in south Manchester, one of the biggest young adult enclaves anywhere in Europe. There is a resident population of over sixty thousand students, plus thousands more post- and non-student types. The churches and chaplaincies are there, but it looks as if they cater mainly for those who attend. There are a few big charismatic groupings, but they are rather hidden away and thrive on attracting young Christians from the older and staider denominations. So where is the hugely visible, on-the-street and unavoidable Galilean Jesus? If he were here now, surely he would be out and about meeting, talking, healing, welcoming and engaging with the masses? Most of them, of course, would reject him or simply walk on by, but some, a significant some, would hear and see and follow.

The challenge is for us to divert some energy, time, cash and people power away from other issues and groups and into our lost generations of young adults. We have, firstly, to stop losing our eighteen- to thirty-year-olds, and then to encourage them to become the essential members of a new mission initiative.

And now, for the sake of those who think that I have lost track of our children, perhaps I can briefly draw attention to a surprisingly large group of 'eternal children' who really are outsiders and with whom we do far too little. They are the people with learning disabilities. Christian groups such as L'Arche and Causeway Prospects do some wonderful kingdom work with such people, but most of us simply ignore them. Yet here are human beings just like us who respond passionately when the words and works of Jesus are opened up to them. Anyone who works with them and their carers will be blessed richly in return.

Men

What would the church look like if we modelled Jesus' awareness of and welcoming evangelism to women in our work with men?

In *The Death of Christian Britain*, Callum Brown has written persuasively about what he calls the 'feminisation of piety'.[3] He argues that this was a process begun in the nineteenth and continued into the twentieth century, which gradually led to Christianity being seen as a religion which appealed primarily to women. If this is true, and I am sure that it is, then men have taken the place of women and become the religious outsiders. Jesus made a special effort to make contact with and show equal interest in the women of his day. Is this what we should be doing today for the men?

Today the main power-holders in the churches are still male, but they are leading a predominantly female movement, and this gender imbalance has been with us since the late nineteenth century, according to Callum Brown.

What would it take for individual churches, denominations or dioceses and their mission departments to create this new work amongst men? It might mean a broadening out of our world of political correctness and a development of a truly inclusive view of mission. Men are spiritual outsiders, untouched by the good news and undisturbed by the church. The inclusive approach to

---

3 Callum Brown, *The Death of Christian Britain*, Routledge 2000.

women has been a long-overdue step forward for the church; perhaps now is the time to balance it with a more gender-equal evangelism simply by inviting more men, be they young or old, working, middle or upper class, to come and join the party.

We are embarrassed by men and nervous of their masculine hardness and indifference. We are more comfortable working with children and women. Yet Jesus refused to shirk the challenge and found, especially in one-to-one conversations, that inner personal doors were opened.

Men's pub nights, male Alpha courses, curry and lager trips for the boys, mission weekends and retreats aimed specifically at men, church-based football and rugby events – the whole project may not look 'quite the thing' at first glance, but a deeper examination will reveal it as a vital, 'Jesus the evangelist' piece of ministry, as an opening of doors for the outsider.

Any church, of any description or theology, could get its core members together and draw up a list of the poor, the young adults and the men they know. They could then plan some sort of specific initiative towards them in the style of Jesus the evangelist, sharing friendship, social concern, healing and the good news of the gospel.

The point is, Jesus the evangelist did not concentrate just on the insiders, nor did he pour all his energies into those who just happened to turn up. He was proactive and compassionate in his love for and mission towards those on the outside. To him they were not so much the unrighteous, but more the latecomers to the banquet.

Mission-Shaped Church has made us all more aware of both the 'dechurched' and the 'unchurched'. Perhaps we could all open our eyes a bit wider to see the third grouping, the 'on the edge of the churched', from which can emerge a wonderful 'newly churched' bunch of followers of Jesus. Reaching these outsider groups is not just the vocation of 'Fresh Expressions', but of all 'Jesus the evangelist'-shaped churches.

> The task is to become church for them, among them and with them, and under the Spirit of God to lead them to become church in their own culture.[4]

Every single church, be it new and innovative or traditional and ancient, has its own mission field, its own Galilee made up of people in the local community, those who relate to its activities and organisations and all those known by its members and its networks. The task here is not even to make contact with new people, but to make communication with those with whom it is already in contact. They, in turn, will become the ones to make contact with new people.

> The harvest is plentiful but the workers are few. (Matthew 9:37)

'The Christian church is the only organisation which exists for the sake of those who are not yet members.' So said the great and prophetic archbishop William Temple, one of the few people who has been able to hold together a powerful concern for the poor and weak alongside a passion for evangelism. He is a great twentieth-century example for us of someone who understood and followed the practices of Jesus the evangelist, the 'Son of Man [who] came to seek and to save what was lost' (Luke 19:10).

---

[4] Graham Cray (ed.), *Mission-Shaped Church*, Church House Publishing 2004, page 40.

The seekers

Jesus was proactive and full of grace in his going 'outside the city wall' of religion, in his approaches towards the outsiders. In the case of the 'seekers' it seems to be the other way round. They are the ones taking the initiative in looking for and wanting something from him. A deeper reading of the stories, however, shows that although the seekers come towards him, he is the one who has made the first move. He is searching, like a good shepherd, for his lost sheep (Matthew 4:23; Luke 19:1). It is a combination of what we used to call 'outreach' and 'in-drag'.

A characteristic feature of the occasional Gentiles who appear in the Gospels is that they are purposefully searching for Jesus. He is not coming to them, they are coming to him. The pattern is set by the wise men travelling from the East asking, 'Where is the child?' Later on we read of the Roman centurion and the Syro-Phoenician woman, both full of faith, and the Gadarene demoniac who becomes one of Jesus' first evangelists. Right up to the end the pattern continues, with a bunch of Greeks coming to Philip in Jerusalem and saying, 'Sir, we wish to see Jesus.' Even at the cross, there is a final recognition by the Roman guards of who Jesus really is.

Of course, Gentiles were not the only seekers. The mainly Jewish crowds were hungry for healings and curious about the new prophetic 'kid on the block'. Crowds being crowds, however, theirs was a fairly superficial or short-term search, but there were some deep searchers among them. These were the ones who would give a lifelong 'yes' to his invitation to 'follow me'.

- Nicodemus was a Pharisee. He had to guard his reputation and public image, and so he came secretly, at night (John 3:2).

Jesus took Nicodemus's searching beyond the limits of traditional religion and spirituality into the area of personal inner knowing. He spoke to him of eternal life and of being 'born again' (a poetically beautiful and revelatory concept which we have tragically turned into a negative and cringy term of derision). I wonder how many devout, committed, 'still not quite found it' Nicodemuses there are in our churches. Most of us, be we evangelists, pastors, flower arrangers or whatever, can probably think of one or two we know straight away. To have such thoughts is not to be judgemental, but to be caring.

- Jesus' conversation with the woman at the well happens because he makes the proactive missionary move of travelling into her Samaritan village (a sort of 'dechurched' place, John 4:5). It is the longest account we have of Jesus having a one-to-one evangelistic encounter. She is a lonely woman. For her, the communal well is not a place for meeting other women, but a place which emphasises her aloneness. She is a disappointed woman. Her past is full of broken relationships and possibly abuse at the hands of various men. She is an empty woman. Her search for cool water is a metaphor for her whole life of thirsting. Jesus sits and spends time with her. He is sympathetic, perceptive and has the confidence to go right to the heart of the matter. He knows that the answer to her hurt and lostness is to find and receive God at a deep and personal level. Not only does the woman find everything she is searching for in the sensitive Jesus, she also launches straight away into the work of evangelism: 'Many of the Samaritans from that town believed in him because of the woman's testimony' (John 4:39).

- The rich young man is the saddest member of our triptych of searchers (Matthew 19:16). He comes to Jesus asking and wanting, but he is wedded to his wealth. How tragic, to get so close, to find and then to lose it. And how interesting that Jesus does not go running after him: he knows the score. Not all seekers become followers; the rich man is not the only person who has lost someone that day. He has gone away richer, yet poorer. Jesus must have grieved the loss of a transformed life and of another potential follower.

There is no set model of personal evangelism for anyone to adopt by studying these passages. There is no straightforward 'ABC', 'Four Spiritual Laws', or 'Six Simple Steps'. These are one-off encounters in which Jesus treats people as individuals. There is, however, a sort of pattern which has two parts to it. Firstly, everyone is special and Jesus starts where the person is, not where his theory or formula is. Secondly, Jesus is non-judgemental and all-accepting and leads everyone on to the same place. He leads, or attempts to lead, them on to a closeness to God. That is his universal and completely inclusive solution to the human condition.

Seekers in our selfish age

You can trace the path of 'There must be something more' as it winds its way through Western pop music. Here are a few examples from my limited knowledge:

- Does it begin with the Beatles singing of a 'nowhere man', a sort of opposite to the 'Son of man', living for all of us in a 'nowhere land'?

- Or perhaps it begins with the poetry of Bob Dylan. Amid a multitude of searching songs, perhaps his most famous image is that of a rolling stone trying but not quite managing to find its way home.
- The Who are still searching. Back in their heyday they were singing about the 'Seeker', and about 'Tommy' who was desperate to be saved from the grave.
- Meanwhile U2, while being friends and followers of Jesus, 'still haven't found' what they're looking for.
- In recent years Travis have suffered from being constantly rained on, Oasis have stood in the shadow of the 'wonderwall' and Coldplay have cried out to God to give them grace as well as style, as they try to work out where they go from here.
- Dolly Parton has made more progress than most. She realises that she is a seeker and has sought out a preacher. Meanwhile Mick Jagger has gone off in his four-wheel drive to search for the Buddha, though he saw Jesus instead.

Apologies for my old man selection of rock music – mind you, it's not just the pop-singers who are seeking; the pop-novelists and writers are journeying too:

Jack Kerouac, *On the Road*
Robert Pirsig, *Zen and the Art of Motorcycle Maintenance*
Richard Bach, *Jonathan Livingstone Seagull*
Bruce Chatwin, *The Songlines*
Nick Hornby, *How to be Good*
Tony Parsons, *Man and Woman*
Ben Elton, *Dead Famous*
Jonathan Coe, *Full Circle*
Blake Morrison, *South of the River*

All are asking questions, looking for meaning, wanting something better and deeper, and seeking happiness.

It is not that you need the insight of a great singer or writer to be a seeker. These uniquely aware and creative souls are all saying something, not just about themselves, but about a part of the post-Christian times in which they live and some of the postmodern people amongst whom they live and move and have their being. Even poor old Rebus, Ian Rankin's whisky-loving, lonely Edinburgh detective, is on some sort of spiritual journey as he drifts through empty churches and odd friendships with priests. The interesting thing is that both the sequences, one of pop music and the other of pop literature, began in the 1960s. This was the very period, according to Callum Brown, when young people in the West started breaking out of the old world of adult certainties, enjoying extended education and greater affluence, and losing contact with the Christian faith.

So does this mean that we are suddenly living in a new spiritual age, as some have claimed?

> We cannot fail to recognise the growing curiosity there is in different forms of faith and spirituality. Our society has become increasingly characterised by a pluralistic 'pick and mix' blend of belief systems, values and lifestyles.[5]

My own answer to this question is a small 'yes' and a big 'no'. We are, after all, still living in the old, selfish, money-grabbing, materialistic age. Certainly there are searchers and spirituality has at last come out of the closet, but it is still a minority sport.

---

[5] Yvonne Richmond et al., *Evangelism in a Spiritual Age*, page 8.

Jesus seems to have discovered seekers as the odd exceptions, hanging on the edge of the crowd, the ones who seemed to listen that bit more attentively than the majority. He warned that the truly big search was for the things of this world rather than God (Matthew 7:13), and he saw much spiritual growth being crowded out by worldly desire (Matthew 13:22). Strangely, George Orwell found something similar when he went in search of working-class men to overturn the inequalities of 1930s Britain. He came to the conclusion that, given 'fish and chips, silk-stockings, tinned salmon, cut-price chocolate, the movies, the radio, strong tea and the Football Pools,' these men would never rise up in search of something better – they would mutely accept things as they were (*The Road to Wigan Pier*, p. 83).

I suspect that there has never been a 'spiritual age', that wherever you stick the pin into history you will always find that the majority are happy with a basic basketful of material pleasures. In our world it is not religion which is the opium of the masses, but cheap lager, DVDs, overseas travel, nice cars and endless 'footie'. Andrew Marr describes our age as a 'head-on victory of shopping over politics. Of the defeat of visions, and rival idealisms of a new Jerusalem or a second Elizabethan age by a culture of consumerism, celebrity and self-gratification' (*A History of Britain Since the War*).

But the majority never means everyone. There are always the seekers, who can see right through the bottom of the materialistic basket. I think we could say of our times that, although the majority are content to live in a 'nowhere land', there is a considerable minority who are looking for a spiritual dimension, reality or road. These are the ones who are travelling on what Jesus called the narrow and hard path. As we have already seen, in our postmodern culture people are enquiring or entering at three gateways to get on to this path.

- They are drawn to the *spiritual* or sacred. Tarot cards, dream-catchers, meditation, Buddhism, angels, icons, retreats and sacred spaces are all popular.
- Some are desperate for *healing*, be it in body, mind or spirit. Today we are hungry for good health and deep peace.
- Many are longing for *relationship* and community. Acceptance, welcome, friendship, love and a sense of belonging are what we all need in a lonely and privatised world. We have seen them on the television in *Friends*, *Auf Wiedersehen Pet* and *Coronation Street*, and we want to be part of them.

These three gateways each represent basic human needs. That is why they each have a significant, yet minority group of seekers milling around them. They are also what we might call basic core products of the good news experience. Jesus did the spiritual and sacred, healing and peace, and relationships and accepting friendship. He did all three in an evangelising sort of way, i.e. he did not just want people to find the sacred or peace, he wanted them to find the real stuff in him: 'Come to me. . .', 'I am. . .', 'But I say to you. . .' Today his living church can do all three as well, both in an ancient, mysterious tradition and in a bright, contemporary, on-the-street style. In recent years, I have witnessed different churches in Manchester bravely attempting to open up all three doorways. Running a Christian stand at 'body, mind and spirit' events, launching healing services for midday shoppers and workers, and setting up midweek 'drop-ins' to offer both good food and genuine friendship. All are working in modest but effective ways. Too often in the recent past we have lost confidence in what we are essentially about, and have allowed other quack spiritualities to steal our clothes, but things are changing.

Jesus was there for every single individual in the crowd, but he knew enough to know that most of them were not there for him. He gave his all to them as a proclaiming, healing and demon-busting evangelist, but he had a special roving eye for the significant minority, the seekers.

Today's seekers are those who are looking for a bit more – a bit more depth or meaning, or a bit more hope in a darkening future, perhaps a bit more help with their life struggles, or a bit more love from someone. Nick Spencer's little book *Beyond Belief* and Yvonne Richmond's written-up research in *Evangelism in a Spiritual Age* both come to the same conclusion:

> People today have 'big questions'. Sometimes those questions emerge into their lives and demand attention, and this can lead to a re-evaluation of life and life-style. Most of the time, they lie quietly under the surface.[6]

So the key handful of seekers are the ones who have stepped out of the crowd, or been disturbed out of it, and who are aware of their 'big questions'. The biggest of these, according to Nick Spencer, concerns their destiny and the hope for life after death. How interesting, because who has a better answer to that question than Jesus?

Many searchers are people who used to have a faith, or who used to belong to the church. These are the prodigal sons and daughters who bring so much joy to their Father. Melvyn Bragg describes his own returning journey in commenting on the 'Lighten our Darkness' prayer:

---

[6] *Evangelism in a Spiritual Age*, page 18.

> This clear and magnificent prayer speaks both to people who are inside the church, and to people who have – or are trying to rediscover, as I am in a rather solitary, very fragile and tentative way – a faith.[7]

When Gillian Oliver suggested that we had a special 'Back to Church Sunday', I felt instinctively that she was on to a really good idea. Gillian was press officer for Manchester Diocese at the time, and that was where we first tried out the concept. The results of that first event in 2004 were carefully researched, and the model has now been adopted by other dioceses and individual churches. It is increasingly clear that there are significant numbers of lost souls searching for a way back. It is equally clear that 'Back to Church Sunday' is an effective and easy-to-do way of looking for these searchers. To some extent, we can see the whole of Jesus' ministry as a 'Back to God' campaign. It was directed first at the Jewish nation who had lost contact, in a sense the 'dechurched', and then reached out wider to include the Gentiles, the 'unchurched'.

Seeking the seekers

Clergy and laity regularly talk to someone in my position, in a disappointed voice, of how many people attended their mission weekend, special 'guest-friendly' Harvest Festival or Easter services, etc., and of how few came the following week. I always reply, quite truthfully, that in my opinion, if sixty or so people attended the mission and four or five are coming to a follow-up basics course, then that is wonderful. The people coming to the big event are the 'crowd' and those who continue with the

[7] Quoted in James Whitbourn (ed.), *The Best of my Belief*, Triangle 1997.

experience are the 'seekers'. I operate on a 'parable of the sower' principle of 'diminishing interest in the minds of the many, but deepening intent in the hearts of the minority', which I think mimics the way that Jesus worked.

This slimming down of the crowd, leaving a residue of true followers, is illustrated in John 6. It begins with Jesus feeding the five thousand, who then want to make him king (v. 15). It finishes with the words, 'From this time many of his disciples turned back and no longer followed him' (v. 66).

The model looks a bit like this:

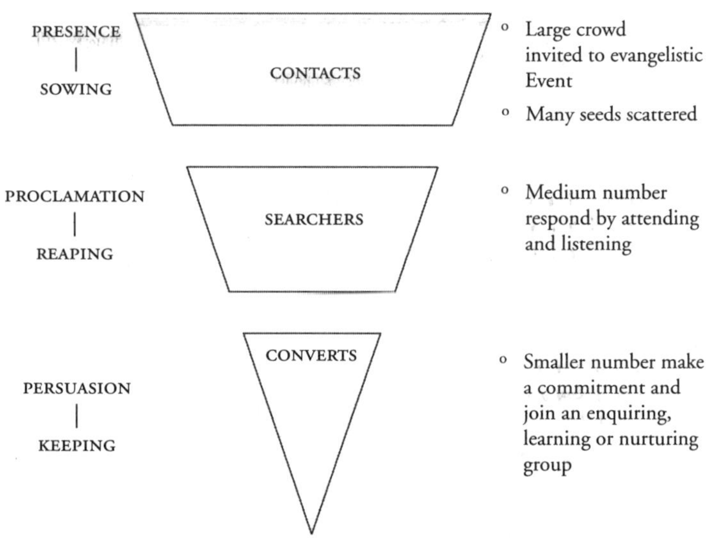

I do not believe it is too fanciful to think of the big presence block as Jesus' Galilee, the medium one as his journey south, and the third, smallest and final one as the gathered companions after the resurrection, as long as we remember to keep all the boxes flexible and fuzzy edged. The people who appear on our church mission map, or who are visited and invited to our evangelistic event, then become our Galilee.

> News about him spread quickly over the whole region of Galilee. (Mark 1:28)

A young priest recently contacted me. He had just moved to his first post as vicar, a tiny church on an old post-war estate. As he began to get known, he was frankly such a kind and pleasant person that he was literally 'good news' in that place. I suggested that he wore his dog collar at all times, engaged in serious listening and offered to pray whenever anyone had a difficulty. A Galilean ministry was developing, providing a platform for inviting people and sharing the gospel message.

Thinking of the local church as having a Galilean ministry might seem a bit traditional in these postmodern times. Not a bit of it. Michael Moynagh describes how today's over-mobile people are often looking for some sort of local belonging, and how the local community actually consists of lots of 'micro' local communities (a bit like Galilean villages), each of which needs its own Christian presence. ' "Rooted" churches will have a great future. These will be churches that are even more local than the local church.'[8]

Twenty or so years ago, I read a simple but very helpful book on local church evangelism written by Gavin Reid. In it I came across what was for me a revolutionary concept: 'evangelism is a seeking out of seekers'.[9] Before this I had been trying somehow to

---

8 *Emergingchurch.Intro*, Monarch 2008, page 76.

9 Gavin Reid, *Good News to Share*, Falcon (Kingsway) 1979, page 36.

make contact with everyone, and to make converts out of them, whether or not they were actually interested in spiritual things. This incisive little phrase immediately rang bells for me.

Having adopted the concept, the next big question was, 'So how do I seek out the seekers?' I began with lots of prayer, establishing deep friendships and an attempt at discernment, at reading the signs. Frankly, this did not get me very far and the idea lay dormant in my mind for several years, until I stumbled across the thought that maybe the easiest way is simply to ask people if they are seeking. I had always operated on the principle that evangelists were people with the big answers. I have now swung over to the position that we are the people with the big questions.

Jesus was a great one for asking questions. He asked Bartimaeus, 'What do you want me to do for you?' (Mark 10:51). To Nicodemus he said, 'You are Israel's teacher . . . and do you not understand these things?' (John 3:10). To a pair of blind beggars he said, 'Do you believe that I am able to do this?' (Matthew 9:28). To Peter he said, 'Who do you say I am?' (Matthew 16:15). He asked the woman at the well where her husband was (John 4:16), and to the rich young man he effectively said, 'Why don't you give it all away?' (see Luke 18:22).

These days I am always asking questions:

- 'Do you believe in God?'
- 'Did you ever go to church?'
- 'When did you lose contact?'
- 'Do you ever think about God?'
- 'What about heaven?'
- 'Have you ever felt alone?'
- 'How did you find the service?'

- 'Why don't you join this group that the vicar is forming?'
- 'We're having a special night at the pub, do you fancy coming with me?'

I ask these questions of my best friends, family, neighbours, occasional acquaintances and lots of people with whom I just come into contact. I reject the prevailing orthodoxy in evangelism circles which says that Christians have no friendships outside the church and must therefore invest months and possibly years in building them. We all have plenty of relationships, but we hang 'Evangelism Keep Out' notices on many of them. We are happy to engage with strangers, but feel shy and fearful with our nearest and dearest.

Jesus' pattern was to go wandering around lots of villages in a relatively small area that he knew well. The great pile of all the people I know or meet is my personal Galilee – I wander around it and keep asking questions. As I ask my questions, I will also try to be a bringer of peace, hope and healing, and, very importantly, I will try to laugh or at least smile with as many as possible.

This is my attempt to put into practice in my world both what Jesus himself did and what he mentored the disciples into doing when he sent out first the Twelve and then the Seventy-two. I listen very carefully to the answers and to the way in which they are given. Often the answer to the question makes it clear that the person with whom I am speaking has no interest, they are not a seeker, their door is well and truly closed. So I do what Jesus told his disciples to do: I knock the dust off my sandals and move on to the next person (Matthew 10:14). Sometimes the answer to the question is positive, or approaching positive, or at least not entirely negative. So I stay and spend time, explore issues, try to share something of my peace, and invite them on to the next step in their journey.

I am attempting to travel around my own personal Galilee just like Jesus did, and to help me in this I have a discipline that I call 'A Seeker a Week'. Actually, it probably works out nearer a seeker a fortnight, so it is a discipline that I aim at but often miss (like all other evangelists, I am much better at talking about it than doing it). 'A Seeker a Week' may involve the following steps:

- Establishing an initial relationship.
- Developing a conversation and asking someone if they are a seeker.
- Spending time with a person who is seeking and inviting them along to the next step on the journey.

Just like Jesus, good evangelists lead and train teams. The usual pattern when building up to a mission is to prepare everyone on the team in how to present the gospel, i.e. how to do the talking. Nowadays I have completely dropped all that and simply ask them to learn three questions and to ask them of all the people they meet at all the different events they attend. The three questions are:

- 'Who are you?' This is about striking up an initial relationship.
- 'Where are you?' or 'Where are you with God?' Suddenly you find out if they are interested, if they are seeking.
- 'Why don't you. . .?' It might be, 'So why don't you become a Christian?' or, if it is too soon for that, 'Why don't you come to the next big mission service/follow-up meeting/basics group?'

Back to the idea of 'A Seeker a Week'. Not only do I attempt to follow this discipline, but I also share it with others, especially other clergy. The response is nearly always, 'I would love to aim at that too, but in my particular case it isn't possible.' Frankly, there are just too many 'buts'.

I realise that this is a bit easier for me because, as a minister, I meet lots of people and I wear a dog collar. So I encourage non-clergy to wear some sort of identifying badge or symbol, or a silver cross on their shirt or blouse. Equally, I really do encourage clergy to play their part and wear their collar. There is a special opportunity and calling on all clergy of all denominations and theologies to be involved in the seeking of the seekers. Those who think they have delegated the task have actually avoided it; those who think they are too busy are indeed too busy.

Neil Short was until recently a vicar of a very busy and growing church in Burscough, Lancashire. He is a constant question-asker. His personal Galilee consists of his parishioners, many people on the edge of his church, fellow members of his golf and cricket clubs – in fact, just about everyone with whom he comes into contact. At some stage he asks them all the same question, which goes a bit like this: 'I don't know if you've heard about this, but every now and then I run a little group at my house for a few people who are interested in finding out a bit more about God. I'm starting the next one in a few weeks. Would you like to come?'

Some say 'yes', some say 'no', but what an effective way of searching through lots of people to discover a handful of seekers. You do not need to have some strange evangelism gift to do this. All you need is a pleasant manner, a sense of vocation and a bit of grit.

Developing a culture of invitation

Is there a strategy for opening the doors for both the outsiders and the seekers, which transposes the model of Jesus the evangelist into our world? I think there is, and it is called 'invitation'.

John Young has been a major presence on the evangelism scene in the UK for over thirty years. He is a prolific writer and has done more than anyone else to introduce and build up the idea of interviewing Christians with an interesting story to tell. He has done this both in evangelistic events and in his widely used 'York Courses'. John was the first person I ever heard using the phrase 'developing a culture of invitation'. As soon as I heard it, I had a sort of disclosure moment: I knew it was of Jesus, and I knew it could work in our world.

Jesus' parable of the banquet (Luke 14:15–24) is all about inviting people to a great occasion full of food and drink, hospitality and welcome, celebration and home-coming. Soon after choosing to follow Jesus, Levi the tax-collector threw a banquet and invited all his tax-collecting friends to come, enjoy his hospitality and meet with Jesus themselves. It is a classic piece of evangelism (Luke 5:27–29).

The great thing about inviting people to enjoyable gatherings is that it is so positive and joyful, and it works perfectly in our culture, whether we are having a small supper party, a night in a local restaurant, or beer and curry down at the pub. It might be a one-off social gathering, or a full-scale mission or festival.

Jesus seems to have loved table fellowship – so much so, in fact, that there are thirteen examples in the Gospels of him eating and drinking with people, usually in their house or on their territory. We see him eating breakfasts, suppers and a midday snack in the cornfields. He seems to have been equally at home with the poor and the rich. He ate with sinners who were drawn to him and Pharisees who ended up distancing themselves, with seekers, friends and disciples. When he sat down with people, the relationships seemed to change: perhaps it was the relaxed nature of the moment, the feel-good atmosphere that was generated, or just the melting of human coldness that often happens when people eat together.

John Dominic Crossan picks out this practice of sharing meals with others, what he calls commensality, as one of the most defining features of Jesus' kingdom ministry. In recent years, the church has been rediscovering the 'kingdom nature' of meals and no one has done more than the members of the great and wonderful Alpha movement to help us all in this rediscovery. More than any other organisation, the church is supposed to be about welcome, friendship, hospitality, shared food and drink and all the warmth of humanity that goes with it. If we follow the pattern of Jesus, I think we can make every meal a sacrament, while still wanting to see all our guests press on to the ultimate shared meal and become part of the eucharistic family.

In Ursula Le Guin's strange and mystical world of *Earthsea*, there is a great house with a hall, the heart of which is a magical table that expands to accommodate all guests. There is always space, welcome and food for an extra one or more. I love this image as a picture of what Jesus' table should be like – whether in our kitchen or our sanctuary.

Evangelists are forever bemoaning the inability or unwillingness on the part of church members to witness and share their faith. We keep coming up with new and better courses and resources to train and stimulate them to this task, but no matter how good the materials we produce, they seem to have a very limited impact. My own feeling is that, frankly, we are never going to get most of our people talking about Jesus. What we can do, however, is to get a good number inviting someone to a carol service, flower festival, party, church outing or remembrance service. John Young argues that all we have to say to a friend or work colleague is: 'We're having a special event at our church. It's going to be really good. Would you like to come with me?' In effect, it is another way of asking someone if they are seeking. Of course many will say 'no', but how many will say 'yes' because they are quite interested, and how many will say 'yes' simply out of good manners and will then come and discover that they *are* quite interested?

Inviting someone to a gospel event is not an alternative to real gospel sharing, and it is not watering it down for those who cannot do the real thing – it actually is the real thing.

A couple of years ago, I got involved with a vicar in Manchester who was encouraging his church to have an invitational mission. It is a modestly sized, middle-of-the-road type of church, very insular, with no memory of missions in the past. So how could he get his non-inviting congregation to reach out? He personally gave every member three invitation cards to each gathering and service. He told them that one was for themselves and two were to give away. It was that simple, and it worked. I was amazed how many guests turned up. I think the fact that he also spent a complete night patiently sharing the vision with his church council and sending up his own hungry and desperate prayers also played a key part. This piece of work strikes me as being rather like Jesus' sending out first the Twelve and then the Seventy-two, or the sending out of the invitation deliverers in the parable of the banquet. As with his own work, it is all about balancing 'outreach' with 'in-drag'.

Invitation gatherings can be built around anything that we can do well. Dave Banbury and Tim Sledge are two evangelists with whom I regularly work. They are both brilliant at creating imaginative and enjoyable events at which they always take the opportunity of presenting the good news. Dave's big things are cool young adults' get-togethers and 'Pints of View' with a bunch of blokes down at the pub. Tim is a high church evangelist who loves chocolate and is a very classy musician. He has created 'Love Chocolate' evenings and musical appreciation nights to which many people can easily be invited. What both Dave and Tim are doing is plugging into popular culture at one end of their cable and Jesus the evangelist at the other end and simply connecting. They are building contemporary 'gospel banquets'. Their work is both messianic, bringing in the kingdom, and incarnational, introducing it in a way people can identify with.

In Manchester Diocese we have been working at developing a culture of invitation over the last few years. It began when a small interdenominational group set up 'Real Christmas', turned the traditional carol service into a huge event and invited the whole city to go along to their local church: simple, but very effective. Since then we have set up a 'Mission Weekend' project and 'Back to Church Sunday', as opportunities for church members to invite people along to their church.

Our latest venture is 'God Friday', a more sedate but deeper version of 'Real Christmas', but this time at Easter. Once again we are running a campaign, producing quality resources and encouraging many churches across the city to hold a user-friendly, low-brow popular-culture hour at the cross on Good Friday night. At every one of these events, the message and invitation of the cross is preached.

We are also piloting a 'Festival of the Four Feasts'. With this we want to enter into the contemporary mood for festivals and wrap it around Jesus the people person. In the course of a few days, a church will hold a 'Levi Meal', inviting a few definite seekers to come together to eat, listen and talk. Next up is a 'Feeding of the Five Thousand', consisting of a big family fun Saturday, followed by an 'On the Shore Breakfast' on Sunday morning before or instead of church, involving the story of the resurrection. Finally, a 'First Supper' is held on the final night, with the bread and wine being offered to any who feel called to come a bit closer to Jesus.

Now here is an idea to both terrify and inspire in equal quantities. Every single Christian, lay leader, parish priest, vicar and pastor has their own personal Galilee, their own life place, full of people. Most of our people are probably part of a fairly superficial non-seeking crowd, but somewhere in there are a few seekers. Most of us do not actually need to go out and meet lots of new people, we simply need to develop our own Galilean ministry, wandering through all the relationships we already have, scattering acts of grace, asking the key questions and inviting people to the feast.

In reaching out to the outsiders and seeking for the seekers, we are gold-mining in our own Galilee. Most of us begin with exciting revivalist ideas of hitting the big one – sticking a shovel in the ground and discovering our own Klondike revival with crowds coming to faith. Sometimes it does happen like that, but not very often, and it does not seem to have been like that for Jesus. For most of us it is much more like panning for gold. Gradually, persistently, we meet, engage with, ask our questions of and invite to the kingdom lots of people, and slowly but surely the nuggets pile up. Much of our energy, hope and work comes to nothing, but some of our seed falls on good soil.

Everyone in the UK lives or works in someone's and some church's Galilee. How many of them ever experience a Jesus-type person coming into their village, asking them the big questions, or inviting them to come and enjoy? You could begin right now by simply making a list of five people you know, and then setting out for your first village.

Invite me in
Don't leave me out,
Give me a chance
To make my own choice,
Don't make your usual assumption
Try me with an invitation,
And maybe, just maybe
I will say 'yes' to your smile.

CHAPTER SIX

From Converts to Disciples

> The ambiguity suggests that we should speak of circles (plural) of discipleship, rather than of a coherent circle. The innermost circle seems to have been the twelve, with Peter and the brothers James and John at its heart. But round the twelve we have seen a wider circle of followers.[1]

The evangelism trade in its present mode began to form in the late eighteenth and early nineteenth centuries in Britain and America. It was a blending together of Methodist-style preaching and American revivalist campaigning. For much of the time it has been largely about producing as many converts as possible. Conversion was seen to be about personal repentance from past sinful activities and the embracing of a basic belief in Jesus. This step of a private change of heart and mind would then ensure the convert of salvation from death to eternal life. The hope was and still is that these converts would then go on to become church attenders, financial contributors and job-doers.

---

[1] James Dunn, *Jesus Remembered*, page 540.

So far so good . . . but therein lies the problem, for this is as far as it often goes for many people. This type of conversion experience, for which I and millions like me have been tremendously grateful over the years, is a great doorway but a pretty thin mansion; it is a wonderful birth but there is not a lot of nurture or maturing. Even when the conversion process is extended from a one-off appeal to a journeying enquirers' course, it still tends to focus on the beginning rather than the continuing of the movement.

Therefore go and make disciples of all nations. (Matthew 28:19)

Jesus was interested in disciples who were deeply transformed so that they could go onwards and outwards and have a deeply transforming impact on their world. We evangelists today are labouring to produce lots of converts, while Jesus worked to create a handful of men and women who each had lots of conversion in their life. His goal was not so much freshers' week as the final graduation ceremony.

The shape of Jesus' ministry was one of massive immediate impact attracting large numbers of people; then, as the movement pushed onwards, the numbers slipped backwards: 'Many of his disciples turned back and no longer followed him' (John 6:66). The parable of the sower painfully yet realistically spells out this whole falling away or sifting through of large numbers phenomenon. Crowds are to disciples what tadpoles are to frogs. You start off with hundreds swimming around in a friendly comfort zone of a pond, and you end up with a few fully developed creatures hopping around in the fairly hostile environment of field or garden.

In order to learn how Jesus the evangelist made disciples, we shall follow the whole process, using Luke's Gospel as our principal (though not only) guide.

Discipleship in Luke

The story actually begins with Jesus himself. Disciples are learners, and Luke gives us a couple of snapshots of the young Jesus learning and developing intellectually and spiritually (Luke 2:40, 52). He was a son/disciple, disciplined to learn and obey his Father's ways and mission plan. As he prepared for his life's work, his baptism was his ordination (Luke 3:21), coming in his thirtieth year (Luke 3:23). The temptations were his testing examination period, sorting out his attitudes towards physical comforts, his subjection to his Father's will and his own ego-drive – testings that were never far away (Luke 4:13). Jesus the disciple prepared well and was ready to begin to recruit his own disciples, filled with the power of the Holy Spirit (Luke 4:14).

Before moving on with Jesus, we ought first to note that he was not the only one in the discipling business in first-century Israel. John the Baptist had his own group of disciples (Luke 11:1), two of whom transferred to following Jesus (John 1:35). There were also other rabbis and Pharisees who attracted followers, or *talmidim*, to study the law, the Talmud and their own individual teachings. Jesus' rabbinic methods were unique. In a world where the follower normally chose his favourite rabbi, just like students today choose their preferred university, he did it the other way round, by choosing his own students: 'You did not choose me, but I chose you and appointed you to go and bear fruit' (John 15:16). It seems as if Jesus' discipleship group lived a much less austere and prayerful life than others (Mark 2:18).

It was in this intense leader/follower, teacher/pupil world that Jesus gradually recruited, taught, mentored, prepared and finally sent out on mission his own group or groups of disciples.

In Luke's account we see Jesus beginning his work completely alone. Immediately there is a response and a gradual gathering of the interested. From among these early enquirers or adopters, he picks out a few individual men and calls them to follow him. First come Peter, James and John (Luke 5:1), followed by the surprising choice of Levi the tax-collector (Luke 5:10). If this had been an ordinary piece of team building, then we might think that the human chemistry for disunity and disaster were there from the beginning, but it did not work out like that. John's Gospel tells the story rather differently, with first Andrew and Peter, then Philip and Nathaniel being drawn to Jesus like bees to honey. Here they are first 'seekers' and then followers.

The fishermen and the tax-man were called to follow Jesus both physically, in his village wanderings, and also missionally, with the iconic images of leaving their boats and nets, balance sheets and office behind them.

> Then Jesus said to Simon, 'Don't be afraid; from now on you will catch men.' (Luke 5:10)

> Being with Jesus and being sent by him seem at first sight mutually exclusive, but they clearly belong together. The Apostles have to learn to be with him in a way that enables them, even when they go to the ends of the earth, to be with him still.[2]

Jesus' call on individuals did not always meet with a positive response. The rich ruler whom, according to Mark, Jesus loved, could not bear to give up his money to follow Jesus, and went

---

[2] Joseph Ratzinger, *Jesus of Nazareth*, page 172.

away a sad man (Luke 18:18–25). Conversely, the Gerasene demoniac volunteered to go with Jesus, but was instructed to remain among his own people and tell them what God had done: a case of following without actually following (Luke 8:39).

Jesus seems to have led these first disciples into a very relaxed and life-affirming way of being. The traditional pattern of radical religious adherents is one of denial and even glumness, rather like mourners at a funeral, but Jesus' followers were more like guests at a wedding (Luke 5:33; 6:1). With him they were like the colourful patches on an old coat, or the sun-filled, youthful new wine in old wineskins.

The Twelve and the Three

As the people movement gathered momentum, so the number of followers or disciples grew, and after spending the night in prayer Jesus called twelve of them to become his apostles (Luke 6:12–13). These were the ones who would not just follow behind, but would eventually go on ahead of him.

At the heart of the Twelve, there was an inner group consisting of Peter, James and John, who have sometimes been compared to the trio of intimate bodyguards that King David had employed. Perhaps Jesus needed his own personal support and encouragement group, or was he already establishing a leadership structure for the future apostolic church? At the healing of Jairus's daughter, these three went alone with Jesus and the parents into the house to witness one of his most significant healings (Luke 8:51). Similarly, when he ascended the mountain for the transfiguration, these were the ones Jesus took with him.

In a strange, but reassuringly human sort of way, these three are guilty of some of the greatest bloomers in the discipleship story. Peter, 'the rock', steps out of the boat to follow Jesus onto the water and promptly sinks. Later he denies knowing Jesus three times before the cock crows. James and John, meanwhile, suggest calling down balls of fire on resistant Samaritan villages (Luke 9:54) and commit one of the creepiest acts of self-centred toadyism ever recorded (Mark 10:35). The fact that these sorts of embarrassing stories have been remembered and retained is itself a pointer to the disciples' self-critical honesty, and to the Gospels' historical accuracy.

Being one of the Twelve must have been an amazing and exhilarating experience, especially during the time in the Galilee. There they were, like rock star roadies, living at the very centre of a celebrity circus, witnessing healings and the driving out of demons on a daily basis and being so close to the mysterious enigma that was Jesus. They were his assistants at the great feedings, students of his wit and wisdom, confidants of his fears and fellow travellers on the road and in the boat.

When Jesus held himself back and sent them out to do the proclaiming and healing, it must have been, at one and the same time, both terrifying and exciting. They went in pairs (never alone) and carried very little material baggage. They were searching for the searchers, the ones who would respond positively, and were warned away from wasting their precious time and energy in places where they were not wanted (Luke 10:1–6). The rationale behind the project was straightforward and twofold. Firstly, there were too many villages for Jesus to visit himself, but he did not want any to miss out. Secondly, as disciples they were learners and doers of their master's will. In doing what he did and preaching his message, they shared in his authority. They returned at the end of their mission thrilled and exhausted, to a teacher who clearly had more confidence in them than they had in themselves. Jesus shared their moment and then took them away to rest up (Luke 9:10).

What would it mean for today's churches if all those in training for ordination or other forms of leadership were expected to undergo a similar preparatory exercise, a piece of hands-on work experience, wandering around proclaiming healing and driving out evil? Perhaps we, like them, should be learning to do it his way.

As Jesus and the disciples left the Galilee and headed south to Jerusalem, the mood changed. The fear factor crept in (Mark 10:32). It was not so much that no one knew what the future held, but more that whenever Jesus tried to talk about it they just could not take it in. Luke's Gospel devotes a lot more space to this 'towards Jerusalem' phase than the others, a full ten chapters, from 9:52 to 19:28. As the journey moved south, Jesus spent less time with the crowds and put more time, energy and attention into a more radical teaching of the disciples (Luke 12:1).

In Jerusalem for the final week, the disciples faced their greatest challenge and produced their biggest failures. They fell asleep when Jesus needed them, betrayed him, denied him and deserted him (Luke 22:45–57). Their response to the resurrection was slow and disbelieving, with not an ounce of expectancy (Luke 24:11). Not exactly the stuff of positive, big faith disciples. Yet that is just what they became as the resurrected Jesus turned around the defeated duo on their way to Emmaus (Luke 24:33), breathed peace into troubled hearts and put deep faith into Thomas (John 20:19–29), and forgave the wretched Peter (John 21:15).

The story seems to be one of the Twelve's constant dependence on Jesus. Occasionally, however, such as at the transfiguration (Luke 9:28) and the entrance to Jerusalem (Luke 19:28), the emotional balance shifts. In his vulnerability, Jesus needed their presence, support and wakefulness, especially on his final night (Luke 22:8). The teacher/pupil relationship was two-way.

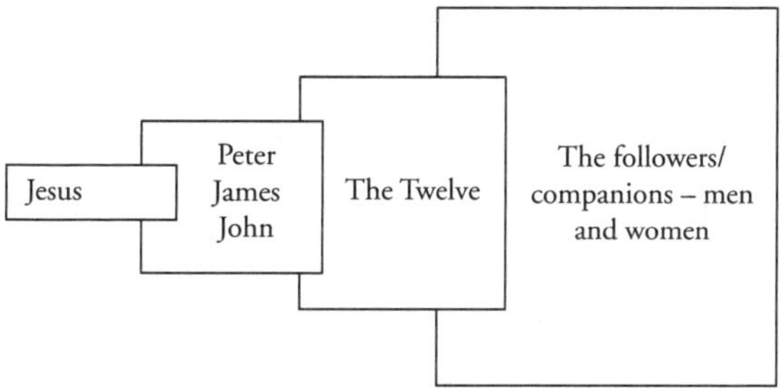

The companions

> They got up and returned at once to Jerusalem. There they found the Eleven and those with them, assembled together. (Luke 24:33)

This post-Easter assembly of men and women are described in the NRSV as 'the companions'. Companions are much more than colleagues or even friends. They are (literally) 'bread-sharers'. Following Jesus they had shared bread with him and with each other, at family meals, at the great crowd feasts of thousands, and (some of them, at least) at the 'Last Supper'.

So the Twelve were not the only disciples or followers of Jesus. To discover more, let us skip back to the Galilean crowds. Luke divided his crowds into two camps. In one camp there were those who came to get something from Jesus. Then there were those who went beyond this initial, consumerist stage and actually became learners. The parable of the sower, which comes towards the end of the Galilean period, explains it all. The story was told to the whole crowd, but only interpreted to the disciples. Here Jesus separated the 'utterly unmoved', the 'mildly interested' and the 'quick convert' from the 'long-haul follower' (Luke 8:4–15). This last grouping represented the ones who made up the second camp, who continued to follow him (Luke 14:25) and sang him into Jerusalem (Luke 19:37). It was from this crowd that Jesus sent out a second mission group, which this time numbered seventy-two (Luke 10:1). It was a crowd that included supportive women (Luke 8:1–3), who were last at the cross and first at the tomb (Luke 23:35; 24:9).

There were others too, odd individuals, in various stages of discipleship, scattered through the story. Barsabbas and Matthias, who had 'been with us the whole time the Lord Jesus went in and out among us' (Acts 1:21), Nicodemus, Joseph of Arimathea, Mary, Martha and Lazarus, blind Bartimaeus and Jesus' own mother, brothers and sisters were all part of this wider following crowd, this people movement that is impossible to define and pin down.

The story of Jesus and his disciples reaches its final chapter at the ascension. Matthew gives us a scene back in Galilee where it all began, while Luke takes us to Bethany and the actual departure of Jesus. In both we see Jesus handing on his mission to his closest followers. This handing over is powered by a big vision: Jesus wants these followers to go out more widely and in a bigger way than he ever went himself, to the 'ends of the earth' (Acts 1:8), or, as Matthew puts it to 'all nations' (28:19). In Acts the commission is to 'be my witnesses', a fairly conventional job spec for evangelists. In Matthew Jesus gives them a bigger and deeper task, to 'make disciples'.

Jesus the evangelist was not just a gatherer of converts, he was a maker of disciples. And he did not just make disciples, he made disciple-makers. His final piece of believing in and forming of his disciples was to send them out in his name, on his mission and copying his example.

The disciple in relationship

The relationships began when Jesus looked hard and deep into people's faces and asked them questions, offered invitations, or made a call on them to 'follow me'. Or sometimes it was the other way round, with a searching, lost soul full of hunger and need being drawn to his words, actions and living presence. It was a relationship between:

- Teacher and pupil
- Leader and follower
- Master and servant
- Parent and child
- Sender and sent

It was a relationship based on one giving and the other receiving, on authority and obedience, on one demonstrating and the other emulating.

It is hard for me, as a Manchester person, not to see a parallel at Manchester United, first between Matt Busby and George Best and then latterly between Alex Ferguson and Roy Keane. These were formational relationships, with one man being formed in the image of the other. In each case, the elder parental figure saw something special in the younger and then gave himself to developing that potential. In response, the younger learning man offered honour and obedience to his mentor. These were dynamic and massively fruitful relationships, though sadly both broke down too soon and fell short of what could have been achieved.

In our postmodern, commitment-avoiding world and church, we often prefer to talk about spirituality rather than discipleship. Interestingly, we usually use the prefix of 'my', because we like to think we are in control. It is a consumerist 'nip and tuck' relationship, where Jesus becomes a sort of 'religious service provider' rather than a teacher, leader and master. 'My spirituality' makes few demands on me, and hardly ever takes me out of my comfort zone, because it is under my authority and I am at the centre. Discipleship, however, is about Jesus being central as 'my Lord and my God', and about me obeying, learning from and following him.

It is an ongoing, long-term, monogamous relationship – not the monogamy that starts with fire and excitement and then gradually cools down into routine and formulaic piety, but the sort that begins with an initial sense of having found 'the one' and then deepens into devoted and passionate belonging. Why else would the disciples have gone out on frankly impossible-sounding missions (Luke 9–10)? Why else did Peter remain hanging around, even while he was denying Jesus, somehow still tied to the one he loved (Luke 22:54–62)? Why else did they all follow him, even when they were frightened?

> They were on their way up to Jerusalem, with Jesus leading the way, and the disciples were astonished, while those who followed were afraid. (Mark 10:32)

In the Gospel story, each person who began a discipleship relationship with Jesus also entered a whole series of relationships with other disciples. They became a brother or sister in a family. They went out on mission in small teams. They had to soften their self-importance with humility. They became 'companions', bread-sharers.

Today many of us in the 'church growth' world who are concerned to see forward movement and greater evangelistic effectiveness are talking about goals, resourcing, strategies and prioritisation, etc., and quite right too. All these issues, however, are secondary to the need to establish deep and loving discipleship relationships. As a missioner wandering from church to church, I learned a long time ago that the church with the active relationship is always way ahead of the one with the action plan.

Teaching the disciples

> He . . . sat down. His disciples came to him, and he began to teach them. (Matthew 5:2)

Disciples are learners. Having drawn the crowds, proclaimed the 'good news' and gathered in the various groupings of disciples, Jesus spent an increasing amount of time and energy teaching them. Matthew's Sermon on the Mount (chs. 5–8) and Luke's equivalent Sermon on the Plain (ch. 6) represent major collections of teachings which were probably gathered from various occasions in Jesus' ministry. Both are described as major events when Jesus shifted his focus away from the crowds and onto his committed disciples. Matthew's compilation is often portrayed as Jesus delivering a new Torah for a new people. In this portrayal, the Twelve are symbolic of the twelve tribes of Israel, and the new law is based not on a series of commandments, but on the central and all-enveloping imperative to love, love and love.

The 'growth parables', and especially that of the sower, seem to represent or capture best the transition in Jesus' word ministry. At one point we see him predominantly, though not exclusively, working the crowd in a recognisably evangelistic way, and then he moves on to conduct an intense and revealing seminar with his closest followers: 'The knowledge of the secrets of the kingdom of heaven has been given to you' (Matthew 13:11).

Luke is our main guide to this second phase of teaching both the Twelve and the (probably more liquid) wider group of disciples. Much of this in-depth, constantly shape-changing seminar takes place on the road to Jerusalem. Repeatedly we see Jesus working with these real followers as his key group and taking them into a whole range of issues, including:

- Obeying the Word of God (Luke 8:19)
- Real faith (Luke 8:25)
- Self-denial and taking up the cross (Luke 9:23)
- Child-like greatness (Luke 9:48)
- The cost of following (Lukc 9:57)
- The blessedness of being a disciple (Luke 10:23)
- How to pray (Luke 11:1)
- The need to beware of hypocrisy (Luke 12:1)
- Not worrying about life and body (Luke 12:22)
- Rejection of materialism (Luke 12:32; 14:25)
- Sin, repentance and forgiveness (Luke 17:1)
- Increasing faith (Luke 17:5)
- Servanthood (Luke 17:7; 22:27)
- Treasuring children (Luke 18:15)
- The rewards of following (Luke 18:28)
- Avoiding the self-importance of religious leaders (Luke 20:46)
- Generous giving (Luke 21:1)

- Coming hard times (Luke 21:12)
- Not using weapons (Luke 22:50)

The great danger in such a list is that it looks rather like a list of very heavy dos and don'ts. Indeed, this is often how it has been applied over the years, to create a sort of devout but very severe, not to say downright miserable, version of following Jesus. These teachings were not given as a new set of commandments, but as the outworkings of a new way of living – one that was clearly meant to be costly, but that was and is primarily about joy, forgiveness and new beginnings. Jesus' disciples were not burdened with lots of rules and fasting like the Pharisees; they had a new and lighter way of living.

Jesus' own discipleship had begun at his baptism with an experience of shared 'pleasedness' between Father and Son. When he recruited his own followers, it was more like inviting guests to a wedding, or partying at the return of a lost son. The first great sign that these newly enlisted followers witnessed was Jesus changing water into wine. When two of these depressed and disappointed disciples encountered Jesus without recognising him after the resurrection, their hearts burned within them. Later on that same day, and again after the ascension when Jesus had finally departed, the gathered companions were touched by great joy.

Holiness is not the same as heaviness; piety should lead to partying; liturgy should include laughter as our discipleship spills over into dancing.

Just as important as what Jesus taught is the way in which he taught it. Two areas of comment will suffice here, the first about his methodology, and the second about his prioritisation.

Jesus' methodology

In his teaching methods, Jesus seems to have combined the conventional mode of a rabbi with those of a master craftsman and a modern-day sports coach.

- As a rabbi, he had his assembled group of theological students gradually growing into spiritual and intellectual maturity. He taught, and they learned. The words of Luke 9:44 (in the NRSV translation) capture it nicely: 'Let these words sink into your ears.' It is like an earlier version of the much loved grammar school dictum, 'Read, mark, learn and inwardly digest.' (The grammar schools, of course, borrowed the phrase from the collect for the second Sunday of Advent.) The disciples engaged with his unique teaching, they asked him questions of explanation and he answered them back with questions of exploration: 'Who do you think I am?' 'Why do you call me good?' 'What do you think of this?'
- We can view Jesus rather like a great Florentine craftsman of the Renaissance, seeing the potential in young apprentices and drawing them into his workshop. As such, the disciples were sometimes taught theory, but more importantly they witnessed the master artist at work in his healings, driving out of demons and proclamation of the gospel. They observed him working in people's lives, like so many young Michelangelos watching their master Ghirlandaio work the paint. Sometimes it is the other way round: the craftsman watches the apprentices, sharing their frustrations when they make mistakes and their joy when they get it right (Matthew 17:20).
- As a coach, Jesus created a very dynamic group-learning environment. He prepared his students as a united team.

> He built up their confidence with affirmation, bonded them together, warned of dangers, analysed the opposition, taught strategies and inspired them with aspirational goals. Then he sent them out in pairs to play the game, while he watched nervously from the sidelines. At the end of the game he was there to share in their triumph before taking them off to rest and reflect (Mark 6:30–31).

Discipleship is a broad curriculum, not a narrow specialisation. It involves learning skills, acquiring theological understanding, developing spirituality, and building up lifestyle and relationships. More than anything else, however, it is about character formation. Ultimately it is about becoming the right sort of person. As with Jesus himself, the being comes before the doing.

The post-Enlightenment church has always placed great importance on the rabbinic teaching method. Theological college education and the criteria for promotion and preferment adopted by denominations and dioceses all rely heavily on the Western academic tradition. At the local church level, many continue to be tied to traditional patterns of Bible study and a lecturing style of teaching and preaching. There is nothing wrong with this rabbinic method – it is just that by itself it is all a bit narrow, rather like a piano on which you can only use the white keys. Jesus offered a wider and more holistic approach to disciple-making. He used not just book and brain, but also hand and eye, question and reflection, theory and practice.

I was recently asked to do a day's teaching on evangelism with a bunch of ordinands (trainee vicars) and would-be lay readers. Having such a day was itself a major step forward for the diocese in question, and one that should be commended to others. When I and the course tutor suggested at the day's end that everyone could now go home and organise their own 'Levi Feast', i.e. invite a few friends round to talk about Jesus, there was a mind-boggling range of responses. Clearly they were not used to 'on the job' learning.

My first attempt, as a young clergyman, to teach the basics of evangelism was done in a classroom. I planned the six-week course, advertised it and taught it. Everyone enjoyed it. Nothing happened. It was only some time later, when I worked with four of those who had been on the course, helping them to set up and run their own evangelistic home meeting, that learning began. You cannot learn to swim by reading a book: at some point you have to get into the water. Working with those 'willing four' was for me a bit like helping them to set up their own football team. I recruited the team, prepared them for the game, watched from the sidelines and then discussed it with them afterwards.

In recent years there has been a move towards apprenticeship or mentoring. It is important for all effective and ministering disciples, be they bishops, Sunday school teachers or church treasurers, to see the potential in others and then share their own experience and ability with them. For evangelists, who have often been 'lone operators' and have allowed others to admire rather than learn our tricks, this is a real imperative. We need to find and equip the next evangelists, we need to find female ones, and we need to find young ones.

Jesus' priorities

The second remarkable feature of Jesus the disciple-teacher is the way that he prioritised the task. He found large amounts of time which he gave to a relatively small group, by taking them away from the much larger, immediately needy and demanding Galilean crowd (Luke 6:20; 9:10). As in his individual searching out of and ministering to the searchers, so with his work of teaching, we see Jesus regularly turning from the 'big crowd, spread thin' scenario to a 'small learning group, lay it on thick' approach.

In the early days of my own evangelism, I tended to place almost all my attention on gaining converts. My pattern was to gather a few searchers, take them through the first steps of becoming a Christian and then parcel them off to a couple of mature church members to form an ongoing house group. Sometimes the group swam and sometimes it sank. This was sloppy delegation on my part. It left me free to go and find another bunch of searchers, but it left the initial job only half done.

After operating this fairly hit-and-miss system for some time, I came under the influence of Howard Astin. Howard was one of the first, and to my mind one of the very best, adopters of the cell church model in the UK. In his own church he developed the methodology of punctuating weekly house or cell church meetings with a monthly gathering for his group leaders. At these leaders' meetings they would practise VHS, or 'Vision, Huddle and Share'. Such gatherings were a vital part of the emergence of a whole new group of leaders. There he was able to disciple his disciples, sharing plans and pastoral concerns and offering support. In this way a much more effective long-term and in-depth work was equipped to bear fruit. In our own case, we never went the full distance and became a cell church, but we did pinch some of its brilliant insights into producing and equipping leaders.

Clergy, organisational heads and evangelists have just the same discipleship needs as those they seek to serve, but we often forget this or arrive at a place in life where we are just too busy to attend a course, read a book, or go on retreat. This 'too busy place' is a dead end. We can only give out what we have first taken in, and the more energy we burn, the more we need to feed. The best teachers are those who are still learning, the best leaders are the ones who are still humble enough to recognise that they themselves need to be led. Leaders, clergy, influencers and evangelists in particular who have a real tendency to be too independent all need what they recommend for others. We need lifelong mentoring, spiritual guidance and the close presence of those who are strong enough to correct our waywardness. Discipleship is not like going to college. There is no graduation ceremony; it is a lifelong business.

In his evangelism, Jesus took the long view. He was patient and thorough, treating men and women as individuals, not just as part of a crowd. His goal was not a lot of people with some God inside them, but some people with a lot of God inside them. His evangelism was not just initiation, but transformation.

Two of my all-time favourite movies are about discipleship. They both approach it from the angle of a young, free-minded teacher leading a group of pupils out of the conventional learning straitjacket into a new, more colourful and exciting place. In both cases the personality, feel and vision of the teacher is the vital element. In the first example, *The Prime of Miss Jean Brodie*, the work ultimately breaks down because the teacher is more egotistic (fuelled by her own values) than charismatic (fuelled by God's values) and wants to control her pupils for her own ends. This tendency to create disciples in our own image and for our own purposes, to reproduce our own attitudes, strengths and weaknesses, is a familiar scenario and temptation for many of us involved in discipling others. In *Dead Poets Society*, the teacher, played by Robin Williams, is an inspirational idealist who goes completely beyond the acceptable and numbingly dull limits of a very institutional school. The pupils learn new things in a thrillingly life-expanding sort of way. When tragedy strikes with the death of a student, the teacher is made the scapegoat. His pupils desert him to protect their own position, but finally return to him in a cathartic moment as they stand up on their desks before the school's head and declare the disgraced teacher to be the captain of their lives. I have no idea what was in the mind of the movie's makers, but it feels very much to me like a 'Jesus and his followers' story.

The discipleship journey

Disciples do not come like flat-pack furniture with mass-manufactured identical parts and a universal set of easy-to-follow instructions, all waiting to be put together in a single afternoon. They are individually craftsman- or craftswoman-produced. They are gradually formed, durable creations. Each one is unique in his or her raw materials, design and intended use. They are as much loved as built in their formation, beginning as servants and becoming friends (John 15:15).

Looking at the work of Jesus, the formation process or journey seems to have had three stages, which we can label as 'Come', 'Follow' and 'Go', or, for those who prefer, 'Birth', 'Nurture' and 'Adventure'. In the first stage the hungry or searching person is a needful seeker, in the second a disciple, and finally becomes an apostle.

> Come to me, all you who are weary and burdened. (Matthew 11:28)

This is surely one of the great Gospel texts, yet it is rarely used by preaching evangelists. Perhaps this is because it puts all the emphasis on men's and women's need, on Jesus' inclusive acceptance and grace. The only expectation placed on people is that they take the first step and come. The words gather up so much of what has been happening up to this point in Matthew. There has been lots of coming by the broken, the poor, the lonely and the outcasts. Each one who has come has found his or her needs met. Jesus' great evangelistic 'good news' was that 'God's kingdom has drawn close'. He has himself come as a friend of sinners, as a shepherd searching for his sheep. All that the lost have to do is to come and receive.

Evangelists have traditionally done two things with Jesus' 'come'. Firstly, we have added on to it a heavy word about repentance and have generally forced people into an inward-looking moral inventory of their lives, past and present. In other words, we have concentrated on people's sinfulness, while Jesus was more concerned with their needfulness. Secondly, we have often stopped after the 'come', thinking that our job was done, whereas we should have realised that it was just the end of phase one. This word 'come' is a great offering to everyone with need, and a wide, sweeping gathering in of all who are interested. But it is only the beginning.

'Come, follow me,' Jesus said. (Matthew 4:19)

At the time of writing, there is a whole string of television shows where people offer their best and are then ridiculed or seen to fall short. *X Factor*, *Britain's Got Talent* and *Strictly Come Dancing* are just about the most popular. The ultimate, however, is certainly *The Apprentice*, where every week the watching millions get themselves ready for the big moment when Sir Alan Sugar stares stonily into a nearly-good-enough's face and delivers the ultimate put-down, 'You're fired!' How different is Jesus' invitingly warm and constructive lift-up, 'You're hired!' His is an inclusive vision, seeing the potential in one-talent people as well as in those who can boast the full ten.

If 'come' is the first phase of the dance, then 'follow' is the middle section. The call is to stick close to Jesus, to make his direction their direction, his choices their choices, to keep up with his momentum, to be charged by his urgency. It is too easy to shrink this dynamic movement word about following into a much-reduced call to inner moral repentance. The turning around and starting afresh is not just a cleaning up, or a private psychological purification, but a much more exciting stepping out to follow Jesus. Of course, as he made clear in his teaching of his disciples, this following will include making moral choices, but they should be seen as footsteps within the bigger picture of journeying with the leader.

Such following is costly. It leads into conflict, it tears disciples away from the securities of their old lives, families and friendships, and it means taking up the cross (Matthew 10:34–39). Following Jesus on his journey literally involved crossing frontiers of fear as the disciples went with him from the comfort zone of Galilee to the threatening unknown of Jerusalem (Mark 10:32).

These twelve Jesus sent out. (Matthew 10:5)

Becoming a faithful, Bible-reading, prayer-meeting-attending, money-giving, committed church member is not the goal of discipleship. Neither is developing a healthy spirituality or regular liturgical involvement. These are all steps along the way, milestones on the journey from spiritual birth through adolescence to maturity. Adulthood is about apostleship: we can only say that we have grown up when we have gone out. Apostles are 'postal people'. They are sent out into the community by the word 'go'. Their task is not to invent or write their own letters, but to deliver the communications, messages and invitations of the sender.

All the time that the disciples were with Jesus, they were taking part, as in an apprenticeship, in his own great going out from heaven to earth. As part of this, they had their own two great going out experiences. The first came at an intermediary stage in their following, when Jesus sent out first the Twelve and then the Seventy-two (Luke 9:1; 10:1). They went out:

- In small teams
- With few possessions
- Armed with his authority
- To proclaim, heal and drive out demons
- Staying in people's homes
- In every town and village
- To focus on those who responded positively
- To walk away from the negatives.

In his own going out on mission, Jesus operated in three types of venue. His initial location was often the synagogue, and from there he would regularly move out of doors to a larger space such as a hill-side or the lake shore. In and around these public spaces, however, it looks as if he often did his best work in private homes. It is here, on their own territory, that people are often at their most confident and relaxed, but we the evangelists are at our most uncertain and vulnerable. How interesting, then, that in sending out his disciples Jesus does not talk about hiring the village hall for big meetings, or even about holding an outdoor barbecue, but places all his emphasis on going into people's homes (Luke 9:4; 10:5; Matthew 10:12). Now I have not done any research on this one, but I have a pretty strong feeling that in the past, clergy, pastoral workers and even Sunday school teachers did a lot more home visiting than we do today. I have an equally strong feeling that, although much of this home visiting was greatly welcomed and well received, it was not very evangelistically focused. Today we are desperate for people to attend our gatherings and services. Before we try to get them to cross our threshold, maybe we should first cross theirs.

The mission which began in Simon's house (Mark 1:29), the evangelistic gathering at Levi's (Luke 5:29) and the healing visitation to the home of Jairus (Luke 8:51) all show Jesus himself operating in this important and most intimate of venues. We have already seen the importance of shared meals in his ministry; put the two together – home and table – and we find shared humanity and personal relationships can also be the theatre of mission.

Today we have the big gathering, we talk of transforming cities (although to Jesus they were places of rejection), we use a whole range of communication gadgetry, we embrace the media and publicity campaigns, yet we so often miss the heartbeat of the small, local and personal.

Looking with a fresh eye at Jesus' sending out of his followers, John Dominic Crossan argues that it is a huge misunderstanding to limit this apostolic mission to the Twelve alone and to one particular moment in time. He proposes something much broader and continuous, a network of 'healed healers' regularly coming and going, involving men and women and with Jesus always at the centre (*Jesus: A Revolutionary Biography*, p. 109). I find this a compelling and exciting picture which seems to find echoes in the stories of Legion and the woman at the well

(Mark 5:19; John 4:39). It is a picture of a movement that is not evangelist-dependent but evangelist-assisted.

The second great sending and going out came, as we have already seen, at the end of the Jesus on earth story. For him Jerusalem had been the climax of the journey, but for them it would be just the beginning. What had been Jesus' mission from the Father became theirs, and remains so to this day. To get the full impact of this great sending out, you have to read the relevant pieces from all four Gospels (Matthew 28:19–20; Mark 16:8, 15; Luke 24:47–48; John 20:21). This time Jesus sent them out to:

- Go to all the world
- Proclaim repentance and forgiveness
- Make disciples
- Baptise and teach
- Remember he is with them
- Wait, to be first clothed with power from on high.

He sends them out to do it his way in their world.

Learning about going is much more than just a theoretical exercise. There is a place for inspiring sermons and motivational Bible studies, but no one ever learned to ride a bike by reading a book or watching a PowerPoint presentation. Eventually we all have to get a bit saddle sore. At some stage we have to open up our church mission field map, say our prayers and then actually go out. As we have seen, we can start by first going to the various groups on the map, to the fringe, the local community and all those with whom some sort of friendship has been established. This sort of going, armed with a simple invitation, a simple question, an offer of caring help and a promise to remember and pray, is an initiative of grace. As well as the local church mission map, we can each draw up our own personal one. Here we simply plot our various relationships and 'go out' searching for the searchers and inviting people in.

'So how do I get my people interested in evangelism?' Without a doubt, this is the heavyweight champion of all the questions that church leaders ask missioners. And the answer is, 'You get people into it by doing it.' Now let us be honest, most churches never have a mission week or weekend, it is only the minority who will set up an evangelistically minded 'Songs of Praise' or pub night, and it is even fewer who will get round to organising an enquirers' course. But it is only by doing it that we learn to do it. It isn't enough to buy boots and a map: we become good at going by going out, and going out regularly. Most churches need to have a mission or run a group for searchers, just to learn how to do it. Such events should be part of the annual cycle of normal life, not just occasional forays.

I recently encountered an ordinand in training to be a vicar, who had been sent out by his theological college to help with a community project. Sadly, there was no suggestion in the student's brief that articulating the 'good news', offering healing or driving out demons might be part of that going out into the community. It was pretty clear that this rather shy Anglican found sharing the works of Jesus easier than sharing the words. The future shape of someone's ministry was forming, and he looked a bit like a trainee drummer who only had one drumstick. Despite what everyone seems to think, evangelists are not the ones who find it easy, they do not have an endless supply of inner boldness; they are simply the ones who do it, and the more they do it, the better at it they become.

The discipleship journey is a bit like the one that the salmon follow to their breeding grounds. It is long and demanding and many drop out along the way. John gives us a poignant but very human insight into one such incident: 'From this time many of his disciples turned back and no longer followed him' (John 6:66). The main 'turning back' points are the transition phases, from coming as a needful seeker, to following as a disciple, to going out as an apostle. The challenging questions then for us are, 'Can we help an interested searcher into genuine conversion?' 'How do we gently yet firmly help a new convert into deep learning?' 'Will we have the patient persistence to lead a follower out of their comfort zone and into the world?'

William Booth, the great nineteenth-century revivalist and founder of the Salvation Army, actually began his ministry of evangelism as a Methodist. He looked back to the pioneering work of John Wesley and realised that the essence of his effectiveness was not so much in his altar calls as in his discipleship class meetings: 'Under God, Wesley made Methodism not by converting sinners but by making well instructed saints.'[3]

Too often the evangelism trade has devoted most of its time and energy to the 'coming', a modest amount to the 'following', and just a few leftover scraps for the 'going'.

Cost, vulnerability and calling

In talking about 'come', 'follow', 'go', we have at some point to consider cost and vulnerability. Jesus himself told the large crowd who were following him to stop and, like a man preparing to build a tower, or a king going out to war, to 'count the cost'

[3] Roy Hattersley, *Blood and Fire*, page 217.

(Luke 14:28). Perhaps the largeness of the crowd is the clue to the fact that they were not taking into account what being a follower really involves.

The cost is everything, but before we get too severe and miserable about this, we also have to remember what Jesus said about the rewards of following him, the blessedness that he bestows and how his yoke is easy and his burden light (Matthew 11:29). Speaking for myself, as a would-be disciple who has given much up but still has plenty of giving up yet to do, it feels as if I have put down emptiness so that I can pick up fullness. I have left behind routine, so that I can follow purpose. I have rejected greyness, so that I can live in the rainbow. I have emptied my pockets of pennies, so that I can fill them with pound pieces.

It is when we go out to the world that we are at our most exposed, our most easily hurt or embarrassed. It is then that we are vulnerable. That is why so few do it – it is the significant minority of disciples who go out to minister peace and justice in the local community, bring healing to the neighbourhood and proclaim the good news to the poor. Many of those who do this find that in their most exposed situations tragedy is visited upon them.

I have often heard my old friend John Holmes speak of his own vulnerability and occasional sadness. Each time I have been deeply moved. He spent years working and giving his all to God in a demanding but growing inner-city Leeds church, where the progress was often 'two steps forward and one step back'. It was there that he lost a baby son. John and his wife Rosemary had been united in costly discipleship and were suddenly united in an even deeper vulnerability.

John is simply the finest parish priest/clergyperson/pastor (the label is irrelevant in this context) I have ever known. He pioneered the now trendy idea of the 'evangelical/charismatic/Catholic vicar-cum-evangelist'. Basically, more than anyone else I know, he has been there, done that and worn out the T-shirt. Despite all his years of experience, he still retains a naïve, enthusiastic and almost boyish vulnerability for the things of Jesus. He has never learned to grow a thick and protective skin. He is still going out in mission to the world, still sometimes being disappointed, hurt and rejected, and still being wonderfully fruitful.

There is no vulnerability bypass for those who go out.

> My Father, if it is possible, may this cup be taken from me. Yet not as I will, but as you will. (Matthew 26:39)

It was frightening for Jesus, fear-filled for his followers, and is still intimidating for us today. That is how it is.

Today's talk of mission and evangelism is continually peppered with the words and concepts of 'gift' and 'gifting'. No matter how much we spiritualise it, this sort of language will inevitably lead to such questions as, 'Am I gifted at evangelism or healing?' and, 'Am I good at it?' In other words, too much use of the gift idea puts all the emphasis on individual evangelists and their effectiveness, or lack of it, and is in danger of building them up as religious celebrities. As we have already seen, the concepts of 'evangelist' and 'evangelistic gifts' arose late in the New Testament period. In the Gospels, the mission is shared to a greater or lesser extent by all the followers of Jesus, and effectiveness is gradually learned, developed and brought to fullness by learning and doing together. It is something in which all of us can and should be involved at some level. In all his discipling, Jesus never enters 'Gift World'. Instead, he sees the need, shares the burden, sends his people out and expects them to obey. His is the world of compassion and vocation: 'The harvest is plentiful but the workers are few' (Matthew 9:37). This does not make the early church's model of gift and ministry redundant, we do not have to choose between the two, but it does give it a balancing emphasis.

For all of us involved in the great evangelistic adventure, and in doing it his way in our world, discipleship is a double-sided coin. On one side, we are ourselves called to be child-like disciples. On the flip side, he wants us to work with him to make disciples, gathering the crowd, spotting the searchers, helping them to become followers and then springboarding them out as apostles. It is all a bit like the childhood game of 'Follow My Leader'. Do as I do, walk where I walk and take over when I drop out.

> And surely I am with you always, to the very end of the age. (Matthew 28:20)

Please do remember
The words of your sender,
Please do remember
And always be a listener.
Please do remember
The ways of your leader,
Please do remember
And always be a follower.
Please do remember
The hopes of your teacher,
Please do remember
And always be a learner.

Please do recall the sense of your call.
Please don't ever forget, or it will all end in regret.

CHAPTER SEVEN

Jesus Grew a Church

> Did Jesus intend to found a 'church'? The question is hopeless. Of course he didn't; of course he did.[1]

Of all the bits and pieces involved in the great sprawling reality that is the Christian world, it is the 'church' that has the worst image. No matter how hard it tries, it never quite gets it right. Whatever it says, whoever it befriends and wherever it goes, someone somewhere will be very unhappy and they will make their unhappiness vocal and possibly quite vindictive.

In recent years the attack has come from the likes of Richard Dawkins, Christopher Hitchens and Philip Pullman. Together they form a sort of media-savvy 'Grumpy Old Atheists' movement with their own 'Dark Materials' style of dogma.

As for my own tribe, the poor old Church of England, it just feels as if the media have always got it in for us. They basically have three big stories. Story 1 is that we are declining almost to the

---

[1] N.T. Wright, *Jesus and the Victory of God*, page 275.

point of disappearing. Story 2 is that we are having another major row and are on the threshold of schism. Finally, they have Story 3, which is about naughty vicars putting their hands in the till or on someone else's wife. Of course there is some accuracy in all these storylines, but none of them tells the truth of how large, united and faithful we really are.

Much more damaging, however, is the widespread and never-ending criticism that comes from within. We have the liberals, constantly wanting to drive a wedge between 'kingdom', which is good, and 'church', which is usually seen as bad. We have the evangelicals, endlessly going on about decline, in order to prepare the way for their latest messianic rescue plan. The Catholics are forever bemoaning our loss of holiness, while the charismatics are continually reminding the rest of us about our need for renewal. The negativity, disillusionment and cynicism of the insiders are far more corrosive than the sticks and stones of the 'professional unbelievers'. Such attitudes feed our insecurities, while undermining our self-esteem and hopes for the future.

In all of this the church is a bit like the England football team. The criticising has become part of our psyche. The individual criticisms are usually valid and based in reality, but the more we highlight the church's sins, the more we lowlight its strengths. The more we talk it down, the deeper it sinks.

Of course the church is a failure. The idea of a bunch of ordinary people setting out to emulate the warmth, love, compassion and life-transforming impact of Jesus was always doomed from the start. Of course the church is disunited, torn by political intrigue and personal ego, hypocritical and impure. Given that it is made up of ordinary, half-seeing and self-centred human beings, how could it ever be anything else? So yes, the church is a failure. But what a beautiful and heroic failure we are!

It is far too easy to magnify the negative and to belittle the other and positive side of the coin. The sacrificial living, financial generosity, joyful welcoming, faithful prayer and worship, waves of forgiveness and utterly courageous mission that are all lived out by so much of the church are too easily lost from sight. In fact, it is not as clear-cut as 'two sides of a coin'. The reality is much messier, as a Jesus-like persona continually struggles to emerge out of a darker human swampland.

The important question then becomes, 'Is the "Beauty and the Beast" that is the church the creation of institutionalising, power-hungry men (and in the main they have been men), or is it the child of Jesus the evangelist?'

Jesus and the church

The first thing to note about Jesus' teaching is that the word 'church' only appears on his lips on two occasions. Both appear in Matthew's Gospel, and there is much dispute over whether he actually used the word himself, or whether it was ascribed to him by a later story-teller or editor.

The first instance is that of the conversation at Caesarea Philippi (Matthew 16:18). Here Jesus commits himself to a joint church-building project with the disciples. Connecting with Matthew 7:24 and 26:61, we see that the role of the disciples is that of foundation-forming obedience, while the role of Jesus is that of the initiative-taking architect and leader.

The second instance comes in a teaching seminar story (Matthew 18:15–17). Here Jesus is wanting to safeguard the unity of the church and introduce a sort of forgiving, self-healing process into its life. In both cases the Greek word *ecclesia* that we translate into 'church' points not towards a building or formal organisation, but towards a 'gathering' or 'congregation', a voluntary coming together of free people. It is a political term originating in the ancient Greek democratic city gatherings. There all free adult males were seen as being equal and were expected to take seriously both the privilege and the responsibility of joint decision-making.

When it came to putting his church-building intentions into practice, it looks as if Jesus' first plan was one of renewal of the Jerusalem-centred Judaism of his day.

- The setting up of the twelve disciples, symbolising the twelve tribes.
- The redrafting of the Mosaic law in the Sermon on the Mount.
- His practice of regularly preaching in synagogues.
- His conflict with the scribes and Pharisees.
- The final challenging pilgrimage to Jerusalem and the temple.

These all seem to be part of a conscious attempt to fulfil the prophetic vision of restoring the heart of Israel.

The religio-political structures and leaders rejected his mission, but a significant minority of the lowly 'pew-fillers' responded. A new people movement emerged, like a pearl out of the shell. This was probably as much a spontaneous response to Jesus' preaching and healing as a planned organisational construction.

> The gospels do not report any public announcement by Jesus of his intention to found a church . . . or any programmatic call to join a new community.[2]

---

[2] Hans Küng, *The Church,* Continuum new ed. 2001, page 73.

Tom Wright, however, imagines a bit more creativity on Jesus' part:

> The evidence points, I suggest, towards Jesus intending to establish, and indeed succeeding in establishing, what we might call cells of followers, mostly continuing to live in their towns and villages.[3]

It is this spontaneously emerging new style of Israel that Lloyd Douglas recreates in his novel *The Robe.* Here the Roman centurion present at the crucifixion travels throughout the Galilee in the guise of a textile merchant. On his journey he meets with a whole range of Jesus' followers. Some were healed by his hand; others were captured by his words. They continue to meet secretly for fellowship and prayer, and to live out the mission and lifestyle that he inspired in them. They are the first generation of the church.

Here, then, are a few of the highlights from the teaching and example of Jesus the evangelist concerning what it means to be a gathered and spiritual community, i.e. a church.

- Mark 1:29–31. Jesus heals Simon Peter's mother-in-law, affirming the importance of family relationships.
- Mark 3:35. He defines the ultimate type of family relationship in terms of people's obedience to God.
- Matthew 13:32. The kingdom is like a mustard seed that grows into a tree, which offers welcome and hospitality to the 'birds of the air' (Gentiles and outsiders).
- Matthew 19:14. Jesus emphasises the priority place of children, or at least childlikeness.

---

[3] N.T. Wright, *Jesus and the Victory of God*, page 276.

- Luke 12:49–53. Being baptised by and following Jesus will bring discord to some families.
- Luke 14:26. Following Jesus comes before love of family.
- Luke 15:1–32. The getting lost and found again of the single sheep, coin and son are not just private, individual experiences. They are also about being part of the wider group.
- Matthew 20:28. Being part of his community is about serving, not being served.
- Matthew 20:29–34. Two blind men are healed and then become part of the 'following community'.
- John 13:3. Jesus washes his disciples' feet.
- John 13:34. A new commandment for the disciples is that they should love each other.
- Luke 22:17. He shares his body and blood in the form of bread and wine at the Last Supper.
- John 19:25–27. On the cross Jesus builds a new, deep relationship between his mother and the 'disciple whom he loved'.

It is clear in all of this that Jesus was not some sort of personal guru offering individualised salvation and spirituality (a trap into which our Westernised evangelism often falls). His words and works were about creating communities, changing communities, and opening doors for the 'lost' into welcoming communities. These were real, breathing, organically together communities, not loosely tied clubs or networks. The vital building bricks are relationships. Such relationships begin in our communion with God and spill over into our congregating and communing with each other. This is why the opening of the Eucharist is so vital. Sadly, it is often seen as just the beginning of the service and is quickly passed over without much notice. In fact, it is much weightier than that, for it is 'The Gathering'.

How ironic that The Beatles, who, more than any other pop group or rock band, recognised the importance of all-inclusive love and warmth, also produced the ultimate pop music picture of loneliness and lostness with their *Sergeant Pepper* album. It is a collection of songs which, taken together, offer a bleak and yet truthful version of what we might call 'ordinary life'.

In recent years, television audiences in America and the UK have been watching *Lost*, a story of ordinary, everyday people lost on a tropical island. They do not know where they are, why they are there or where they are going. In some respects it is a bit of an update on William Golding's *Lord of the Flies*. In both cases the island strikes me as a metaphor for the whole planet, and it is not just a handful but an entire population who are lost.

Sergeant Pepper, *Eleanor Rigby*, *Lost*, *Lord of the Flies* and a thousand other songs, serials and books all point to the need for a new formation of people living together in harmony. The *ecclesia* of Jesus, the 'gathering' that he created, is the answer to that need.

Growing the church in our world

It is like a vine, a field of wheat, a flock of sheep, a growing seed. . . All these images are organic; all have growth in their DNA. They are images of life and, as we all learned from our earliest science lessons, all living things grow. Growth and health go together, and healthy growth is about quality and quantity. Healthy living things get better and bigger. These are all images used by Jesus to talk about his work, his kingdom, his followers and his mission.

Ultimately they are images of the – or perhaps we ought to say *his* – church.

When the church is living out and copying the root values of Jesus, it should have both a theology and a reality of growth. It should be growing more like Jesus and should be growing the number of people who want to grow more like him. Today we may have a theology of growth, but for the church in the West we have a history of decline. It should be that our theology holds and creates our future history. Sadly, at the moment it looks as if our past history is gripping our theology by the throat and choking us to a slow death.

Or is it? When it comes to assessing trends of growth or decline for the contemporary church, we have to bear in mind that throughout the world as a whole the church is growing at a breathtaking speed. It is only in the West that it is shrinking. And even here there are two schools of thought.

Firstly, there is the traditional version of constant numerical decline. Peter Brierley's report *The Tide is Running Out* appeared in the year 2000. In it he offered a statistical analysis of British church attendance trends, which he summed up with the overwhelmingly depressing phrase, 'We are bleeding to death.' Most see this downward slope beginning after World War I and continuing on inexorably. Callum Brown's *The Death of Christian Britain* challenges this dating and sets the big pendulum-swinging moment in the mid-1960s with a drift away from the churches of middle-aged and younger women. On the other hand, the novelist Ian McEwan, a prescient observer of time and cultural mood, describes the early 1960s as 'a time when religion had generally faded into insignificance'.[4]

---

[4] Ian McEwan, *On Chesil Beach*, Vintage 2008, page 45.

Writing in *Redefining Christian Britain*, Jane Garnett describes a sort of mutual alliance around the 'church decline model' between secularist sociologists and evangelistically minded evangelicals.[5] For the secularists it fits into their atheistic version of history, while to the evangelicals it offers support in their drive to return to what they would see as a purer, more biblical, evangelising church.

The Fresh Expression movement is a clear example of how church decline can be over-stressed in order to gain support for a new initiative. The stated aim is that we are developing a mixed economy with new and traditional forms of church side by side. There is, however, a tendency for Fresh Expressions people to sometimes write off the contemporary value and prospects of 'traditional expressions'. Thus encouragement is shouldered out of the way by discouragement and co-operation gives way to competition. What we actually need is a mutually respectful and supportive relationship between 'fresh' and 'refreshed' expressions of church.

Nevertheless, we have to accept the figures of ongoing decline. In one respect they are unchallengeable, but in another they are only part of the reality from which we start to build or renew.

There is also a second school of thought which needs to be listened to if we are to get a balanced view. Here the names of Robin Gill, Edward Bailey and Grace Davie are all significant. Robin Gill has argued that in the 'golden age' of full churches, from whence we began our downhill slalom of decline, those churches were never quite as full as we imagine. Certainly churchgoing in the nineteenth and early twentieth centuries was stronger than today, but not as strong as we have often thought. Perhaps we are beating ourselves too harshly. Meanwhile, Edward Bailey,

[5] Jane Garnett, *Redefining Christian Britain*, SCM Press 2007.

sociologist and clergyman, has written persuasively about the long-term persistence of what he calls 'implicit religion'. Perhaps things are not quite so clear-cut after all.

Most interesting to my mind is Grace Davie. She presents two hypotheses. In the first one she talks about 'believing without belonging'. After examining the 'European Values Studies' (EVS) of 1981, 1990 and 1999, she concludes:

> I am hesitant about the unqualified use of the term secularisation even in the European context, a marked falling-off in religious attendance has not resulted, yet, in a parallel abdication of religious belief.[6]

Her second hypothesis or concept she calls 'vicarious religion'. By this she means that many people in the local community, who have ceased to be regular attenders, still highly value their local church, their local minister, church school, occasional offices and major festival times, etc. Far from being indifferent to its future, they actually want to see it continue and will, from time to time, make use of it, and some might even return to it.

In other words, the church is not the disappearing city under siege that we have often thought ourselves into being. Lynda Barley's *Churchgoing Today*, in which she analyses recent Anglican attendance figures, reminds us that the 2001 government census revealed that 72 per cent of the population in England and Wales still consider themselves Christian (p.10). She also points out that there are considerable numbers of midweek regulars who never show up on the 'Sunday count', a growing number of people in Fresh Expressions, and a swelling body of monthly attenders, the

---

[6] Grace Davie, *Europe: the Exceptional Case*, page 5.

scale of which is not reflected in our traditional counting system. Her conclusion is that, 'Churchgoing is not in terminal decline. It has an important place in Britain's communities and not just for special occasions.'

Far out on the opposite wing to the pessimists there are some groups of super-optimists. They are the revivalists. As someone who was brought up spiritually in the heady days of the 1970s charismatic movement, I was taught to expect, pray for and work towards revival. I am still waiting. Today the stories originate from North America rather than Wales and the Hebrides, but the prayers and the hoping are just the same. Now, it may well be that past revivals were as great as the stories tell us, and it may well be God's will to visit us with one again in the near future. But I cannot see anything like revival in the ministry of Jesus and, as the whole point of this project is to emulate him, I'll just keep getting on with it.

We could simply leave pessimists to embrace one school of thought and optimists the other – and revivalists to pray for yet another. True understanding, however, usually comes from a synthesis of two or more apparently conflicting positions. Putting these together, then, we can hazard the following statements:

- The church has been on a long-term journey of numerical decline.
- We are probably still on this road, but the slope may well be flattening out and is actually beginning to go back uphill in some places.
- Churches generally are far too pessimistic about their future.
- There is still a widespread, deep and warm receptiveness to our presence and mission throughout society.

- We have to grow the church, and we have to do it now.
- When we move into evangelism mode, say our prayers and trust in God, things seem to happen.

As someone who has spent the last thirty-six years struggling for growth and effective evangelism in the church, I am convinced that, taken together, these statements represent a pretty good situation in which to be planting the growing seed.

Growing the church the Jesus way

According to Rick Warren and *The Purpose-Driven Church*, there are five dimensions to a growing church. A church grows:

> Warmer through fellowship.
> Deeper through discipleship,
> Stronger through worship,
> Broader through ministry,
> Larger through evangelism.

We might argue about the order here, but I suspect most of us would agree that he has captured the Jesus version of growing the church. My intention here is not to offer a fully developed strategy or outline plan for achieving such growth. (Those seeking this sort of vital help might like to look up the work of Leading your Church into Growth. This is a nationally based organisation which offers courses and resources to church leaders.) What I do want to do, however, is to suggest four characteristics or values that derive from Jesus and that are all lived out by growing churches today.

A united church

> In my business, togetherness is not just a nice concept that you can take or leave according to taste. If you don't have it, you are nothing.[7]

Ask any political leader, football manager or parent and they will tell you, 'Disunity leads to disaster.' A united team is better than one with bags of talent. A together family is happier than a rich one. A church which has oneness will be more Christ-like and more Christ-effective than one which has lots of gifts and resources but little grace and relationship.

Our problems are not new or unique. Disunity, ego and petty rivalry are never far away from the stories of Jesus and his disciples. Difficulties with a supposedly rival exorcist (Luke 9:49), the Mary and Martha squabble (Luke 10:40), the request of James and John (Mark 10:35), the long-term unease with Judas (John 6:70) and the emergence of the 'disciple whom Jesus loved' as a possible leadership rival to Peter (John 13:23) are all revealing incidents. How disturbing and yet comforting to realise that they were just like us. No wonder Jesus made such a big play for unity.

> A new command I give you: Love one another. As I have loved you, so you must love one another. (John 13:34)

He gave them not only a new commandment, but also a new 'coming together meal', the ultimate uniting act:

> Take this and divide it among you. (Luke 22:17)

---

[7] Sir Alex Ferguson, Manager of Manchester United Football Club.

His ideal for his disciples was that they should all live as students with the Father alone as the one teacher (Matthew 23:8).

Disunity can be about theology, as different factions argue for what they think is right. Jesus, however, establishes unity itself as a theological issue, as the right way for people to live. More often, though, division is actually about personalities, competition, hurting long memories and manipulative relationships.

If a church is truly an organic life form, then disunity is a break in a branch, a wound to a limb, an uprooting of some of the wheat. It causes pain, creates weakness, leaves the whole open to infection and allows precious blood or sap, our 'water of life', to slip away.

Of all the sad scenes in *The Lord of the Rings*, for my money the saddest one concerns the break-up of the 'Fellowship of the Ring'. A small missional community of just nine characters is brought together and charged with the task of getting rid of the ring. Theirs is an uncomfortable unity, not surprising when it had to hold together men, hobbits, a dwarf, an elf and a wizard. Despite all the strains, the fellowship holds until Boromir, a proud and strong prince warrior, introduces his own agenda. He wants to keep the ring to strengthen the men of Gondor. The fallout is all about distrust, failure to share the big truth and the loss of the strength which is created by unity and common purpose. If Tolkien had wanted to write a completely happy fairy story, he would have omitted this part of the tale, but he was far more interested in how people really are.

In contrast, *Band of Brothers* is a story of enduring unity under great pressure. It is the true account of Easy Company, part of the American 101st Airborne Division in World War II. The story begins with their gruelling training, which starts to weld them together. From there we follow them through their participation in the D-Day invasion of Europe and on through a series of battles to the end of the war. With strong and loving leadership, a great sense of what they are about and a gritty determination, they stick together, share each other's pains, joys and failures and discover strength in their brotherhood. It is a compelling picture of what life, togetherness, mission and shared struggles must have been like for Jesus and his band of sisters and brothers.

David Watson inspired and led the great work of evangelism and church growth that happened first at St Cuthbert's and then moved on to St Michael-le-Belfrey in York. When he came to write up the story, he was brave enough to describe some of the great and painful fallouts that they had. Looking back on these incidents, he wrote:

> It never helps to apportion blame. The whole sad saga was a vivid and painful reminder that, however 'renewed' individuals or churches may feel themselves to be, we are still sinners, in constant need of the Lord's forgiveness, patience and love. We still hurt one another, sometimes unbelievably so, and still have to go on forgiving one another, as much as seventy times seven.[8]

A healthy church is a growing church, and a united church has a very good chance of being both.

When the Eucharist, Holy Communion or Lord's Supper is strongly at the heart of the church as the family meal, when it is extended beyond the formal worship to include many other shared meals and get-togethers, then there is a place for unity to

---

[8] David Watson, *You Are My God*, Hodder & Stoughton 1983, page 148.

happen. When difficulties are used to bring people together rather than to drive them apart, then unity breeds. Add to this the word of unity in preaching and discussion in an open and loving way, and people can be inspired by the big vision. Finally, when the church leaders are keen to model the path of wholesome relationships rather than petty rivalry, then unity has a chance.

A missionary church

> The Son of Man came to seek and to save. . . (Luke 19:10)

> He sent them out to preach. . . (Luke 9:2)

> Therefore go and make disciples of all nations. (Matthew 28:19)

Jesus was a missionary. He gave birth to a missionary community and sent them out on a mission to the world.

No one surveying the overall state of our church today could really describe it as 'missionary'. We are stuck somewhere in the middle ground between maintenance and mission. Most of us are nearer to one than the other.

I regularly do an exercise with church leaders in which I ask them to quantify all the discussion times from their council and committee meetings. The results are always the same. In every case, and I do mean every case, they report that they spend more time talking about money than any other subject. Buildings and equipment, getting through the 'annual round' and 'who does what' are the next big subjects. Mission and evangelism are on the edge of the agenda. The same applies to denominations and dioceses, where the big discussions are usually dominated by the 'three Bs' – buildings, budgets and bureaucracy.

So how hard would it be, not so much to put evangelism on the agenda occasionally, but to make it a central and staple item? I recently found myself leading a workshop for about twenty vicars. They were drawn from all traditions with one common denominator: they all wanted to see real growth in their churches. When I asked them to work in pairs to identify the biggest single blockage to this growth, they all came back with the same answer – that the members of their church did not have the stomach for missionary evangelism. Some of them were honest enough to note the same deficiency in their own make-up. They also felt that the same lack of hunger and vision was missing in their superiors. The organic 'needing to be healthy to be growing church' is lacking in two vital elements: vitamin E (evangelism) and vitamin G (growth) are both missing, or are there in only very small amounts.

The situation is not terminal, however. Jesus talked about growth beginning from the smallest of starts, a single mustard seed (Matthew 13:31). Even those churches which seem to be most lacking in evangelistic zeal invariably have at least two or three people who still have the passion. This tiny number begins as something small, then becomes a modest presence, and eventually something significant. The gospel has an inbuilt capacity for growth. It can overcome barriers, outgrow weeds and thrive in most environments. All it needs is a bit of space and feeding, some light and water and a generous helping of quality time from the gardener.

In 2004 the Church of England produced the *Mission-Shaped Church* report, one of the most prophetically disturbing and exciting moments of our last few years. It is having a huge impact within both Anglican and Methodist churches, giving birth, amongst other things, to the 'Fresh Expressions' movement. More than this, however, it gives a purposeful shove to our entire missionary endeavour:

> It is therefore of the essence (the DNA) of the church to be a missionary community. 'There is church because there is mission, not vice versa.'[9]

In Manchester Diocese, wanting to avoid unnecessary divisions, we are trying to locate 'Fresh Expressions' shoulder to shoulder with 'Re-Freshed Expressions' of church. The clear distinction is not between new or traditional ways of being church, but between missionary or non-missionary. At the moment I am involved with a project called Seven, working with about forty or so young adults drawn from across Manchester. We are a 'Fresh Expression', but not an expression of church because we are not yet missionary. We are a largely spirituality, teaching and friendship expression at the moment. A few have come to faith, but we have not yet got the big 'E' into our bloodstream. In contrast, we have a whole clutch of small, traditional parish churches in Manchester that are experiencing fresh life and growth under the leadership of a new generation of evangelising priests. These 'Re-Freshed Expressions' cover the whole range of churchmanship and can often be found in some of the most difficult parts of the city.

The key area of classification, as I said above, is between missionary and non-missionary modes of church. I have been to a café church which was in fact all café and no church, and a parish

---

[9] *Mission-Shaped Church*, page 85.

church which was all church and no parish. Mission church lives out the real, authentic, joy-loaded, transforming life of Jesus. But it does it in the community, not the cloister.

Now is it me, or is there a genuine missionary ending to Alan Bennett's play *The History Boys*? It has been a smash hit on both sides of the Atlantic and in 2007 it was released as a film. The actual boys featured are a bunch of bright sixth-formers studying together to gain entrance to Oxford University. The real teaching is offered by their beloved tutor, Hector. Hector has a deep love of literature and the beauty of words, and it is this more than anything else that he wants to share with the boys. The final scene in the play provides a typically 'Bennettesque' biblical allusion. The boys have all gained their Oxford places, but Hector has tragically died in a road accident. Then, at their last gathering, he appears again to them and charges them to go out into the world and pass on the love of language that he has passed on to them. It would be great fun to watch the play with a bunch of Christian sixth-formers or students, or perhaps with a church council or group of elders. The viewing could be followed with a few teasing-out questions and the suggestion that maybe they are not so much the 'History Boys' as the 'His Story Boys'.

Jesus was an evangelist who knew exactly what he was about. In understanding himself, he understood his mission and no one was going to pull him away from it:

> I must preach the good news of the kingdom of God to the other towns also, because that is why I was sent. (Luke 4:43)

This is not the job spec of a religious leader who does a bit of evangelism from time to time. It is, rather, the career choice of a purpose-driven, community-building missionary.

An incarnational church

When the Son of God became the Son of Man, and the Eternal Logos began to speak with a northern, working-class, Galilean accent, it was the greatest 'dumbing down' in the history of the universe. He gave up sacred tradition, cultural excellence, aesthetic good taste, intellectual elitism and his own personal and perfect preferences and became 'common'.

Nobody likes dumbing down. We prefer it the other way round, with the common people stepping up. We think it best that they learn to appreciate our traditions, to become in effect a bit like us, adopting our cultural, moral and religious norms. This is nowhere more true than in the realm of our worship and liturgy. Whether we are:

> high Anglican,
> preachy evangelical,
> coolly Soul Survivor,
> warmly Spring Harvest,
> esoterically Taizé,
> ritualistically Roman Catholic,
> alternatively pebble-counting,
> PowerPoint with potpourri,
> deeply icon-loving,
> or Wild Geese flying,

we all expect the outsider to come in and learn our ways. The idea of us giving up something of our cherished, wordy services, lengthy procedures and favourite music is rather out of the question.

> All spoke well of him and were amazed at the gracious words that came from his lips. (Luke 4:22)

Whether in Galilee's *Coronation Street*, or in Jerusalem's *Bonfire of the Vanities*, the mass of the common people heard, understood and valued what he had to say.

The Church of England has a historic tradition of 'Common Prayer', i.e. worship that is supposed to serve and work for the 'common people', phrased, according to the preface of the 1662 Prayer Book, in the 'vernacular'. So perhaps in a moment of rare honesty those of us who are Anglicans could all admit that our current prayer book should not be called 'Common Worship', but 'Quite Posh Worship'.

'Dull', 'lengthy', 'boring' and 'weird', are just some of the words used by so many outsiders, seekers or even new converts to describe their first visit to a church. There is a whole crop of modern novels from the likes of Nick Hornby to Blake Morrison that use these very words when their characters go to church. But this is not just a modern literary view: you can trace the same trail in Tolstoy and Proust, Charles Kingsley and George Eliot, Dickens and Hardy. Now, 'weird' I can live with – maybe it is just another way of describing mystery – but surely, to make God 'dull' and 'boring' is some sort of sacrilege. In fact, some churches are so aware of this type of popular response that they attempt to screen off enquirers from their regular services.

As an Anglican clergyman in training, I spent five years at theological college attending chapel twice a day and studying, amongst other things, 'Liturgy and Worship', yet I cannot recall a single lecture with a title such as 'So how can we make it alive, attractive and totally engaging?' In the Church of England we have a whole division committed to liturgy and more aspiring liturgists than ever before, so when is the Liturgical Commission going to organise a series of seminars on 'Making worship work for ordinary people'? There are no descriptions of Jesus leading times of worship, services or vigils in the Gospels, but there is a very strong sense that whenever he met with people to do 'God stuff', there was life, reality, engagement and vitality.

A common observation of those who study growing churches is that they all, regardless of their particular tradition, have quality worship which works for ordinary people.

The same sort of incarnational questions hang over all our shared life, attempts at communication and missionary endeavours. From our magazines to our meetings, our preaching to our posters, our vocabulary to our vision, the questions are: 'How like Jesus' way is this?' and, 'Whose world does it live in?'

As we have already noted, Grace Davie has spoken of us no longer living in a culture of obligation, where people come and participate out of a sense of duty. Instead we are now living in a world which is all about personal choice. Here people choose to come if they like what they hear and will come again if it was good the first time. In other words, everybody is free to do what they want with their time and life. A growing church will be an incarnational church which encourages people to choose to come, and to come again. Some like the choral tradition, but most would probably prefer worship songs. Some listen to Radio 3, a lot more tune in to Classic FM, but the biggest single audience is for Radio 2. What can we learn about our music from this, or has the question not occurred to us yet?

> In a society that prizes choice, church will be isolated if it treats everyone the same.[10]

---

[10] Michael Moynagh, *Emergingchurch.Intro*, page 66.

A range of great incarnational bridges have been built over the years between church, the local community and the wider world. I am thinking of such things as the popular festivals of Christmas, Easter, Harvest and Remembrance. There are other, more 'folky' religious get-togethers such as Valentine's Day, All Souls and the local church's open day or patronal festival. These are occasions which touch the human spirit in all its experiences, from love to pain, happiness to grief, and loss to eternal hope. They provide a local space where people can find the spiritual. Weddings, baptisms, house blessings, school beginnings and leavings, illnesses and funerals are all doorways. The trusted local church in the local community (our vicarious being there, and being wanted to be there) has a unique place and vocation in these situations to be 'heard gladly by the common people'. Some of this may not be part of our planned church agenda, but it is very much part of people's life agenda, and that is the point. Somehow Jesus the evangelist managed to make the two work together. The process is called 'incarnation'.

In 1999, I was part of an evangelising team in the city of Bradford that set up a Christian pub. It was just about the most difficult, but also the most deeply moving project with which I have ever been involved. It was difficult, because it took us into a strange and uncomfortable world. It was deeply moving, because I saw a bunch of Christians giving their all, and a pub full of lost souls being touched by the love of Jesus, and loving it. Ultimately the enterprise was not a long-term success and we had to cease trading after three years, but we had lots of little victories along the way.

The pub was called The Cock and Bottle and it had one of the roughest reputations of any pub in Bradford. Because we were determined to be incarnational, we sold real beer and had a really good time. Every Saturday night we ran a disco, and I noticed after a while that one of our DJs always played techno-style dance music. The problem was that our usual Saturday night crowd were mainly middle aged. They were into The Beatles, Simon and Garfunkel, The Rolling Stones and Robbie Williams. It was a classic stand-off: Dave the DJ versus the paying public. It was the incarnation issue. We could have been some great medieval cathedral, producing our sort of music beautifully, or a pulsating renewal fellowship with endlessly repeated worship songs, doing it all for ourselves. Eventually, Dave the DJ realised that Jesus the evangelist came first, so he started playing the music that people liked.

> A missionary church seeks to shape itself in relation to the culture in which it is located or to which it is called.[11]

A positive church

Positive people make things happen. Negative ones have a tendency to magnify their problems, predict their failure and bring about their own downfall.

Those of us who teach evangelism and church growth and write books about them sometimes make it all sound a bit too straightforward. We can give the impression that it is all a bit like building with Lego – simply follow the plans and click all the bricks neatly into place. Real life, of course, is not like this, largely because human beings are not as neat and predictable as Lego bricks.

Then, as if making it look easy was not enough, we usually come across as these amazingly cheerful, positive and enthusiastic communicators. Meanwhile, those who have to listen to and endure us are the normal run-of-the-mill, doubting, insecure pray-ers and

---

[11] *Mission-Shaped Church*, page 81.

tryers, who have had some successes and quite a bit of failure in the past. The circus is misleading. There are no easy systems; no one ever discovers 'the answer' and most evangelists are tortured on the inside with their own internal fears and low self-esteem.

As we have seen, Jesus never reduced the work of evangelism and church growth to an easy-going, formulaic, straightforward 'follow the maker's instructions' sort of programme. In his own mission he constantly had to face up to his own disappointments, rejection and – yes, let us use the word – failure. In the growth parables, he taught his followers and all future church-builders to expect thin soils, interferers planting weeds at night, dead branches that need pruning, trees that bear no fruit and sheep that get lost. Nevertheless, they are still called the parables of *growth*. Why? Because, despite all the problems, barriers and false dawns, Jesus still anticipated the growth of his kingdom and the fruitfulness of his people.

> This is what the kingdom of God is like. A man scatters seed on the ground. Night and day, whether he sleeps or gets up, the seed sprouts and grows, though he does not know how. (Mark 4:26–27)

Today, many churches and church leaders are infected by over-negative doubts and insecurities about their own ministries and effectiveness. We are pessimistic and fearful when we look to the future. Without actually putting it into words, we have bought into the predictions of secularism rather than the promises of salvation. Too many in the churches are like the Men of Gondor in *The Lord of the Rings*. There are still plenty of us and we still have a citadel, but we feel it is only a matter of time before we fall, or at least gently decline and fade. The need now is for authentic, realistic and truthful affirmation. We need not discouragement, but encouragement, courage within. We need to be lifted up, not brought low.

Attempting to teach Wendy to fly, Peter Pan said, 'You just think lovely wonderful thoughts, and they lift you up in the air.' The story continues, 'For no one can fly unless the fairy dust has been blown on him.' In this connection, I like to think of the words of Jesus as the 'wonderful thoughts' and the 'fairy dust' as the gift of the Holy Spirit, which we will think more about in the next chapter. This is positive thinking taken to a new level, with the result that we are 'lifted up in the air' and begin to fly.

The positive thinking of Jesus' followers is optimistic, but more than that it is hopeful – full of hope. Our hopes for the growth of his church and the effectiveness of his evangelism is based soundly on seven great foundations:

- Vocation / Calling – he has chosen us to do it.
- Promise / Abiding – he has promised to be with us.
- Spirit / Empowering – his gift to us.
- Kingdom / Growing – his DNA in us.
- Story / Reminding – his church history leading up to us.
- Example / Teaching – his churches and evangelists encourage us by doing it.
- Context / Relating – his world and people are closer to us than we think.

In his foreword to *Mission-Shaped Church*, Archbishop Rowan Williams said:

> I have regularly been surprised and deeply heartened by the widespread sense that the Church of England, for all the problems that beset it, is poised for serious growth and renewal.

Amen to that.

Bob Jackson's *The Road to Growth* is probably the most important book about church growth to appear in recent years. In it he talks particularly about the Anglican Church being in a 'cycle of decline', wherein 'diminishing numbers, deteriorating finances and a decreasing workforce all impact on each other to produce a self-perpetuating downward spiral' (p.7). Despite this painful but honest analysis, he is optimistic about our future, if we do the right things: 'What is needed is a strategy for generating a new cycle of growth in which delight, new birth and hope begin to take over.' Here he is surprisingly close to Callum Brown when he eschews management makeovers and calls for a 'destiny shaping turning point' for the whole church.[12]

May I suggest that this new strategic future is found in our past, in the DNA of the kingdom and in the model of Jesus?

> The kingdom of heaven is like a mustard seed, which a man took and planted in his field. Though it is the smallest of all your seeds, yet when it grows, it is the largest of garden plants and becomes a tree. (Matthew 13:31)

If this new strategic beginning is to happen, it will probably happen in individual churches, although it could be made to work for a whole denomination or diocese. Either way, it needs to happen fast, in what Martin Luther King once called 'the fierce urgency of the Now'.

Part of my work involves seeing and sharing ways forward in church growth, stimulating, equipping and training local churches.

---

[12] *The Death of Christian Britain*, page 7.

I regularly hit a brick wall of opposition, distrust or suspicion. To some it is 'theologically shallow', to others it is just not spiritual enough, while to others it is all about management techniques and not enough about the kingdom. It can, of course, be all of these things, but not when it is done the Jesus way, for then it is a thing of love, flowing from the missionary heart of God to the needy lives of his people.

The essential thing to remember about church growth is that it is not actually about the church. It is all about individual people finding their way to God, and their world being transformed.

Anne lives a *Sex in the City* type of life in New York. She is the heroine in *Anybody Out There?*, a 'chick lit' novel by Marian Keyes. Now this kind of book is probably not read by many evangelists – we are all too high minded for that, or perhaps just too old. Nevertheless, it is very influential throughout the Western world, being read by millions of largely middle-class, young adult women, and some men, and Marian Keyes is one of its high priestesses. Back to the story: Anne's new husband, Aidan, has died and she is desperate to find some sort of hope and meaning in her lostness. Anne is a searcher. She describes her spiritual condition in the following way: 'I didn't even believe in God. I didn't not believe in God either.'[13] She had earlier yearned for some sort of connection, but not with the 'dull God' of her teenage years. She had found the 'dull God' in 'dull churches'.

My heart goes out to Anne, and to the millions like her. I long for her to find the real God, who is the exact opposite of dullness. I want her to find him, not because we need her membership, but because she needs his divine relationship and our human fellowship. She needs a church in her cultural world, at the heart of her

---

[13] Marian Keyes, *Anybody Out There?*, Penguin 2007, page 224.

city and at the end of her street – a missionary, united, incarnational and positive church, which is doing it his way.

We believe in one holy catholic and apostolic church.
And we have got one.

It is big in Brighouse
and small in Littlehampton,
high in Highbury
and low in Lowestoft,
Celtic in Cornwall
and alternative in Altrincham.
We have got evangelicals in Edinburgh
and Roman Catholics in Reading and Canterbury,
liberals in Liverpool
and charismatics in Cheltenham.
In Oxford there are Orthodox
while the Baptists are in Bath,
there are the youthful in Yarmouth
and the elderly in Oldham,
Anglicans in East Anglia,
Methodists in Manchester,
house churches in Housesteads,
congregationalists in Congleton,
and the United Reformed Church all over the United Kingdom.

All trying to do it his way in our world
and most getting much better at it.

CHAPTER EIGHT

Jesus and the Father

Didn't you know I had to be in my Father's house? (Luke 2:49)

We have looked at Jesus the man, listened to his message and picked out some of his methods. It is now time to dip into his inner spiritual life, his praying, his pursuing and his power receiving. So far we have been thinking almost entirely of what he did for others. The question now is, who did it for him?

My first stab at a title for this chapter was 'Jesus' Spirituality'. This would have employed a word and concept, or clutch of concepts, that I love working with. Spirituality is ultimately indefinable, but that is OK, because most of the best things in life and certainly the best things of God are just that. Spirituality is about my inner places, my deepest me, my history and hopes, my essence. But it is not just about me. It also reaches out to the 'other', to the transcendent, to God. It is about the spiritual humanity and spiritual deity. It only begins to happen when the two 'poles' of the inner spiritual me and the outer spiritual God connect. Father Richard Rohr, the

Franciscan spiritual writer, has a lovely expression to describe the result of this connection:

> Spirituality is about when you discover that the inside of things is bigger than the outside.[1]

So here is my problem with many contemporary ideas on spirituality: what is supposed to be a 'me' and 'God' word has often lost half its meaning and become just a 'me' word. This narcissistic humanising of spiritual life is a reflection of the me-centred cultural whirlpool of a greedy consumerist world. The 'selfish gene' has struck again. So people talk increasingly of 'my' spirituality and, even worse, 'my' spiritual needs. They look for like-minded folk to set up their own 'us'-centred groups, visit the local spiritual supermarket and fill their houses with their self-selected spiritual odds and ends. It is a 'spirituality' lifestyle that is picked up by Christians almost as much as by New Agers.

The popular writer Paulo Coelho is a typical example of this trend. He has written many novels, of which the most famous is *The Alchemist.* It is a spiritual fairy story, with difficult journeys, good and evil, lost origins, buried treasure and a happy ending. It is part of the 'finding the real you with a bit of help from some vague but kindly, unnamed godly presence' kind of spirituality. It is all a long way from the spiritual teachings of Jesus. He called on people to make life-defining choices just like a builder deciding where to build his house. He expected obedience from all his followers and established forgiveness and love as the hallmarks of a true spiritual life. And for him this life was about

---

[1] Interview for the *Church Times*, 25th January 2008.

pain as well as pleasure, sacrifice as well as satisfaction, and commitment coming before comfort.

What should be a beautiful two-way love affair has become for many a rather ugly self-obsession. Writing in the 1930s, Martin Buber produced *I and Thou*, one of the great classics of spiritual writing. There he talks about the choice before all of us, whether to live 'I and it' relationships, which are utterly self-centred and materialistic, or to live in a deeper, truer way where 'the other' is a personal 'you'.

> Spirit is not in the I but between I and You. It is not like the blood that circulates in you but like the air in which you breathe.[2]

Jesus' spirituality was never a 'me' and 'my' thing, but always an 'us' and 'ours' one. 'It takes two to tango', as the saying goes, and the epic dance of his life involved his own human spiritual nature gripping and in turn being gripped by the Spirit of God. The whole thing was not so much a ritual or religion as a relationship.

Jesus' relationship with his Father

My intention here is first to tell the story of Jesus and his Father, and then to draw out the lessons so that we can do it his way in our world. It is a story with three parts, a slow beginning, a big middle and a climactic ending.

The beginning all builds up to the baptism and the words of a proud Father who has watched his Son being born, growing up and preparing for the task ahead:

---

[2] Martin Buber, *I and Thou*, Clark 1959, page 89.

> You are my Son, whom I love; with you I am well pleased. (Luke 3:22)

This is the affirmation of a loving parent that all children long to hear. It acknowledges both an educational journey completed and a mission about to begin. Not only does Jesus hear his Father's words, he also receives the Holy Spirit. His own 'spirituality' is insufficient by itself – he needs that which is above to descend upon him.

Luke's Gospel gives us three brief glimpses into the thirty years leading up to this baptismal launch. First during his primary years and then again as a young man, Jesus is described as growing strongly in body, mind and spirit in relationship with the Father (Luke 2:40, 52). In between these two summary verses we have the story of the twelve-year-old Jesus in the temple, replying to the enquiries of Mary and Joseph with the words, 'Didn't you know I had to be in my Father's house?' (Luke 2:49) Three snapshot glimpses into the formation of a deeply spiritual man.

After the baptism Jesus goes out into the wilderness, where the devil's temptations are about breaking the 'Father-Son' relationship. Afterwards he returns to the Galilee and begins his work. In both cases, Luke describes him as being 'filled with the Spirit' (see 4:1, 14). In the second of these two instances he adds the concept of 'power'. This is the chemistry of true spirituality: take a willing and obedient human spirit, add a generous dollop of the Holy Spirit, and the result is *dunamis*, explosive power.

> As the Father has sent me. . . (John 20:21)

The 'big middle' of the story is all about the Son being obedient to the Father's will. Jesus was a driven man (Mark 1:38).

His guiding principle was to see what the Father was doing and then to join in with him (John 5:19). Throughout his ministry he treasured and kept alive the 'Father-Son axis', committing time alone to it (Mark 1:35; 6:46). It was a relationship recognised first by the 'Geiger counter' antennae of the demons rather than the dullness of men (Mark 5:7; 6:3). The Father-Son relationship is seen perhaps at its most intimate and at the same time its most inclusive in the words:

> I praise you, Father, Lord of heaven and earth, because you have hidden these things from the wise and learned, and revealed them to little children. (Matthew 11:25)

He led his followers into a relationship with God by which, when they obeyed the Father, they became Jesus' brothers and sisters (Mark 3:34). He taught them to pray intimately to a shared Father (Matthew 6:6), and even gave them their own 'Our Father' prayer (Matthew 6:9–13). Unlike the Pharisees and even the followers of John the Baptist, he wanted his disciples to have a joyful spiritual life (Mark 2:19). He wanted their trust in their Father to be deeper than their worldly worries (Matthew 6:26) and for them to discover the generosity of him who prefers bread to stones and fish to snakes (Matthew 7:9–10).

Not surprisingly for one who had such a strong sense of being a child of God, he wanted to protect children and the 'spiritual child' in others (Mark 5:41; 9:21, 42; 10:14–15). Children were very special to Jesus. He wanted them to have their own access and special level of care.

The final week is the last part of the story, and it contains some strange and poetic echoes of its beginning. Jesus' cleansing of the temple and restoration of it as the Father's house of prayer reminds us of the visit of the twelve-year-old to the temple. His final words from the cross, 'Father, into your hands I commit my spirit' (Luke 23:46), are almost like a giving back of the Father's own words from his baptism. In between these two events we find strong echoes of the wilderness temptations in the Garden of Gethsemane when Jesus prays, 'Father, if you are willing, take this cup from me; yet not my will, but yours be done' (Luke 22:42). Jesus' spirituality was all about his relationship to the Father, and the essence of that relationship was obedience.

Ultimately, the 'Son' became the 'Lamb', but unlike the other 'Son-Lamb' story of Abraham and Isaac, this time there was no substitute to be found hiding in a bush.

I recently discovered what I think is just about the most moving sacrificial lamb story that I have ever come across, and interestingly, it comes from the Muslim tradition. I read the story in *The Kite Runner*, a novel by Khaled Hosseini. Twelve-year-old Amir is the son of a rich man in Kabul, and Hassan is his closest and devoted friend. Hassan is also the son of his father's servant. When Amir is being chased by the local gang led by the psychopathic Assef, Hassan takes his place and is subjected to a brutal rape. Secretly Amir watches it all from a safe distance and sees in his friend's despairing face the same look that he has seen in the sacrificial lamb just before it is butchered:

> That look of acceptance in the animal's eyes. Absurdly, I imagine the animal understands. I imagine the animal sees that its imminent demise is for a higher purpose. This is the look.[3]

[3] Khaled Hosseini, *The Kite Runner*, Bloomsbury 2004.

When I read this story, it moved me to tears and moved me closer to the cross.

During his ministry, Jesus had drawn his disciples into his own Son-Father relationship. After the resurrection, he sends them out on a Father-Son mission. On the earlier mission to the Galilee he had lent them his authority; this time, on a longer and wider adventure and without his human presence to support them, he promises the Holy Spirit:

> The Counsellor, the Holy Spirit, whom the Father will send in my name, will teach you all things and will remind you of everything I have said to you. (John 14:26)

They are to receive the same anointing of power that he received at the beginning of his mission (Luke 24:49; Acts 1:5), so that Pentecost was in effect their Jordan. The same process or journey of discovery is described rather differently by John. This time the wind comes from Jesus' breathing, but once again the Spirit is linked to mission (John 20:21–22).

That is the story of Jesus' spirituality. It is a story of a relationship between Son and Father. It is a story of spirituality flowing into mission. Thinking about the sort of spiritual life led by evangelism-type people (a much wider category than 'evangelists'), I see three big issues standing out. They are 'preparation and launch', the 'day to day', and 'mission'.

Preparation and launch

In one respect the whole of Jesus' childhood, teenage years and young adulthood was a preparation for his ministry which began when he was thirty. As we have seen, he was continually growing during this period. His growth seems to have been spiritual, intellectual and social. He grew to be a godly person, an intelligent person, and a people person. Judging by the level of focus and impact displayed in the first phase of his work, he also grew to be a very missional and evangelistic person.

Much ministerial preparation in the Western church today is strong on the intellectual and often very strong on the spiritual and liturgical. Its weakness is the social and the missional, and the evangelistic is often completely absent. In other words, we prepare men and women for the library and the sanctuary, but not for the world. Many ministers and pastors come out of theological college with no training at all in how to lead people to God, how to practise the threefold ministry of proclamation, healing and exorcism, how to combine community work with community evangelism, or how to create worship that works for non-religious people. In fact, some come into ministry not just lacking the basic skills, but not even believing in such things.

David Watson was arguably the single most influential evangelist that the English church has produced since World War II. He was also an Anglican vicar. In his autobiography, *You Are My God*, he describes his training for ministry. He recalls it as being all too focused on academic and at times very dull theological teaching. However, there were two great positives in his story. The first was his relationship with a very young David Sheppard, who took him under his wing, mentored him, prayed and read the Bible with him. The second was his time spent helping out on many youth camps. These gave him his first opportunities to lead Bible studies, give short talks and attempt to lead enquiring teenagers closer to God. As we have seen, Jesus did not just teach, he actually mentored his disciples and he put them into mission situations to learn how to do it.

It is just this sort of preparation that we need to offer today, but we are still a long way off. I was recently in a conversation with a leading Anglican training expert and made the suggestion that we offer training in basic evangelism skills. The atmosphere of our whole conversation suddenly cooled. I was left feeling that I had trampled onto someone else's territory and suggested something that was not in 'good taste'.

So now for three quick positives:

- For the last twelve years I have been part of the 'Leading Your Church into Growth' team. This consists largely of clergy who have grown churches, evangelists and missioners. We work together to offer teaching, experience, resources and consultancy to clergy and lay leaders. The project grew out of the discovery that the overwhelming majority of clergy in the Church of England have never been helped in the twin areas of church growth and effective evangelism. We have since learned that the same sad state of affairs applies to many other church leaders too. It is both encouraging and alarming to hear so many who come on our courses saying, 'I should have been taught all this twenty years ago.'
- At one time evangelists used to evangelise. Now more and more they are equipping others to do it. Daniel Cozens, J. John and Ian Knox all led the way. They began by taking on board 'young apprentices' and have gone on to build whole training schemes affecting many lives. Rob Frost did a similar and huge work for the Methodist Church. Meanwhile, Andy Hawthorne and the 'Message' have not just had a massive

impact on thousands of Manchester young people, but have also called, taught and given 'on the job experience' to many other budding youth evangelists.

- Some years ago, I was employed as the 'adviser in evangelism' by Bradford diocese. While I was doing this, my colleague Christopher Lewis, who was responsible for training curates, came up with a brilliant idea. He said that he wanted all the curates to experience the 'doing' of evangelism, so would I gel them all into a team and take them on a parish mission once a year? They did the practical with me and the spiritual and theological reflection with Christopher. This is a very workable system that I would recommend to other denominations and dioceses.

This might seem a long way from spirituality and relationship. It is not. It is all part of the integrated, whole life and being of those of us who are trying to do it the way of Jesus the evangelist.

In Jesus' case, the next part of the package after his preparation was the powerful and mystical experience that came upon him at his baptism and launched his mission.

> And the Holy Spirit descended on him in bodily form like a dove. (Luke 3:22)

The water of the Jordan, the voice of the Father and the descent of the Spirit: this is a big moment to launch a big mission and it is most famously pictured by Piero Della Francesca's well-known painting, 'The Baptism of Christ'. Here, to capture the trinitarian nature of the event, the artist has created a central focus to the picture around two triangles consisting of the outstretched wings of the dove, the outpoured water and the head and upper body of Jesus. The theology is in the geometry. In the painting's background an unknown man is already stripping off his clothes. He is a spiritual searcher, a repenting lost soul. He is queueing up to be baptised by Jesus – the mission is about to begin. But Jesus will baptise people not just in water, but in the Holy Spirit (Mark 1:8).

For most of us, receiving the Spirit tends to have a fade-out factor in our fractured lives – it begins in passion and depth, but becomes a bit dry and shallow. For Jesus it had a permanency: the Spirit came down and was to 'remain on him' (John 1:32). As well as this permanency, John the Baptist's assessment of the situation was that Jesus was given the Spirit 'without limit' (John 3:34). There was a lot of Spirit to give! Clearly it is impossible to describe fully what happened between Jesus and the Spirit at the Jordan, but what we can say is that Jesus had a big charismatic experience to equip him for a big charismatic job.

John Wimber loved to talk about Jesus' work of 'power evangelism' and of our continuing his example:

> Power Evangelism is a spontaneous, Spirit-inspired, empowered presentation of the gospel. Power evangelism is that evangelism which is preceded and under-girded by supernatural demonstration of God's presence.[4]

Jesus' baptism was all about his empowering for a powerful mission.

These days, big experiences are out. The pendulum has swung. Now we are all into journeying and slow, gradual progress. But as with evangelism, so with spirituality, most of the best journeys

---

[4] *Power Evangelism*, page 46.

begin with, and occasionally include other, significant one-off moments. What we need is not a pendulum, swinging from one pole to another, but rather a see-saw which holds them together in a dynamic balancing act. They were both there in Jesus' life, the beginning and the continuing, the big launch and the ongoing footsteps, the deep experience and the daily engagement.

For the disciples, as we have seen, the big experience came at Pentecost, but there is a strong feel throughout the Acts and the rest of the New Testament of further receivings and fillings.

Jesus' baptising of his disciples in the Spirit was about power made sacramentally recognisable in the form of wind, fire and breath. I am continually and aesthetically intrigued by wind turbines. Some days I find them ugly and plastic mechanical intrusions into the landscape. At other times they appear to be beautiful, part machine, part animal and part flower. The difference is in the movement. When they have it, they are alive; when they lose it, they may still be the same turbines with all the same dimensions and structure, but they look dull, heavy and ineffective. They move when the wind blows. In John's Gospel, Jesus breathed onto his disciples, and in the Acts, God blew on them. For individuals and for the young corporate church, it was an experience of the Spirit, promised by Jesus and provided by the Father – a big charismatic and trinitarian experience.

Day to day

> Oh dear Lord, three things I pray,
> To see thee more clearly,
> Love thee more dearly,
> Follow thee more nearly,
> Day by day.

In the Western tradition, we tend to think in terms of months and years when it comes to development, building and evaluating. We stretch time out into *chronos.* In contrast, Jesus seems to have lived his spiritual life and operated his mission plan (these were, of course, two parts of the same thing) in a more immediate and spontaneous rhythm of taking a day at a time. This was *kairos* time, time focused into the immediacy of the 'now'. This is exactly how the Genesis story of creation envisages God operating. We see hints of Jesus' daily rhythms at various points in the story (e.g. Mark 4:35; Luke 4:42) and observe him teaching others to live a day at a time (Matthew 6:34). The proposition that he also worked to a long-term vocational plan does not conflict with this vision of daily living – quite the opposite, in fact. It is the big plan and strong sense of overall direction that build the platform on which he can live and work in the 'now'.

> What are days for?
> Days are where we live.
> They come, they wake us
> Time and time over.
> They are to be happy in:
> Where can we live but days?[5]

The danger of always living in the long term is that we never experience the immediacy of early morning vision, the pleasing vigour of daily labour and the satisfaction of evening's reflection. Long-term *chronos* missioners tend to treat individual days like the odd coins in our pocket: they count for little, and sometimes we waste them like a general with too many soldiers or a millionaire

---

[5] Philip Larkin, 'Days'.

with too much loose change. Days are not pennies, they are pounds. Each one is so valuable and offers so much scope. If we set out with a three-year mission plan to evangelise an area, build a church, run a youth project or train a whole diocese or district, then we have 1,095 days to work with. Despite what many of us think, it is not that we do not have enough days, but rather that we waste too many.

Jesus' day-to-day prayer life looks like a son opening his heart to his father. Sometimes he is relaxed and confident, but at other times he is lonely and frightened. I have this feeling that sometimes his early morning times with his Father were like that moment when we lie in bed, pull the curtains back and simply enjoy the early morning sunlight and birdsong. Perhaps at other times it was more like pulling the bedclothes over his head and wishing it would all go away. Wherever he was on the 'feelings spectrum', he wanted his Father to come in and jointly occupy that place.

It was the German theologian Joachim Jeremias back in the 1970s who famously focused on Jesus' prayerful use of the term 'Father'. He argued two things from it. Firstly, that it was utterly unique within Judaism: no one else had the audacity to talk to God in this way. Secondly, he said that it denoted a special degree of warmth and intimacy enshrined in the use of the term *Abba* to replace the more formal and traditional language of prayer. Following his work, much has been made of the word *Abba* in Bible teaching and popular renewal music. It has to be pointed out, however, that in all the uses of the term 'Father' by Jesus, the actual word *Abba* appears only once, in Mark 14:36.

Later theologians have questioned the 'absoluteness' of Jeremias's claims, but there is still an acceptance of his central thesis, that in addressing God as 'Father', Jesus was taking prayer to a deeper and more personal place:

> It should not be supposed that Jeremias has been disproved completely: there is a striking phenomenon to be observed in the prayers of Jesus.[6]

When Jesus began his prayers with the word 'Father', he was speaking from his open heart straight into the heart of his Father, the one who knew him the best and cared about him the most. It was the language of honesty and spontaneity, of laughter and tears – it was love talk.

So often our prayer life shrivels down to just intercession or asking. We come with our long lists of requests, perhaps before a mission or during a healing service, like the little boy in the fish shop with all his needs written out for him on the back of an envelope. Or perhaps we are all the time just wanting more and more, like demanding teenagers punching their own personal code into their own personal Link machine. This so easily becomes the kind of prayer which is filled with endless words, religious expressions and terminology. Suddenly it is not the real me being with God, but me nervously and hurriedly trotting out all the stuff that I have picked up from a hundred prayer meetings or books of liturgy. There is, of course, a real and important place for hungry and desperate requests to be made to a Father who wants to give: 'Ask and it will be given to you; seek and you will find; knock and the door will be opened to you' (Matthew 7:7). But when prayer turns into, or becomes taken over by, our neurotic anxieties, something of the broadness and deepness of being with God gets lost.

---

[6] N.T. Wright, *Jesus and the Victory of God*, page 649.

Jesus establishes the ultimate blueprint for prayer in the Sermon on the Mount:

> Our Father in heaven,
> hallowed be your name,
> your kingdom come,
> your will be done
> on earth as it is in heaven.
> Give us today our daily bread.
> Forgive us our debts,
> as we also have forgiven our debtors.
> And lead us not into temptation,
> but deliver us from the evil one.
> (Matthew 6:9–13)

One simple prayer that says it all. It is addressed to 'our Father' – the relationship is opened. Then come six succinct clauses. The first three are utterly worshipful, looking at God. The second three are humanly needful, focusing on ourselves as we lay our requests at the foot of his bountiful table. Our familiarity with the words disguises their profound depth and inclusivity. Most of the time we rattle through them like reciting our telephone number. A better way is to wait a while before we begin and then to speak the words slowly, pausing after each line to think, ruminate and explore.

The Gospels show us Jesus spending time alone in prayer at key moments of his ministry. This is not quite the same as a daily regulated prayer time. However, in the light of these examples and of the more matter-of-fact way in which he speaks to his disciples about their prayers (Matthew 6:5–15), it is not exactly a leap into the unknown to think of him praying on a daily basis. Devout Jews of his day would have prayed three times a day, at daybreak, sundown and in the middle of the day at the hour of the sacrifice being offered at the temple. He may well not have felt constrained by this formal practice, but it would be odd to think of him as praying less than his contemporaries.

In Mark 1:35, we see Jesus praying in anticipation of a full day of demanding work. To complement this, we are then shown him praying at the end of an exhausting and emptying time, in this case the feeding of the five thousand (Mark 6:46). On the first occasion he was presumably looking forward, perhaps nervously, and needing guidance, wisdom and energy. My own guess, as an evangelist, is that he was previewing the whole day in his heart, opening it up to his Father, expressing his hopes and fears and wanting to build up his faith. The second story looks like him cooling down, replaying it all, dwelling on the positives and the negatives, giving thanks and enjoying the deep and satisfied rest of a tired man who has done a good job. So there is praying in anticipation, prayer-empowered action and prayerful reflection. It is a good model for us all to adopt.

In both of these before and after moments, Jesus went to a special place, at a special time and into a special aloneness. The mountain was his favourite place, not because it was closer to God or because he was seeking a mountain-top experience, but because it took him away from other people. There were no distractions, no conversations, no e-mails, no mobile phones and no radio. Out of a busy life, he carved his own space/time bubble and there were only two seats in it, one for his Father and one for himself. Spirituality needs private spaces, whether we follow a Catholic sacramental path, or an evangelical 'quiet time' approach, or, best of all, a combination of the two. Many like to furnish their private space/time with icons, worship songs, texts, crucifixes or Taizé chants as a source of enrichment. Whatever we find personally helpful is fine, but the carving out of a private clearing in the overgrown busyness of our lives is an essential for all of us. I have various special places. One is in the cathedral where I work (oh, for more churches to be open through the day!), another one is on a walk. I have one in my own home and another one in a favourite retreat house where I sometimes go. Part of my personal space is the cup of tea that I like to wrap myself around at the heart of my privacy.

In a busy time of ministry, prayerful aloneness is often the first thing to be squeezed out. In Jesus' case, the opposite seems to have happened. The less time he has to himself, the more time he needs with God; the more he gives out, the more he needs to take in. As he becomes pressed by ever more demands on his energy, he has himself to make ever greater demands on the Father's strength (Luke 5:15–16). As Bill Hybels has famously reminded us, 'it was not so much that he was too busy to pray, but rather that he was far too busy not to pray.'

Luke 6:12 gives us another through-the-keyhole image of the praying Jesus. This time he was not so much active as very thoughtful. He was thinking long and hard about his disciples and about which ones to choose to make up the 'Twelve'. The pattern is the same, away from people and close up to God, this time for a full night of prayer. Many churches, evangelism teams and mission groups have discovered the deep value of nights of prayer. Most of us tend to find them a bit daunting beforehand, but surprising and even enjoyable when they actually happen. Whenever I have organised them, I have always included plenty of tea and coffee breaks for the sake of the weaker spirits, i.e. myself. Who knows, maybe Jesus took a thermos and sandwiches with him on his big night. It is not just that a night (or, to be honest, in my case a half-night) does something to God, in the 'impossible to understand' way that prayer always does, but it does something to us too.

Jesus' great prayerful concern for his disciples is captured in John 17. Here he is operating as an evangelist-cum-midwife-cum-elder-brother. He is not content to run an evangelistic mission, lead people to faith and then leave them to get on with it while he moves on to the next place. These men and women are far more to him than mere converts: 'They were yours; you gave them to me' (John 17:6). But his ownership does not mean that he can manipulate them or take them for granted: it is actually a source of caring responsibility. This is a responsibility in which he has a working partnership with the Father. He prays:

- for their protection from the evil one,
- for their survival in a hostile world,
- for their unity,
- and for their continuing joy (John 17:11–21).

It is difficult for travelling evangelists to have this sort of prayerful concern for those we bring to faith. We do not operate the way Jesus did, with a long-term investment in the lives of our disciples. Having said that, I know of some who do have a system of follow-up prayer. It works in a more general way, but given that we have a caring God who, according to Jesus' prayer, also has a big stake in the well-being of our converts, I think we can assume that it does still work. For those operating in a more settled situation, John 17 provides a wonderful blueprint for ongoing prayerful love and responsibility.

In the Garden of Gethsemane we see the praying Jesus at his most desperate. He was frightened. His feelings were running high and he was utterly lonely. Even his disciples, whom he had specifically asked to support him, let him down. This is the one occasion when we see him use the *Abba* word.

> *Abba*, Father . . . everything is possible for you. Take this cup from me. Yet not what I will, but what you will. (Mark 14:36)

This was, as Mark tells us, distressful and agitated prayer, not triumphalistic, comfortably accepting or peaceful prayer. Jesus was awash with all the discomfiting feelings from which we often suffer, but, unlike many of us, rather than suppress them he let them pour out. This was 'hurting prayer'. It was, to use a much over-used word, an 'awesome' half-night of prayer.

There are two poles in all this living out of a daily prayer life, and it is too easy for them to become separated. One pole is fervent activity, with lots of rushing, doing and evangelising. The other pole is contemplative. This is all about waiting, being and receiving. There are very few men or women who can hold the two together in a creatively dynamic way. Jesus the evangelist was one who could and did.

My experience of evangelism people is that we tend to be very strong on the activity pole and weak on the contemplative. Add to this the realisation that most of us are strategically goal-orientated, and suddenly we are in trouble. We easily become addicted to work, to busyness and to achieving, and, as with all addictions, the more we get the more we want. What we need is not the same as what we want, however. What we desperately need is to sit down, find stillness, stop doing and wait on God. This, of course, is exactly the advice that Jesus gave to his disciples:

> Stay in the city until you have been clothed with power from on high. (Luke 24:49)

Most of us are so bad at this that we need someone to help us do it. We need a spiritual guide, line manager or support group who will not just ask us about our achievements, but will have the strength to ask us the much more difficult question about our prayers. Of course the opposite is equally true. There are plenty of those who have a temperament which leads them naturally towards stillness, who need to add more urgency and action to their inner depths, but not many of them are evangelists.

When it comes to spirituality, there is something in all of us that craves to be, and to be seen to be (Jesus was wise to this one too – Matthew 6:5), a holy and saintly soul. Whether our hero is a Smith Wigglesworth or a Teresa of Avila, we all have someone we would love to be like. The blunt truth is that most of us never will be like that person. These are exceptional people, gifts to the world, and the overwhelming mass of the rest of us just do not have that extra mystical 'M' gene in our DNA. We can all, however, be like Forrest Gump. In the movie, Forrest Gump is not a greatly talented Olympic athlete. He is a simple jogger, a dogged, persistent 'Steady Eddy'. He simply keeps on keeping on. He discovers both a physical and psychological healthiness in the rhythm of running, and, very importantly, he gets there in the end. In fact, most of us are not even runners: we are walkers. Arthur Wainwright, the great English fell-walking man, once said:

> One should always have a definite objective, in a walk as in life. It is so much more satisfying to reach a target by personal effort than to wander aimlessly. An objective is an ambition, and life without ambition is aimlessly wandering.

Jesus certainly seems to have had plenty of definite purpose and ambition to his spiritual walk. But before getting too narrowly programmed, I would want to add what Bishop Gordon Mursell, a veritable spiritual sage, says:

> The Christian spiritual tradition has an astonishing vitality and inventiveness, enabling those who make it their own to see life not as a pre-determined routine, or even simply as a journey, but as something at once attractive and challenging: an adventure.[7]

When it doesn't work

The temptations, and their promised return (Luke 4:13), indicate that Jesus was troubled by self-doubt and temptations of egoism. Meanwhile, as we have seen, keeping the disciples on the straight and narrow caused him real problems. Despite this, however, it looks as if his spiritual life worked very effectively, which is just as well given who and what he was. For us there is no better pattern to follow, but what about the phases in our lives when it does not work very well, when the stream just dries up, or when the bright light dims to a grey sense of routine, or when we keep pedalling, but the wheels stop turning? These are often the times when our aspiration for spiritual reality leads to a sense of guilt and failure.

For most of my life I have struggled with the spiritual disciplines, struggled to believe in God and in myself. I have lived whole

---

[7] Gordon Mursell, *The Story of Christian Spirituality*, Lion Hudson 2001, page 10.

chunks of my ministry feeling that God was away on some lengthy sabbatical, or busy with my friends and colleagues, all of whom seemed to be enjoying normal and healthy spiritual lives. The thought of having a warm ongoing relationship with the Father is usually more of a chimera than a reality for me. Or perhaps I ought to say a 'felt' reality, because what is real and what we 'feel' to be real are not always the same.

I am sure that I am not the only one in the 'kept behind after spiritual school' group. In fact, I have regularly discovered that others involved in the work of evangelism tend towards a weaker spirituality. It may well be something to do with our excitable 'up and down' temperaments, our insecurities, fear of failure and the bad treatment that we often receive from inside the church. In my own case, a lifelong friendship with the 'black dog' of depression has created much gloom, and things are certainly not helped by the fact that I spend far too much time and energy trying to lead others to God, and not nearly enough time allowing myself to be so led.

There is something rather comforting in discovering that those we most admire share in our weaknesses. Studdert Kennedy, better known as Woodbine Willie, is one of my greatest heroes. I love him – born a northerner, committed to the poor, he was a passionate life-long evangelist whose temperament oscillated between fun and gloom. He coped with his own doubts by being even more committed.

> What he did was to pledge the whole of himself to the proposition that in fact it was true. Faith, he was never tired of saying, was a gamble. He bet his life, as he said, upon one side in life's great war.[8]

---

[8] William Purcell, *Woodbine Willie*, Hodder & Stoughton 1962, page 222.

Anyway, I have learned a few things about surviving the evangelist's 'dark night of the soul', so here are just five hopefully helpful thoughts.

- My doubt is not a problem and certainly not a threat to God, but it is to me. If I stop believing in him or sensing his presence, it does not affect the reality of his presence at all, because he is God – but it does make my life a lot more difficult. Maybe that is just how it has to be, or maybe it isn't. It actually took me many years to realise that all my doubts actually say more about me than they do about God.
- I have to be open, honest and full-blooded with God. There is nothing anywhere about prayer involving me being 'nice' to God. He is a big boy, he has been around the block quite a few times and he can look after himself. It is OK for me to shout and rail at him from time to time. More than anything else, he wants me to be honest; like any true father, he wants to relate to the real me, not a mask of sweet piety.
- I need special people, not lots of them, perhaps just one or two. As an insecure evangelist, I am desperate for all the encouragement in the world. I need to be loved, remembered and listened to. I do not need lots of advice or Bible verses offered, I can do that for myself, but I do need a good listening to from time to time. I need those one or two special friends or colleagues who love me enough and are strong enough not to be swayed by my big talk, who can look me in the eye and probe into the inner me, who can relate to the small frightened child inside me. Like most evangelists, I am surrounded by those who would love to be that special person and many of them are

in different ways, but to find the really special one, I have usually had to go out and search.

Jesus also needed others around him – at the transfiguration (Matthew 17:1), the entry to Jerusalem (Matthew 21:1) and his weakest moment in Gethsemane (Matthew 26:36). These look to me not just like teaching occasions, but like points of real dependency.

- Just do it anyway! Faith is not about certainty. It is about going on and doing it when we are uncertain. The more I go on living as if he were there, the more it all seems to work out best. When desperately searching for his own personal faith, John Wesley was advised by Peter Böhler the Moravian to 'preach faith till you have it, and then, because you have it, you will preach faith.'[9] It is a bit like living in a great big casino. I have placed my bet, all my chips are stacked up on the big 'G', and I am not going to change it.
- Finally, faith is both a gift and something that can be grown. It is organic: put it in the right soil, give it a bit of food and water, protect it from the worst of the icy draughts, see it gets plenty of sunshine, and it will grow. Oh, and don't forget to talk to it.

And so, on to the last of our three reflections on Jesus' spiritual life.

Love-of-others spirituality and mission

> Almighty God,
> We thank you for feeding us
> With the body and blood of your Son Jesus Christ.

---

[9] Quoted in Roy Hattersley, *John Wesley*, page 130.

> Through him we offer you our souls and bodies
> To be a living sacrifice.
> Send us out
> In the power of your Spirit
> To live and work to your praise and glory.
> Amen

Every single week, in England alone, over a million Anglicans say this prayer and hundreds of thousands of Christians in other denominations and groupings say something very similar. It is a wonderful and complete piece of liturgy which is all about doing it his way in our world. It is corporate spirituality, feeding on word and sacrament and then going out to share the gospel, in the power of the Spirit.

Sadly, we have to ask, which of us do actually 'go out'? I wonder how many of us during this prayer think, 'The service is now ending,' when we are meant to think, 'The service is now beginning.'

In the case of Jesus, his spirituality and his experience of the Holy Spirit all flowed directly into his love for people. It was the Spirit who led him to Galilee for the beginning of the work (Luke 4:14). His sense of being anointed by the Spirit formed his missionary focus (Luke 4:18).

> His awareness of being uniquely possessed and used by divine Spirit was the mainspring of his mission and the key to its effectiveness.[10]

The Spirit empowered him to perform signs of wonder and to drive out evil spirits (Matthew 12:28) and it was this same Spirit that he promised to his followers (John 14:16).

---

[10] James Dunn, *Jesus and the Spirit*, Eerdmans 1997, page 54.

For Jesus, spirituality was never a thing in itself, for himself, it was not a source of enlightenment, inner peace or greater joy to be kept in his own heart – it was always about loving and sharing. The Holy Spirit was never just a blessing, never an 'ego-enrichment', but always an evangelistic empowerment.

Now here is an old-fashioned Sunday school lesson that ought to be taught afresh to all of us. The Sea of Galilee and the Dead Sea are both great lakes and are both supplied with fresh, life-giving water by the inflow of the River Jordan. The Sea of Galilee is alive and clean, while its more southerly sister is toxic and dead. Why? Because the Sea of Galilee has an outflow and the Dead Sea does not.

The same is true of churches and individual Christians. We can have terrific spiritual inflow, but if we have no missionary, loving outflow we shall self-poison. I often wonder if this is the source of so many of our interior disputes. Whether it is the national church arguing and splitting up over sexuality, or individuals leaving the local church because the flower stand is in the wrong place, it may be a case of 'the devil makes work for idle souls'. Spiritual energy, prayer, Bible study, enthusiasm and commitment that should all go into building up the kingdom are often being used to break up the church.

This movement of spirituality into loving outflow was wonderfully brought to life in the ministry of Alexander Boddy, one of the most important yet lesser known mission priests of the nineteenth and twentieth centuries. Boddy was the vicar of Monkwearmouth in Sunderland from 1884 to 1922. There he combined a 'social gospel' concern for the industrial poor with a constantly evangelising church-growth mission. Hundreds became Christians and hundreds of desperately poor miners and steelworkers were fed. Quite apart from his amazing missionary work, he went on to introduce the Pentecostal movement to Britain in the initial years of the twentieth century. Only now is the full extent of his ministry beginning to be fully recognised.

In 1892, he and all his brother clergy were asked by the then bishop of Durham, 'What will bring the gospel to bear more effectually upon ordinary life?' While others commented about visitation schemes and better preaching, Boddy replied, 'Meetings of clergy simply to pray for a greater filling by the Holy Ghost for service.'[11] This was how he described his first great Pentecostal blessing:

> It was on the 21st of September, 1892, at about 8.40 in the morning, in All Saints' Church, Monkwearmouth – my church in Sunderland, that the Holy Spirit in infinite love came upon me, when I was taking part in the Communion Service.

This was his big anointing moment, which he kept alive over many years of daily spirituality and the loving of his people.

So who am I as a spiritual person, and what sort of spiritual community am I part of?

> Refined cathedralesque liturgy oozing with history and symbolism,
> Strong mind- and heart-shaping Bible studies,
> Great celebrations of charismatic excitement and blessing,
> Ancient Celtic freedoms rediscovered,
> Contemporary mould-shattering journeys into the Alternative,
> Inspirational mega-crowds of young people on fire,
> Endless 24/7 chains of unbroken and devoted intercession.

---

11 Gavin Wakefield, *Alexander Boddy*, Paternoster 2006, page 62.

And is it

> inward or outward
> fulfilling or emptying
> getting or giving
> mine or his?

Rick Warren says that 'A church's health is measured by its sending capacity, not its seating capacity'.[12] The point applies to individuals as well as whole congregations. Whatever our big spiritual thing may be, the really big thing is about our loving of others. The 'I and Thou' has to become an 'I and Thou and Them'. These are the big truth questions in all of this:

- Do we flow like a life-giving, fresh-water river out of our sea and into the desert of modern life?
- At what point do those of us who chanted, talked, listened, clapped and were on fire actually go out and share it or him with the world?
- How does our contemplation, our vigorous Bible reading, turn us into evangelisers?
- If our rituals feed us with the body of Christ, help us to see the alternative Jesus and renew us in his Spirit, then how soon will we start to do it in his loving way in our world?

Everybody needs a hero sometime. I've had several in my life. They have taught me, corrected me, inspired me and simply shown me a better way. The most important was Denis Shepheard (with a name

---

12 *The Purpose-Driven Church*, page 32.

like that he just had to be an evangelist). Denis was like a spiritual bus station: the love and reality of God flowed in at one end of his life and flowed out to the world at the other. He was a working-class, cockney, funny, warm vicar-cum-evangelist, constantly working alongside Sheila his wife. From Denis I learned much about sharing Jesus – the tricks of the trade, as it were. But what I really learned, and what has stayed with me, had to do with knowing and loving Jesus. It is not ability or even gifting so much as the reality of this relationship which helps me to attempt to do it his way in my world.

Holy Spirit of the Father,
Promised gift of the Son,
Breath of life,
Follow me in my aloofness
Find me in my lostness
Feel me in my weakness
Fill me in my emptiness
Freshen me in my tiredness
Fuel me in my powerlessness
Forgive me in my forgetfulness
And when I lose you,
    neglect you
    move on from you
    or am just too busy to ring you
Please do not forsake me in my humanness.

AND FINALLY

Incarnation

Urban regeneration
Rich and poor exploitation
Islamic aggravation
Sexual liberation

Enviromental degradation
Capitalistic exploitation
Community devastation
Young and old alienation

Football saturation
TV constipation
Nip and tuck operation
Shop till you drop masturbation

Spiritual exploration
Church life deterioration
Multi-faith education
Peter Kaye for ordination

Race and sexism transformation
Use of war as politicisation
Fear and insecurity throughout the nation
Me, mine and myself orientation

And in us, Jesus, with his words of salvation.

And finally? Jesus is not the final word on evangelism. There is, of course, the amazing adventure of the young church in the Acts of the Apostles. There is the life and work of Paul, theologically developing the 'good news' and taking the message to modern-day Turkey, Greece and Italy. There are the missionaries of the early centuries, first to the Roman Empire and then beyond it to India, North Africa, south-eastern Europe and the northern Celtic fringe. There are the medieval friars and preachers and the Reformation restorers and renewers. Patrick, Boniface, Francis, John Wesley, General Booth and Billy Graham . . . the names go on and on. They were lifeboatmen to the drowning, midwives to those wanting to be born, finders and guides for those who were lost.

Jesus was not the final word on evangelism, but he was the first. Proclaiming the 'good news', healing the sick and bringing peace to the possessed, he scattered his seed. He touched thousands of the needy, invited outsiders to become insiders, led some into deep and life-transforming discipleship, established the first Jesus communities and finally sent out the converted. Jesus, the root, the paradigm, the inspiration for all of us.

Today there are still evangelists, but the work is far too important, far too big and far too exciting to leave it just to them. They, along with everyone else who is involved in the 'Jesus movement', are called to be an evangelising people, to do it his way in our world.

Dear Lord Jesus
Who was sent by the Father
To walk the pathways of Israel
And to touch its people,
Help us today
In our world,

To share your message with the lost,
To show your love to the hurting,
To shine your light into the disturbed.

That they might hear truth

find healing

sense peace

And be touched by you

In the name of the sending Father. Amen.

Bibliography

Abraham, William, *The Logic of Evangelism* (Eerdmans, 1996).

Arditti, Michael, *Easter* (Arcadia Books, 2001).

Barley, Lynda, *Churchgoing Today* (Church House Publishing, 2006).

Bosch, David, *Transforming Mission* (Orbis Books, new ed. 1992).

Brierley, Peter, *The Tide is Running Out* (Christian Research, 2000).

Brown, Callum, *The Death of Christian Britain* (Routledge, 2000).

Buber, Martin, *I and Thou* (Continuum, new ed. 2004).

Church House, *Mission-Shaped Church* (Church House Publishing, 2004).

Crace, Jim, *Quarantine* (Viking, 1997).

Crossan, John Dominic, *Jesus: A Revolutionary Biography* (HarperSanFrancisco, 1994).

Davie, Grace, *Europe: The Exceptional Case* (Darton, Longman and Todd, 2002).

Dodd, C.H., *The Founder of Christianity* (Collins, new ed. 1971).

Donovan, Vincent, *Christianity Rediscovered* (Orbis Books, new ed. 2003).

Douglas, Lloyd, *The Robe* (Hodder, new ed. 2007).

Dunn, James, *Jesus Remembered*, vol. 1, *Christianity in the Making* (Eerdmans, 2003).

—, *Jesus and the Spirit* (SCM Press, 1975).

Finney, John, *Finding Faith Today* (Bible Society, 1996).

Fletcher, Richard, *The Conversion of Europe* (HarperCollins, 1997).

Frayn, Michael, *The Human Touch* (Faber & Faber, 2006).

Fredriksson, Marianne, *According to Mary Magdalene* (Hampton Roads Publishing Co., 2003).

Garnett, Jane, *Redefining Christian Britain* (SCM Press, 2007).

Graves, Robert, *King Jesus* (Farrar Straus Giroux, 1981).

Haddon, Mark, *The Curious Incident of the Dog in the Night-Time* (Vintage, new ed. 2004).

Hosseini, Khaled, *The Kite Runner* (Bloomsbury, new ed. 2004).

Jackson, Bob, *The Road to Growth* (Church House Publishing, 2005).

Jung, C.G., *Memories, Dreams, Reflections* (Fontana, new ed. 1995).

Kazantzakis, Nikos, *The Last Temptation* (Faber & Faber, new ed., 2001).

—, *Report to Greco* (Faber & Faber, new ed. 2001).

Küng, Hans, *The Church* (Burns & Oates, 1967).

Lodge, David, *Therapy* (Penguin, reissued 1996).

MacNutt, Francis, *Healing* (Ave Maria Press, 1975).

Maddocks, Morris, *The Christian Healing Ministry* (SPCK, rev. ed. 1995).

McEwan, Ian, *On Chesil Beach* (Jonathan Cape, 2007).

Moltmann, Jürgen, *The Way of Jesus Christ* (SCM Press, 1990).

Moynagh, Michael, *Emergingchurch.intro* (Monarch, 2004).

Mursell, Gordon, *The Story of Christian Spirituality* (Lion Hudson, 2001).

Nolland, John, *The Gospel of Matthew* (Authentic Media, 2005).

O'Collins SJ, Gerald, *Jesus: A Portrait* (Darton, Longman and Todd, 2008).

Orwell, George, *The Road to Wigan Pier* (Penguin, new ed. 2001).
Osborne, Roger, *Civilization* (Jonathan Cape, 2006).
Pannenberg, Wolfhart, *Jesus: God and Man* (SCM Press, new ed. 2002).
Ponsonby, Simon, *God Inside Out* (Kingsway, 2007).
Pope Benedict XVI, *Jesus of Nazareth* (Bloomsbury, 2007).
Prichard, Caradog, *One Moonlit Night* (New Directions, reprint 1997).
Reid, Gavin, *Good News to Share* (Falcon Books, 1979).
Richmond, Yvonne, et al., *Evangelism in a Spiritual Age* (Church House Publishing, 2005).
Savage, Sara, Sylvia Collins-Mayo, Bob Mayo and Graham Cray, *Making Sense of Generation Y* (Church House Publishing, 2006).
Singlehurst, Laurence, *Sowing, Reaping, Keeping: People-sensitive Evangelism* (Crossway, 1995).
Spencer, Nick, *Beyond Belief* (London Institute for Contemporary Christianity).
Wakefield, Gavin, *Alexander Boddy* (Paternoster, 2006).
Warren, Rick, *The Purpose-Driven Church* (Zondervan, rev. ed. 1996).
Watson, David, *You Are My God* (Hodder & Stoughton, 1983).
Whitbourn, James (ed.), *The Best of My Belief: Private Prayers of Public People, Chosen for BBC Radio 4* (Triangle, 1997).
Wimber, John, with Kevin Springer, *Power Evangelism* (Hodder & Stoughton, new ed. 1997).
Wright, N.T., *Jesus and the Victory of God* (SPCK, 1996).
Yancey, Philip, *The Jesus I Never Knew* (Zondervan, new ed. 2002).